Sustaining the Borderlands in the Age of NAFTA

Sustaining the Borderlands in the Age of NAFTA

Development, Politics, and Participation on the US-Mexico Border

Suzanne Simon

Vanderbilt University Press
Nashville

© 2014 by Vanderbilt University Press
Nashville, Tennessee 37235
All rights reserved
First printing 2014
First paperback edition 2016

This book is printed on acid-free paper.
Manufactured in the United States of America

Library of Congress Cataloging-in-Publication Data on file
LC control number 2013007846
LC classification number HC137.M46S55 2013
Dewey class number 388.972´107—dc23

ISBN 978-0-8265-1960-3 (paper)
ISBN 978-0-8265-1959-7 (cloth)
ISBN 978-0-8265-1961-0 (ebook)

To the memory of my father

Contents

Acknowledgments   ix

Introduction   1

1 Democratizing Discourses   15

2 Space and Place in the Borderlands   40

3 Investigating Waste   60

4 Environmental Justice as Place-Making   93

5 Environmental Organizing and Citizenship on the Border   125

6 Transnational Networks and Grassroots Splintering   150

   Conclusion   185

   Notes   193

   Bibliography   203

   Index   217

Acknowledgments

It seems a bit cliché to say, "There are too many people to thank" for their support and advice in the writing of this book, but there is a reason for clichés. There are too many people and institutions to thank. I apologize in advance if I have overlooked any names, institutional or otherwise.

First, I must thank the many people of Matamoros who shared with me their time, compassion and, occasionally, interest. I am sorry to have reduced all of them to "border activists" in this text, when they all were and are so much more than that. Were my writing skills better, or my anthropological imagination more expanded, I might have been able to paint their lives with a more nuanced palette. Nevertheless, this book would not have been possible had certain people not taken me into their fold and allowed me, generously, to know something about their lives. At the time that I conducted the fieldwork and in the immediate aftermath of data review and writing, I suffered the not atypical anthropological hubris of thinking that I had done some good—or at least that I had not caused any damage—in the course of my fieldwork. Now, with years of ethnographic data perusal and writing under my belt, as well as a lot of experience teaching anthropology, I am not as convinced of that. When I went to conduct my fieldwork, I knew that I would one day leave the fieldwork site, just as assuredly as the fact that I had gone there in the first place. As much as I always tried to be clear about that, I'm not sure it was always understood. In any event, the anthropological footprint is evident in this work and I have not tried to sweep it away.

I have many faculty at the Department of Cultural Anthropology at the New School for Social Research to thank for the excellent and rigorous anthropological training I received: Bill Roseberry, Kate Crehan, Harry West, and Steve Caton, among others. Most notable, of course, were those who would eventually become the members of my dissertation committee: Deborah Poole, Rayna Rapp, Adriana Petryna, and Eli Zaretsky. While life moves on and one loses touch except for the occasional conference encounter, I am deeply indebted to these people for having had faith in the importance of this study, particularly at a time when "the border" had fallen out of anthropological fashion. Debbie Poole has remained a wonderful source of both support and inspiration through the years, and faithfully answers the annoying reference letter requests I still sometimes send. I will always be indebted to her for the faith that she has shown in my intelligence and promise, even if I feel as though I have lived up to a fraction of what she had hoped for. Adriana Petryna ripped out the page where I describe Rosalia, Sierra Club representative, and me standing at the banks of the *Dren Cinco de Marzo* and said, "Start your book here!" I did not understand that admonition because I was always more comfortable with theory. After wrestling with the book and rearranging it for too long, I finally started the book at the point she recommended. It flowed much more smoothly after that. Other first time book authors and PhD students should take note! Rayna Rapp is Rayna Rapp . . . larger than life and forever an inspiration. I teach my methods classes nowadays partly with excerpts from her book—*Testing Women, Testing the Fetus*—and I enjoy having the chance to visit with her there. I credit all of these people with most of what I know about anthropology, and I am proud of the tradition that we represent.

However, I would be remiss in not mentioning a longstanding intellectual mentor and, now, good friend, Arturo Escobar. Arturo introduced me to anthropology as an undergraduate and, to continue with clichés, made me fall in love with it. He revolutionized the way that anthropologists and others think about development; he is a lovely person, to boot. I hope that this book is some small contribution to rethinking "development," even if it approaches it in an oblique fashion. Because of the setting, development was tucked into NAFTA and the side accords as ancillary justification. I likely would not be where I am today were it not for the faith that Arturo invested in me early on, and I will forever be indebted. Thank you, Arturo.

I will always be grateful that my first book was published with Vanderbilt University Press, where I have found the staff to be consummate professionals, as well as cheerful, supportive, and patient. The people with whom I have had the most contact deserve special mention. My acquisitions editor, Eli Bortz, expressed initial enthusiasm for this project and oversaw the review process with extreme judiciousness and insight. The managing editor, Joell Smith-Borne, has an extraordinary eye for detail, is the consummate professional, and was an utter delight to work with. I will always be grateful to the copyeditor, Jennifer Kurtz of Abshier House, for her ability to review and correct a manuscript with a fine-toothed comb and for her astute editorial suggestions that improved the overall quality of this book.

Casey Walsh conducted fieldwork in Matamoros only shortly before me. When I would listen, he tried to offer advice, and he always offered support. He is one of the most professional and generous academics I know and was always ready to lend a helping hand.

Many institutions and foundations have found this research interesting and supportable at different times. These include the Social Science Research Foundation (International Dissertation Research Fellowship), the Center for US-Mexican Studies, University of California, San Diego (Research Fellow), and the Institute for Conflict Analysis and Resolution (Postdoctoral Fellowship). I am grateful for all of this support that allowed me to simply research and write, without teaching or committee obligations.

I met many people along the way, at these and other institutions, that deserve special mention. At the Center for US-Mexico Studies, I had the luxury of intellectually co-habiting with a number of other Mexicanist or Mexican scholars, as well as others. Long term friendships that were formed during that year include those with Deborah and Patrick Boehm, Maria Tapias, and Xavier Escandell. I am happy to report that two new lives also came into being during that year, and I will always remember the joy that little Ava brought to our writing circles.

At the Institute for Conflict Analysis and Resolution, I encountered quite a robust group of intellectuals for which I was hardly a match. I learned a lot; everyone could learn a lot from this institution. I was given unconditional, patient, and generous support for my research by all and also learned from that group of scholars in ways that I am still counting. Certain names must be singled out, not just for their intelligence and support, but also for the humor they brought to the workplace every day: Kevin Avruch, Marc Gopin, Susan Hirsch, Terrence Lyons, Agnieszka Pacynska, Dan Robotham, Rich Rubenstein, and Wallace Warfield. While all were supportive (even when they did not need to be), I am especially grateful for Agnieszka Pacynska's similar interests in "dual transitions," Marc Gopin's suddenly alert interest in "legal pluralism," and the little that Kevin Avruch and Susan Hirsh were able to teach me about conflict analysis through an anthropological lens (the steep learning curve was on my end, not theirs). I am especially grateful for the friendship that Agnieszka and I have been able to maintain through the years, and have been happy to watch her and Terrence's lovely Nell grow up, if from afar.

At the School for International Training (SIT), where I went to teach sustainable development for two years, I met a different, but equally unique, group of scholars and students. SIT is an unusual and very special institution within the landscape of American academia. As a graduate institute, its level of theoretical rigor is high. It is mission-driven in an unorthodox, practitioner-oriented fashion. For decades, SIT has embraced the type of theory-practice and community-based learning models only recently embraced by other institutions of higher education. The students there were so inspiring and challenging, I wish I could list them all by name. In the absence of that, I would like to mention the participants of a seminar I conducted on trade liberalization, democratic transitions, and Latin America. Most did not know that I was using that seminar to theoretically hatch the premise of this book; nor did I know at the time. I very much appreciated the insights of Francisco Burgos, Katie Chandler, Claudia Petra Leiva, Colleen O'Holleran, Rebecca Rieber, Korto RS, Salena Tramel, and Ricardo Vargas. I also admired many of the faculty at SIT, but some deserve special mention and not just for support that they (knowingly or not) offered to me at different times: Kanthie Anthukorala, Charles Curry-Smithson, Sora Friedman, Maliha Khan, Nikoi Kote-Nikoi, Rich Rodman, and Jeff Unsicker. Nikoi has become a dear and trusted friend through the years. I hope that he, like Arturo, can see his dream of a radical re-thinking of development realized. The same is true for Kanthie; she will always be a true sister in spirit. Neither of us is good at maintaining long distant relationships, not least because there are always other things to do.

Josiah Heyman provided an early review of this manuscript. I am extraordinarily grateful for the time he took to perform a faithful review, offer constructive criticism, and highlight the merits of the book—namely, the role of NAFTA in Mexico's "dual transition." This assiduous review process was repeated with two anonymous reviewers at Vanderbilt University Press. In all cases, I was professionally honored by the fact that I had produced a book-length manuscript of sufficient merit that top-notch scholars took the time to pore over it. I appreciate the support for the overall thesis, as well as the careful and meticulous comments made throughout. I also thank Miguel Centeno for inviting me to give a talk at the Princeton Institute for International and Regional Studies and encouraging me to think about the environmental side accord as more than window dressing. A ten-minute conversation can make a world of difference.

Within the University of North Florida's Sociology and Anthropology Department and the university at large, there are a number of friends and colleagues I would like to mention. All have helped me through the years, sometimes in ways unbeknownst to them, other times not. First and foremost, I must mention Gordon Rakita. Gordon has an extra tank for supporting other colleagues. He brings humor, concern, impossibly high academic standards, tireless motivation, and intellectual enthusiasm to the office every day. He is one of the best colleagues I have ever had, period. Another colleague that brings support and irreverent humor to the office every day is David Jaffee. I am endlessly grateful for his patience and support; the second floor corridor of the Social Science building has lit up since his return. At a close third (if only because he usually comes for the night shift, when most of us are long gone) is Rick Phillips. He never batted an eye at the lengthy time it took for me to finish this manuscript, is always filled with irreverent humor and, like everyone else listed here, is a top-notch scholar to boot. Last, but not least, is Rosa de Jorio. We are always wrestling with time to have coffee, but I have great admiration for the ways in which she continues to advance cultural anthropological frontiers and maintains the highest level of theoretical rigor, even while wrestling with all the challenges of career and life. I would like to thank specifically those who were just being themselves, offering direct support or even offering support when they did not know they were doing so: Keith Ashley, Alison Bruey, Charles Clossman, Jennifer Spaulding-Givens, Ronald Kephart, Herbert Koegler, Sasha Milicevic, Deb Miller, Ronald Lukens-Bull, Erin Soles, Adam Shapiro, Buzz Thunen, Jennifer Wesley, Jeff Will, David Wilson, and Pam Zeiser. You are all kind, patient, and generous. I would also like to thank my undergraduate research assistant, Elizabeth Sanchez, for her timely help with assembling an initial index, formatting the bibliography, and performing a range of other necessary and important tasks.

Finally, there are a few more people that must be mentioned who do not fit into the above institutional categories: Salvatore Arena, Anne Galvin, Dena Hawes, Kristin Hayden Heller, Erin Koch, Mariana Palpade, Juhi Roy, Michele Rubino, Dan Tardona, and Antonio Zavaleta. Antonio let me do *curanderismo* research for him on the border when my SSRC funding dried up and has become a trusted friend because a kindred spirit. UNF generously provided me with research assistance near the end of this project. I would like to thank Elizabeth Sanchez for her careful fact checking and indexing skills.

I would like to thank my family. This includes first and foremost, my trusted brothers, Bryan and Jeff Crane, their families, and my abundance of nieces. I will always be grateful that one of the four was born on my birthday. Then there is my extended family: I thank the Duvals, the Cooks, and the Tigretts. You all continually teach me what family is and should be. I would especially like to thank Ella Duval. She has provided patient support and guidance through many years, and I am very grateful to her for her generous heart.

I would also be remiss if I failed to mention my favorite four-legged creature, Ruida. She has unselfishly warmed my lap and heart throughout the writing of this book.

Finally, I would like to thank my stalwart, lifelong companion and friend who has taught me how to live, Suska Matsik. She is in these pages, whether she knows it or not.

I have chosen to keep the dedication of this book brief and to the memory of my father. My father, James Lee Crane, was a man of principal and integrity. I loved him dearly. He was also a working class man who died young. Had he been born in Mexico, rather than in the United States, he might have been subjected to the conditions I describe here. It is only in retrospect that I have realized how much his spirit lives on through me, in this book, and in the spirit of Rosalia. I will never be able to repay the debt I owe to Rosalia for sharing her life with me and make no pretense to do so. Similarly, I can never thank my father, as unappreciated as he was, for being the person he chose to be.

Any errors in this book are my own.

Sustaining the Borderlands in the Age of NAFTA

Introduction

It was a warm spring morning and I stood on the banks of the *Dren Cinco de Marzo* with Rosalia (former leader of a local workers' justice organization and current president of an environmental justice organization called Las Caracaras[1]) and Marisa, a representative of the Sierra Club's *Beyond the Borders* Program. The *Dren* was a wide and open canal that carried rainwaters, industrial waste, and sewage from the center of Matamoros to the brackish Laguna Madre. At the time, Marisa was coming to Matamoros every couple of months in an effort to develop a working relationship with Las Caracaras. I was an anthropologist conducting fieldwork there from October of 2001 until March of 2003. Las Caracaras was being groomed to receive a seed grant from the Sierra Club, even as Marisa struggled to understand the enormity of border pollution problems. Together, the three of us labored to understand why nothing had changed since the signing of the North American Free Trade Agreement (NAFTA) and its corollary side agreements on environment and labor. On this particular day, we had driven out to the point where the *Dren Cinco de Marzo* passed by the municipal dump in an effort, once again, to provide Marisa with a graphic illustration of the kinds of environmental pollution problems with which Las Caracaras was struggling.

We stood at the banks of the *Dren* and surveyed the area looking north, south, east, and in our immediate vicinity. We had driven through the dump in order to arrive at this bend in the canal. The bend indicated the place where the canal sidled up to the trash-strewn edges of the city dump. It then continued southeastward from there, snaking lazily through the poorer *colonias* of Matamoros; in the other direction, it moved in a straight shot—looking much like a landing strip or a highway—toward the *maquila* parks.

Lay investigators all of us, we took in the sights of litter alongside the bank and children playing in garbage heaps just outside of the shacks in which they presumably lived. It was well known that inextinguishable

1

fires regularly burned deep inside the dump's garbage heaps. Plumes of smoke could almost always be seen lurking around the peaks, the way puffs of clouds or fog cling to the highest peaks of a mountain range. What kinds of toxic fumes might be released with these fires was any-one's guess. Indeed, the purpose of NAFTA's environmental side accord had been to provide data to answer the kinds of questions about risk that we asked ourselves on that day. Questions of burning polyurethane and polycyclic aromatic hydrocarbons aside, more unsightly—and disturbing—was the mountain of animal bones almost two stories high only twenty feet from where we had parked. The pile was a spooky white-and gristle-colored mass with the foul, if now faint, stench of decompos-ing flesh. The pile of old bones sat precipitously next to the *Dren,* doubt-less tumbling into it at times. Garbage and old plastic bags bobbed in the water as iridescent froth gathered at the canal's edges. We walked out to the middle of a dilapidated bridge so we could look straight down into the filthy mess, even as the stench knocked our collective heads back.

Rosalia was giving us an audio tour to accompany the disconcerting surroundings. She pointed in one direction and explained that the *Dren* passed directly through the industrial *maquila* park before it arrived at the dump. Indeed, on another occasion, I had visited the Industrial Park with Rosalia and Ava, former head of the local Comité Fronterizo de Obreros (CFO), when they had pointed out to me the precise locations in which the *maquilas* were alleged to discharge their wastes into the ca-nal. On previous occasions, the two of them had surreptitiously collected water samples at the discharge locations, but then they had no way to get the waters tested. Rosalia and other members of Las Caracaras hoped to establish a system whereby the Rio Grande and other waters could be systematically collected by them at the grassroots level and tested through local "citizen-scientist" (Irwin 1995) alliances. Rosalia explained this with her quick, clipped speech, as she pointed in the direction of Colonia Verde,[2] where she lived, and the dozen other neighboring *co-lonias* through which the *Dren Cinco de Marzo* made its winding path before dumping into the once pristine Laguna Madre to the south of the city.[3]

NAFTA's Agreement on Environmental Cooperation,[4] (commonly called the environmental side accord, environmental side agreement, or ESA), which went into effect on January 1, 1994, was created precisely to address and resolve the types of environmental pollution that we wit-nessed at that moment. Indeed, the spectacle of unmitigated pollution on the border had been pivotal to the creation of the environmental side accord and, eventually, to NAFTA's passage. NAFTA subsequently came to be called, by some, the "greenest trade treaty in history" (Thomas and Weber 1999, 134) and heralded an era of optimism that one could have one's cake and eat it too: unfettered free trade coupled with environmental and labor protections. The NAFTA side agreements also marked the first time in trade treaty history that dispute resolution mechanisms or "soft law" (Abbott 2001) procedures were put in place to allow civil society constituencies to petition or complain in the case of environmental or labor law violations. Mumme has noted that the environmental accord's citizen petitioning processes were "designed to trigger investigations of alleged non-enforcement of domestic environmental laws" (Thomas and Weber, 2). This "trigger" design of the side accords, and their civil society inclusion mechanisms, were also part of a greater optimism accompanying Mexico's (and by extension, all of Latin America's) seeming transition to both formal and substantive democracy. This NAFTA optimism swept far beyond the borderlands to encompass anticipations of hemispheric integration involving "sustained and deep liberalization" (Estevadeordal et al. 2004, 4; cf. Deere and Esty 2002; Wrobel 1998; Simon 2007) and suggestions that "many governments in the region see an FTAA [Free Trade Area of the Americas] as the next beacon of hope in the long and arduous road of economic reform along which they have been traveling" (Estevadeordal et al. 2004, 6), as noted by FTAA proponents in one of the few scholarly documents on that topic.

This embrace of deep and sustained liberalization and privatization was only one aspect of the optimism engendered by NAFTA and its progeny, however. From another angle, the inclusion of civil society mechanisms within new trade treaties was anticipated, most optimistically, to resolve the perennial, global stand-off between trade and non-trade interests, meanwhile simultaneously producing the mechanisms that would ensure genuinely democratic participation on the part of Latin American publics "in transition" (Deere and Esty 2002; Esty 2001; cf. Barenberg and Evans 2004). Esty's statement captures that sensibility:

> The commission [North American Commission for Environmental Cooperation] has also demonstrated its value as a forum for engaging environmental groups, other NGOs, and civil society more broadly in an ongoing conversation about what environmental issues matter

and how the three countries of North America might best address them (2004, 263–264).

By all accounts, the NAFTA environmental side agreement and its corollary institutions (the Commission on Environmental Cooperation, the Border Environment Cooperation Commission and the North American Development Bank) should have provided the institutional means to rectify the environmental contamination problem that Rosalia, Marisa, and I observed on that day at the dump. According to long time Matamoros resident and environmental activist Rosalia, however, environmental contamination continued to be severe and, in some ways, had worsened with time. Ultimately, from the organic and chemical matter that festered in the *Dren Cinco de Marzo* to the mysterious calcium sulfate that was a byproduct of Quimica Fluor and used to "pave" the city streets, the contents and possible toxicity of environmental surroundings in Matamoros were mystifying and stubbornly opaque. The disconcerting question was one hauntingly posed by Ulrich Beck (1992) some years before: What were the invisible risks of this environment? How did the almost insolent invisibility of these environmental risks compound the generalized sense of environmental threat and, occasionally, terror as the area's fairly macabre anencephaly cluster (discussed in Chapter 3) demonstrated? Who really knew what was in the water, the air, the soil, the food? Who could be trusted to honestly portray and address contamination issues in this border city? In a manner prototypical of the "popular epidemiology" and "citizen-science" alliance movements already being discussed and studied within the corridors of academe (cf. Brown 1997, 1987; Fischer 2000; Irwin 1995), the environmental accord was intended to encourage trust, dialogue, and information sharing across various cross-border grassroots and professional groups, thus ostensibly contributing to both the long-term demystification and resolution of border pollution problems. Dialogue was to be premised on the accurate collection and dissemination of scientific data on border pollution problems, yet both participatory structures and science have fallen short in their capacity to demystify border environmental and social problems.

This book has a two-fold purpose. First, it attempts to provide an ethnographic portrait of life on the border through the eyes and experiences of two different Mexican border groups. One group consists of members of the environmental justice movement, Las Caracaras. The second group consists of a set of workers from Spektra plant who filed a petition under the labor side accord of NAFTA in order to have workplace grievances addressed. The ethnographic chapters of the book weave together the experiences of both of these groups as they engage petitioning processes instituted by NAFTA, cross border organizing possibilities, and their own aspirations to forge a better life for themselves. This book provides a partial accounting of the experiences of predominantly Mexican actors as they navigate the new social, legal, and cross-border organizing terrain put in place in response to the NAFTA debates and the environmental and labor side accords. I approach the accords as grids that, once laid across the border landscape, have encouraged the emergence of specific forms of cross-border organizing, investigations, and aspirations (cf. Staudt and Coronado 2002).

The second goal of this book is to highlight the environmental and labor side agreements of NAFTA as case studies that investigate the local level effects and efficacy of including environmental, labor, or human rights protections within trade treaties. Although the treaty's "greenness" is an important part of this story, I am equally interested in exploring NAFTA's novel discursive and practical linking of free trade, democratization, and sustainable development. The side agreements of NAFTA were inextricably tied to the possibility and promise of flushing corruption from Mexican political culture and completing the country's transition from authoritarianism to democracy (Simon 2007). Chapter 1 argues that sustainable development's stress on grassroots or community participation provided the conditions of possibility for NAFTA's novel linking of free trade and democratization.

At the time of its signing, NAFTA seemed to initiate a new trend in which environmental, labor, human rights, or other non-trade issues might be protected within the texts of trade treaties themselves (see Deere and Esty 2002; Estevadoral et al. 2004). These protections ultimately rested on civil society input. The side accords—with their accompanying commissions, petitioning mechanisms, and dispute resolution procedures—were put in place to encourage ongoing dialogue with Mexico's growing civil society. The protections built into the side agreements of NAFTA became the new standard which, however sincere or cynical their intentions, FTAA negotiators were subsequently required to meet.

The line of inquiry manifested in this book requires sidestepping the familiar criticism that the side accords were merely window dressing or intentionally toothless mechanisms, as many advocacy groups suggest. Discourses shape and produce material reality in fundamental, concrete, and sometimes irreversible ways. I bracket the question of whether the true intent of the side accords was to encourage greater justice possibilities for Mexican and other populations and, instead, simply look at what they have done. The discourse of "Mexican corruption" was particularly influential in producing the side accords and in linking the accords with both sustainable development and political reform or democratic consolidation at the level of the grassroots political culture. If we resign ourselves to saying that the accords were simply legal building blocks that allowed NAFTA to become a reality, then we must simultaneously acknowledge that the discourse around the accords practically and materially produced the contemporary borderlands as we know them today. At the discursive and historical level, then, NAFTA and the side agreements provide the historic and ethnographic context in which this book unfolds. At the practical level, the debate and the resultant accords have also encouraged a great deal of both local and non-local cross-border organizing and advocacy work through unions, NGOs, and other organs of civil society. The bulk of the ethnographic data for the book comes from my participation in, and observation of, two such environmental and labor advocacy efforts.

This book is written and organized in such a way as to illustrate both quotidian features of life for economically disenfranchised Mexicans living on the Mexican side of the border, as well as the new types of transnational advocacy and social movement organizing that cross-cut the area in the wake of NAFTA. Ultimately, the data gathered from the justice organizations, in particular, are intended to test the NAFTA promise that citizens' petitioning processes that were democratically and transparently institutionalized in trilateral side accords would allow voices to be heard "from the bottom up," as well as ensure accountability and visibility at all levels.

The material reveals that the experience of economic liberalization in the form of NAFTA on the border has not laid a foundation whereby actors can pursue their own self-interest in the ways anticipated by the crafters of the side accords. Rather, poverty, inequality, and the absence of basic communication technologies has led many into relations of hyper dependency with more powerful groups which, in turn, has encouraged corruption of a new sort as damaged bodies and environments became part of the bartering process within a general competition for scarce resources. If self-proclaimed descriptions of the side accords' petitioning processes are laden with terms associated with contemporary democratic governance—accountability, transparency, participation, and dialogue—these terms have little practical application in areas so impoverished that the very people hypothetically and textually privileged to engage in these processes cannot practically afford to buy newspapers, never mind have computers and Internet access. The Internet is the primary channel over which the ideal of a rational, transparency, dialogic public sphere is acted out. This means that many are excluded by digital divides, particularly those that have become progressively impoverished under NAFTA and neoliberal conditions. In short, the stewards of this new political order of progressive Mexican democratization occurring from the "bottom up" cannot discharge their duties, suggesting that the political program implicit in the NAFTA side accords discussion has not been entirely successful. The unfortunate consequence is that this experience has reproduced the idea of Mexico as a corrupt third-world nation, even as US politicians continue to deny the corruption, kickbacks, and imperialistic arrogance that have been the defining features of US first-world governance for decades.

As is the case with any ethnography, the data collected here is a reflection of my fieldwork methods. It has become a staple of fieldwork commentary to note how quickly one's original plans fall apart in the field and how a new line of inquiry emerges as a consequence of one's actual encounters during fieldwork. This commentary indirectly refers to how little control many anthropologists have over events as they unfold in their fieldwork setting and how deeply participatory methods can lead one into waters one had not originally intended to chart. This is one of the great advantages of fieldwork. One may plot the project from beginning to end with a rigid scholastic compass, but when one is working in real time with real people and in the midst of already established human relationships, something as simple as one's initial contact in the field can have an ongoing impact on the fieldwork project throughout its duration.

Nothing could be truer in the case of my fieldwork. Because I was (unbeknownst to me) setting foot in a fieldwork setting already littered with rivalries, broken friendships, and local and cross-border networks, my initial contacts played a pivotal role in how the project unfolded over the course of sixteen months. The fact that my fieldwork site was so fractious and cross-cut with political party affiliations, advocacy relations, personal histories, competition over scarce resources and last, but hardly least, the border itself, reveals much about life and advocacy in this region (see, especially, Staudt and Coronado 2002). As will be discussed throughout the book, advocacy on the border is hardly an innocent, seamless, unified, or transparent affair, but one marked by grassroots foibles. This is true elsewhere, of course, but the border seems to add an additional dimension of competition, scarcity, and tension, as well as an urgency to resolve pressing and frightening environmental pollution problems.

There are two interrelated points about my fieldwork methods that need to be emphasized here: (1) the role of my primary informant in the fieldwork, and (2) the different (but overlapping) settings in which I worked and the methods that were appropriate to each. First, Rosalia played a critical role in my fieldwork from beginning to end. In the conventional ethnographic sense, she was the principal informant that provided a link for me with the local community members (including her family and friends) with whom I developed close personal relations. She introduced me to interviewees and was a more or less constant companion throughout the fieldwork. Every day I could go to Rosalia's house on the outskirts of Matamoros and feel that I was welcome there. I am fairly certain that this ethnography can never repay the debt of gratitude that I feel for having a place that I could go to during those sixteen months in which I felt both welcome and tolerated. I doubt that this monograph will contribute much to the amelioration of abuses patiently detailed to me again and again by Rosalia, her family, and others, but I hope that it might have some impact.

In a less conventional sense, Rosalia played a critical role in other unanticipated ways as well. My early association with her led, on the one hand, to extensive contacts in the local community with people among whom she was well received. She opened doors. On the other hand, as time went on, it became clear to me that other doors were closed to me because of our association (and, to a lesser extent, my association with Javier, the person who introduced me to Rosalia). The fact that some people refused to speak with me because of my association with Rosalia provides, again, a window into frictions and tensions at the local border advocacy level. The people who rejected me were activists involved in the workers' labor petition who had previously had working relations with Rosalia until a falling out over resources. This was explained to me quite frankly: "When we hear the name Rosalia [and Javier] we distrust you immediately." Although it may be tempting to dismiss such rejection as mere personal foible and idiosyncrasy (and thus unworthy of ethnographic mention), this rejection and animosity between the two parties reveal how social justice groups split and go their separate ways—particularly when transnational resources are involved (as discussed in Chapter 7).

Second, Rosalia's life as an activist spans the two major topical areas addressed in this book: labor and environmental justice. Thus, while her life is not directly forefronted as oral history or a window into local culture (cf. Mintz 1989), the fact that her life work as a social justice activist and community organizer spanning the gamut from labor to environmental issues demonstrates, to some degree, the ways in which these issues are intertwined on the border. While the labor and environmental side accords, labor and environmental activists, and even this book might portray the two domains as separate, they are organically linked in the life of a woman who has spent the majority of her adult life in a Mexican border city. From Rosalia's perspective, as she told me in no uncertain terms several times, the two are inextricably connected. In fact, in any academic disconnection of the two, one might lose sight of her conviction that both were based on a form of racism: environmental racism and racism in the workplace. In both cases, the bodies being exposed to harsh and dangerous chemicals and living in deplorable conditions were considered dispensable as members of Mexico's poor underclass and border people. Although this ethnography can scarcely do justice to Rosalia's conviction that to disconnect environmental and labor justice issues is to misrepresent the broader issues at stake, it does attempt to illustrate the organic connection between the two domains.

The research questions that I pursued were ones that have become fairly commonplace in a globalized era:

- What are the transnational connections crosscutting this seemingly local problem of environmental pollution and violations of workers' rights?
- To use Tsing's language, how had seemingly universal aspirations toward greater environmental protections gained traction in the local setting?
- How had environmental aspirations conspired to create contemporary labor conditions in Mexico?

- Alternately, how had the seemingly local conditions of space been crafted by transnational and spatializing forces of a symbolic, material, and political nature?
- How was this problematic that I was studying less a feature of local or border culture, and more a nexus of relations, actors, aspirations, and institutions that had emerged around particular issues of both local and global import?

Although this is a fair generalization of how I approached both topics, there are still important differences of method. In the case of my study of the environmental justice movement, Las Caracaras, my approach was a combination of deeply participatory or traditional fieldwork techniques with an applied or activist approach. My relationship with Rosalia, her family, members of Las Caracaras, and the neighbors of different people that I regularly visited allowed me the insights of participant-observation. The strength of the relationship that I forged with Rosalia and others was rooted in the assistance that I gave to them on behalf of their organization, Las Caracaras. Throughout my time there, I lent my skills and organizational support—what, in development terms, is typically called capacity building—so that Las Caracaras could develop a working relationship with the Sierra Club. Organizational and financial support from the Sierra Club eventually allowed Las Caracaras to establish an office and public identity, however tentatively, in Matamoros, and to secure a seed grant to continue their environmental justice work. The deeply participatory and activist components, in this case, were simply two sides of the same coin and, indeed, the applied work that I did on their behalf allowed me to build trust and relations with group members, which eventually resulted in the collection of rich ethnographic data.

My approach with the workers' justice group was quite different, if purely a consequence of ethnographic circumstance. Simply put, while there were many opportunities to participate in the daily lives and organizing activities of Las Caracaras, those opportunities were absent with Spektra workers. Their grievance was a thing of the past and, understandably, most of them just wanted to move on with their lives. Often, when I would sit down for an interview with former Spektra workers, they would query me to see if I had any information about the status of their petition since they had never received any word from the US-based NGO who had aided them with the petition's preparation. My answers, which were largely simply explanations of the labor side agreement petitioning process, later got me into hot water with the petition organizers. Because the workers' petition was a thing of the past, there were no opportunities to attend meetings, be of some assistance, or otherwise spend time with them. If anything, I was a reminder of something that many of them preferred to not think of anymore. Given that many of them worked long hours, had busy schedules and families, and had already invested significant energy in the petition, the time that they gave me for interviews were simple acts of generosity on their part.

Ultimately, the side accords were built on an ideal of transparency, public participation, and sustainable development that had yet to come to fruition in the practical world. Unfortunately, they lent support to a trade treaty that materially prevents the possibility of those ideals coming to fruition. My ethnographic investigations of the tangible real world impacts of the side accords in the place where they were most needed— the borderlands—demonstrate the inadequacy of the agreements to influence change among the populations that need it most. In theory, the accords provide a perfect Habermasian vision of public dialogue and reason. In practice, the poverty and inequalities that NAFTA supported make such informed dialogue impossible.

Organization of the Book

Chapter 1, "Democratizing Discourses," introduces three themes that run like red threads throughout the remainder of the book: democratization and dual transition; conflicts between trade and non-trade interests; sustainable development and participation. Similar to capitalism and other features of modernity, these discourses unfold across a global social terrain ostensibly devoid of substantive local content. In the case of each of the three domains identified above, I describe the specific ways in which these discourses unfolded in the context of the NAFTA debates. This chapter problematizes the concept of dual transitions that has become fundamental to development and neoliberal orthodoxy, and demonstrates that the discourse of dual transition was fundamental to the creation of the side accords and, thus, the (re)production of the contemporary border region.

Chapter 2, "Space and Place in the Borderlands," corresponds to the local setting chapter of most conventional ethnographies. My intention here is to demonstrate how the border region has historically been produced by larger spatializing forces of conquest, state formation, national development, and, eventually, the creation of a *maquila* zone. I briefly review the history of the peoples and places of the border region from early frontier history until the present day and focus on the social, geographic and structural impacts of the *maquila* industry from the mid-1960s onward. The fact that the ecology of the region has been deeply intertwined with its social history has long been acknowledged by environmental historians and border residents, even as the argument that the region constituted a common public health zone (and threat) became one of the building blocks for the environmental side accord.

Chapter 3, "Waste in the Environment and in Workers' Bodies," tackles the question of how the "margins of the state" (Das and Poole 2004) are both discursively and economically productive. I argue that productivity in the margins can be found in environmental and labor wasting processes. Conceptually, this chapter relies heavily on the concept of negative externalities or waste and wasting processes that provide hidden sources of profit and surplus value within capitalist production processes. They are hidden because their actual human or environmental costs (whether it is bodily or ecological degradation) are not calculated into orthodox classical or neoliberal economics. Ethnographically, the chapter also focuses on the investigative activities of both Las Caracaras and the Spektra workers movement.

Chapter 4 explores "Environmental Justice as Place-Making." This chapter argues that, even though the activities of groups such as Las Caracaras are typically captured by the term environmental justice, this label obscures important place-making components of Mexican border environmental activism. For border activists, environmental justice struggles are a natural extension of, and conclusion to, their migrant journeys. The fact that the overwhelming majority of Mexican border residents are migrants from elsewhere (or the interior to revert to a classic center-periphery model) is elided in present-oriented border environmental and policy analyses. Moreover, the simultaneous place-making and environmental justice activities of Las Caracaras members are particularly intriguing because they were aided by the new era of transnational environmental organizing augured by the NAFTA debates. The Sierra Club's "Beyond the Border" program, which epitomizes capacity building as a development strategy, supported Las Caracaras so that they could pressure the Matamoros municipal government into compliance with its existing environmental statutes, and thus try to make Matamoros a better place.

Chapter 5, "Environmental Organizing and Citizenship on the Border," explores both a local instance of cross-border environmental organizing, as well as the city of Matamoros' attempts to comply with the environmental side accord's participatory requirements in the certification and dispensing of a North American Development Bank (NAD-Bank) loan. First, I turn to an oft-noted consequence of the NAFTA debates: namely, the upsurge of cross-border environmental organizing. Building on my observations of a failed, local cross-border coalition-building attempt, I argue that historically embedded, nationalist, racial, and identity-based rivalries on both sides of the border ultimately trumped the NAFTA ideal of seamless ecological stewardship. In spite of the demands for sustainable development and cooperation, border populations are hardly homogeneous; identities matter and they can get in the way of the pursuit of environmental goals. It has often been noted that some of the most intractable obstacles to cross-border organizing are the most pedestrian ones: cultural, linguistic, and territorial obstacles (Barry 1994; Staudt and Coronado 2002). My data supports that claim, but also suggests that these obstacles are disproportionately suffered by Mexican border populations—particularly in relationship to digital divides. In the case study of cross-border coalition building described here, ethnic, local, and border-specific stereotypes were reaffirmed; the bridge that might have been crossed with new environmental awareness was crushed by the equally important weight of history, tension, racism, rivalries, and cross-border suspicions. In addition to describing Las Caracaras interactions with the Coalition against Contaminated Communities (CCC) based in Brownsville, I also describe the former's engagement with the Matamoros Junta de Aguas y Drenaje (JAD) as the city prepared an application for a series of infrastructure building works. The JAD, in this particular instance, was rather uncharacteristically reaching out to the popular classes of the city in order to conform with the participatory requirements for a NADBank loan, which had to be demonstrated to the Border Environment Cooperation Commission (BECC) in order for loan certification to be approved.

Chapter 6, "Transnational Networks and Grassroots Splintering," describes the ways in which local border environmental and labor justice organizations fractured under the weight of transnational resources. I explore the internationally generated political economy of scarce resources that was elided by NAFTA discourses of sustainable development, participation, and transparency. In the case of both Spektra and

Las Caracaras, allegations of corruption and opportunism became rampant once the movements gained cross-border allegiances. Also in both cases, a fairly unified and cohesive attempt at local social movement organizing (based on consensus, transparency, and shared goals) tipped over into more murky, opaque and rumor-laden processes when US-based NGOs became involved. In the case of the workers' justice movement, the petition that was filed under the auspices of the labor side agreement eventually led to suspicion on the part of the workers that their bodies had been doubly bartered: first, by Spektra plant and second, by the NGO that organized the petition. In the case of Las Caracaras, the well-organized grassroots group splintered completely once the possibility of Sierra Club funding became real. This splintering took place along latent lines of friction that became apparent when the possibility of resources became a reality.

Chapter 1

Democratizing Discourses

The NAFTA side accords came into being largely as a function of three global and interrelated discourses. Arguably, the most important of these was dual transition theory as applied to transition governments generally, and to Mexico in particular. "Dual transition" theory suggests that, as an economy shifts from being closed or protected to open and free trade based, a country's political system will also shift from authoritarianism or socialism to liberal democracy. Two additional discourses supported the creation of the accords and the conviction that they would encourage Mexico's democratic transition. One concerned the increasingly visible global conflicts between trade and non-trade interests, and another was the increasingly ubiquitous sustainable development discourse.

Although each of these discourses has its own unique history and trajectory, they wound round, overlapped, and reinforced each other in the NAFTA debates of the early 1990s. The accords were envisioned by their planners to ensure that wealth in Mexico generated by greater free trade would be channeled into regulatory institutions to correct pre-NAFTA labor and environmental abuses. According to the accords' crafters and proponents, the citizen petitioning and dispute resolution mechanisms of the accords would be used by Mexican (Canadian or North American) constituencies, thus ensuring accountability on the part of the state and regulatory institutions, while simultaneously inculcating values of democratic citizenship within grassroots populations utilizing these novel participatory triggers (Mumme 1999, 2; cf. Fox 2000; Simon 2007). According to this logic, the environmental and labor side agreements supported the political arm of Mexico's transition by providing Mexican populations with the formal political tools necessary to coerce their own state into conformity with its written statutes. The trade treaty, in turn, would merely formalize the neoliberal economic arm of Mexico's dual transition, which had been initiated decades before.

This chapter's first section describes Mexico's dual transition and transition theory as it has been applied to Mexico and Latin America more broadly. Nested within the discussion of dual transition is an exploration of contemporary discourses about the importance of transparency to transition processes. Second, the chapter describes the public debates of the immediate pre-NAFTA days and the arguments of both pro- and anti-NAFTA constituencies on both sides of the border. These debates eventually focused on the problem of the non-enforcement of national environmental and labor laws in Mexico. Since questions of Mexican law and enforcement figured so highly in the debates and subsequent creation of the side accords, this section also briefly reviews Mexican environmental and labor laws. The third section is devoted to a discussion of the environmental and labor side accords, as well as their attendant processes and institutions. Finally, the chapter concludes with a brief discussion of participatory, sustainable development. The participatory ideal is especially important to understanding the logic behind the side accords. It supported the dual transitions theory that a full democratic conversion could occur only with democratic consolidation at the grassroots. The side accords were purported to support this consolidation because they required public participation to work.

The "Dual Transition" in Latin America and Mexico

Mexico entered the NAFTA negotiations as a society "in transition" (Tulchin and Selee 2003). The term "in transition" has become a geopolitical catchall to describe the pattern of change in, for the most part, Eastern European and Latin American countries from communism or authoritarianism to free market capitalism and democracy. This sea change largely dominated the post-Cold War world, and was typically theorized by triumphalists as both natural and inevitable. As Centeno notes in the mid-1990s, "Capitalism and democracy appear triumphant. The collapse of the Berlin Wall supposedly signaled not only the triumph of liberalism, but even the end of history" (Centeno 1994, 125–126).

In discussions of Mexico and contemporary Latin America, the topics of democratization, re-democratization, democratic transition, and consolidation have received considerable attention (Hiskey 2005;

Karl 1990; Nef 1995; Olvera 2010). While this transition is considered by some to be wholesale and complete—with formally and democratically elected presidents at the head of each Latin American state—for others the transition is less than complete and even troubling (Olvera 2010; Oxhorn and Starr 1999). In the case of Chile, for example, neoliberal economic policy was instituted under the authoritarian rule of Pinochet, disrupting substantially the narrative that free markets invariably usher in vibrant political cultures (cf. Nef 1995). Struggles for true, lasting, and participatory democracy are necessarily ongoing and evident in the various indigenous and new social movements that increasingly shape the Latin American political cultures (Escobar and Alvarez 1992; Slater 1995). The emergence of a strong and vibrant civil society is evidenced partly by the proliferation of NGOs or global civil society (Fox and Hernández 1992; Friedman, Hochstetler, and Clark 2001; Robinson 2003, 222–226) in Latin America and elsewhere. Nevertheless, while some democratization trends look to indigenous Latin American traditions (Postero and Zamosc 2004; Warren and Jackson 2002), others look northward, particularly in an era in which transnational advocacy has become the rule, rather than the exception. "Politically, Latin America shares a recent authoritarian past with many countries, even as its more recent democratic transitions are joining it with the community of primarily Northern democratic governments" (Friedman, Hochstetler, and Clark 2001, 9). Mexico's grassroots democratization began at least two decades before the NAFTA debates (cf. Fox and Hernández 1992). For this reason, Zárate-Ruiz has described the polemics of the NAFTA debates as, in many ways, a morality play (2001).

    Latin America's economic transition is rooted partly in the neoliberal orthodoxy articulated in the early 1980s with the Washington Consensus (Horowitz 2005, 270; Smith 2002, 472–473; Wrobel 1998, 551). The Washington Consensus encouraged closed and protected economies to shift toward the obverse; namely, toward free trade and "the promotion of production for export, the retrenchment of the state's role in the economy, and the opening of the economy to foreign trade and investment" (Karl 2003, 134; cf. Green 1995). From roughly the end of the Great Depression through the mid-1970s, many Latin American countries favored Import Substitution Industrialization (ISI), which required limited foreign trade, Keynesian economic development strategies (Escobar 1995, 67–73; Harvey 1989, 135–140), and public social services heavily subsidized by national governments. By the end of the ISI period, many of these economies had become inefficient and corrupt, increasingly dependent on foreign aid, and weighed down by bloated state bureaucracies (Duncan 1995).

Latin America's shift toward more open economies coincided with economic globalization more broadly. Beginning in the 1970s, the world witnessed the restructuring of the dominant core capitalist economies according to the principles of flexible accumulation and production (Harvey 1989, 121–197). This restructuring has ineluctably shaped the contemporary era of transnational capitalism. Robinson (2003) distinguishes the new global economy of flexible production and accumulation from the previous world economy by noting that in the global economy, "the globalization of the production process breaks down and functionally integrates these national circuits [of the world economy] into global circuits of accumulation. The distinction between a world economy and a global economy is the globalization of the production process itself" (Robinson 2003, 13). The new global economy has fundamentally and organically reorganized global commodity chains at the level of production, rather than just trade.

Similar to other Latin American countries, Mexico maintained a protectionist economy from the 1940s until the late 1970s and early 1980s, based on both ISI and extensive state-labor corporatist alliances (Cook 1995; Middlebrook 1995, 1989). Politically, the country was governed by the Partido Revolucionario Institucional (PRI) from the 1930s until the 2000 election of the Partido de Accion Nacional (PAN) candidate Vincente Fox. In the early period of PRI rule, President Lazaro Cardenas implemented revolutionary populist goals, particularly through land reform and the creation of *ejidos,* or collective landholdings. The consolidation of PRI rule coincided with a period of relative economic stability; ISI was in place, the economy was growing, and rural resources were being channeled to urban manufacturing to bolster the "Mexican Miracle" (Barkin 1994). Beginning in the 1970s, however, the PRI system began to experience problems on the political front, in addition to the economic front. There were increasing allegations of political corruption, the 1968 Tlatelolco massacre of student demonstrators, and the repression by the Confederación de Trabajadores Mexicanos (CTM) of independent unions. While corporatist alliances between the state and labor had ensured both the support and repression of civil society, as both ISI and PRI rule stumbled, the latter became better known as the "perfect dictatorship." Grassroots efforts toward democratization were underway, strengthening civil society and putting pressure on an increasingly repressive state (La Botz 1995; Lawson 2000; Lorena Cook 1995; Teichman 1997). The PRI's growing legitimacy crisis became full-blown when the government responded inadequately to the 1985 Mexico City earthquake (La Botz 1995, 65–72).

The gradual political demise of the PRI was accompanied by increasing integration into the US economy through trade, export and, finally, *maquila*-oriented production on Mexico's northern frontier. Liberalization of the Mexican economy was pursued first under the de la Madrid administration of 1982–1988 (Middlebrook 1989, 200) and entrenched under Salinas de Gortari (1988–1994), the Harvard trained economist, "modernizing genius" (McArthur 2000, 77), and darling of neoliberal reformers. The *maquilas* of the northern region began to emerge in the mid-1960s and early 1970s and were an early stage in Mexico's eventual complete commitment to free trade: "Mexico's economy, once largely closed and state-directed, has become one of the most open economies in the developing world. Since 1990, Mexico has multiplied its total trade with the rest of the world six times, and trade now accounts for one-third of gross domestic product" (Tulchin and Selee 2003, 6).

Mexico's formal democratic transition is generally equated with the election of PAN candidate Fox as President in July of 2000. In place of the historic *dedazo*,[1] Fox purported to be elected fairly, although even this remains in dispute (Olvera 2010, 85). The 2000 election solidified the notion that personalism in presidential politics was primarily a PRI practice (Morris 2003: 671–672, 1999). Fox subsequently made the pursuit of transparency and the elimination of corruption a centerpiece of his presidency, introducing "new rights of access to information and new institutions for the promotion of transparency" (Olvera 2010, 87), even as his own administration was racked by scandals. The 2000 election bolstered the national narrative (supported by earlier NAFTA debates) that the entire society was in transition from ISI to free trade, darkness to light, opacity to transparency, and authoritarianism to democracy (Simon 2007).

Transparency as discourse, ideal, and practice gained increasing global currency throughout the 1990s (Shore and Haller 2005; West and Sanders 2003). In Mexico, it was and has been inextricably linked with the narrative that equates corrupt PRI rule with a thing of the past within Mexico's "long march to democracy" (Conger 2001). The re-election of a PRI candidate to the presidency in 2012 was supported partly by claims that this was the "new PRI," not to be confused with the party's "dinosaurs." This narrative of dramatic rupture is paradigmatically captured in Jorge Castañeda's prologue to *Mexico's Political Society in Transition* (Castañeda 2003). In an essay in which the word "maturity" figures prominently, Castañeda notes that now there is a "new relationship between Mexican society and its government, a relationship based on trust, accountability, and the rule of law" (Castañeda 2003, 1), and that the country is finally of a political parity with its northern neighbor. He suggests that the mature development of Mexico's political system has been the missing piece in the puzzle of its historically troubled relations with the United States. As he states, "Maturity also means that if disagreements do occur—as they can and most probably will in a relationship as complex as this one—the long term objectives of the bilateral agenda will not be jeopardized. Maturity requires that transparency become the name of the game" (ibid., 3). In this and similar formulations, the terms transparency, accountability, maturity, and democracy are used interchangeably, while ritually contrasted with everything associated with Mexico's past: protectionism, authoritarianism, corruption, opacity and, presumably, immaturity.

Transparency, like sustainable development, figured highly in the creation of the NAFTA side accords. As a political concept, transparency functions in a manner similar to democracy: namely, as both means and end, technique and goal of government. The term has come to function as a buzzword that is interchangeable with "good governance" (Sanders and West 2003, 1). As a rule, transparency in government and society includes free and fair elections, a functioning and non-oppressed civil society, freedom of information, and a free press. Transparency "supports democracy by facilitating access to information that enables citizens to participate in public life, hold public authority accountable to public opinion, counter 'a capture' of public institutions by special interest groups, enhance citizens' confidence in public authority, and improve the performance of public officials" (Stein 2001, 493).

In spite of the term's ubiquity, it has received surprisingly little anthropological or critical scrutiny (exceptions include Shore and Haller 2005; West and Sanders 2003). Transparency discourse, when applied to transition governments, plays on now familiar dyads between corruption and transparency, authoritarianism or socialism and democracy, and protectionism versus free markets, all of which, in turn, are embedded within linear and Eurocentric progressivist narratives (Shore and

Haller 2005). This developmental approach to corruption carries "moral and evolutionary overtones" that add "'corruption' to the list of those negative characteristics that are typically applied to the 'Other,' such as underdevelopment, poverty, ignorance, repression of women, fundamentalism, fanaticism and irrationality" (ibid., 3).

The discourse of transparency (as well as its twin, accountability) had particular salience for the border context in the NAFTA debates, the citizens' petitioning processes of the environmental side agreement, the conflict resolution mechanisms of the labor side agreement, and the border development institutions. In formal terms, the petitioning processes were designed to be open, democratic, transparent, and accessible. The NAFTA side accords employed transparency discourse as part of their justification, but this idealized discussion failed to account for the digital, educational, class, population, territorial, world systems, and visual divides that are a function of the economic arrangements that transparency discourse supports. How can transparency support democracy with access to information and the possibility of holding public authorities accountable if the target border populations cannot access the documents and procedures necessary to make this happen?

Trade, Conflict, and the "Mexican" Problem of Non-Enforcement

While Mexico and other Latin American nations were undergoing dual transitions, trade-related conflicts increasingly occupied the global stage. In the 1980s, protectionism was increasingly viewed as a regrettable historical artifact, with the path forward now unanimously grounded in the logic of free trade's invisible hand, comparative advantage, and economic integration. The trade-environment debate (Esty 2001; Harris 2000; Thomas and Weber 1999), sparked regionally by the 1991 US embargo on Mexican tuna imports, drew particular attention to these clashing agendas, as well as to proposed mechanisms for preserving the best of each for a seeming win-win. There were increasing conversations about the possibility of harmonization and civil society inclusion as trade negotiators, policy-makers and academic observers cast nets beyond mere markets reforms (Deere and Esty 2002; Estevadeoral et al. 2004; Esty 2001; Macdonald 1998) and debated the criticality of soft law mechanisms as critical to global governance (Abbott 2001; Rodríguez-Garavito 2006).

By the time the Salinas presidency and the first Bush administration began NAFTA negotiations, the economic and political stage had already been set by Salinas and his PRI predecessors (Kopinak 1995, 30). The *maquilas* on Mexico's northern border were the most tangible manifestation of the country's foray into economic liberalization. By the time of the NAFTA debates, Mexico had been rejecting ISI for over a decade. NAFTA would merely formalize that opening and deepen regional integration. As Chambers and Smith note, "NAFTA offered President Carlos Salinas de Gortari an opportunity to institutionalize and perpetuate his neoliberal economic reforms" at a time when international pressure for democratization was increasing and "Mexico no longer looked like a paragon of political civility" (Chambers and Smith 2002, 9, 10). The revelation that Salinas and the first President Bush were actively pursuing a trade deal produced pitched battles on both sides of the US-Mexico border, as well as in Canada. These battles were shaped by the irreconcilable interests of pro-neoliberal, free trade, and globalization constituencies, on the one hand, and anti-neoliberal, anti-free trade, and anti-globalization constituencies, on the other. These competing economic and cultural ideologies trumped nationalist sentiments among opposition groups, laying a firm foundation for the post-NAFTA cross-border advocacy era.

On both sides of the border, pro-NAFTA constituencies pushed economic growth as a path to a better life (Dreiling 1998, 234). Business interests engaged in a "multi-million dollar pro-NAFTA lobbying campaign" (García Urrutia 2002, 80; MacArthur 2000; Warnock 1995, 155). NAFTA support in Mexico came from elite economic interests, as well as the Mexican Confederation of Workers[2] (Englehart 1997, 326; Graubart 2005). The Salinas administration aimed to convince Mexican populations that all would benefit from NAFTA (Wise 1998, 5, 15). A 1991–1993 national level survey found that lower to middle class urban sectors anticipated an improved quality of life under free trade conditions (Davis 1998).

Throughout the negotiations, Mexican environmental, civil society, labor, and other human rights resistance and advocacy groups worked together under the broad Red Mexicana Ante el Libre Comercio (RMALC) umbrella. Resistance came especially from poor and indigenous sectors already disenfranchised by the "*proyecto salinista*" (Peña 1993). Although the Salinas administration tried to give the appearance of countrywide support for the trade treaty (Oppenheimer 1996), the

Zapatista movement entered the world stage and burst that bubble on January 1, 1994. As Harvey notes, "The fact that the uprising occurred on the day that NAFTA took effect symbolized that it was the effects of free trade . . . that lay at the root of the problems. Furthermore, it appealed fundamentally to notions of the rights and dignity of labor, of indigenous and regional ways of life, in the face of the homogenizing forces of commodification based by state power" (Harvey 2000, 74).

This popular activity was part of the civil society groundswell that was part of Mexico's democratization from below (Dreiling 1998, 237) and was nested within larger advocacy agendas, such as strengthening civil society and protecting human rights (Brooks and Fox 2002, 53; Graubart 2005, 109–110; Hogenboom 1996; Lorena Cook 1997). Environmental opposition in Mexico never grabbed the public's attention as much as the environmental front did in the United States, however, due partly to the rising influence of US environmental NGOs on domestic politics (Hogenboom 1996, 992). Mexican border environmental groups had been combating *maquila* industry racism for some time, viewing *maquilas* as foreign institutions that took advantage of the lower socio-economic status of Mexican border migrants within Mexico and internationally, and polluting the environment wantonly in a manner consistent with environmental racism (Carlos Vasquez 1993). These groups opposed NAFTA; the debate strengthened and expanded the cross-border environmental networks already in place (Bejarano 2002; Kelly 2002).

By the early 1990s, there was ample evidence of border zone environmental pollution (Barry 1994; Brenner et al. 2000; Kelly 2002, 1993; Moure Eraso et al. 1994a; Peña 1997; Simon 1997), as well as the extensive exploitation of *maquila* workers (Abrams 1979; Fernandez-Kelly 1983; Kourous 1998; Loustaunau and Sanchez Bane 1990; Moure-Eraso et al. 1994b; Peña 1997). *Maquila* labor conditions were arguably representative of sweatshops worldwide: "In the South, the exploitative labor conditions and the unfulfilled promise of employment and growth have turned *maquilas* into an icon of the failure of late twentieth-century neoliberalism" (Rodríguez-Caravito 2006, 64). Additionally, environmental degradation of the borderlands was perceived by NAFTA opponents to augur similar degradation throughout Mexico under the terms of the treaty. This galvanized environmental, labor, and human rights groups in Mexico, the United States, and Canada to protest, warning of "the negative impact a neoliberal-oriented NAFTA would have on social values, like labor rights and environmental standards" (Graubart 2005, 106). US environmental groups argued that NAFTA would encourage business to further pollute the region (Mayer 2003, 99; McFayden 1998, 2) and other Mexican states into which *maquila* industrial parks might be introduced. In sum, the NAFTA debates were situated within larger debates about global economic development and the fate of the US-Mexico border became a "stand in" ideal (Heyman 1994) for critiquing neoliberalism worldwide (Dreiling 1998, 226).

At the beginning of the debates, *maquilas* and corporate greed received the lion's share of the blame for environmental destruction and worker exploitation, but the Mexican government was eventually brought into the loop—particularly by US NAFTA opponents. The trope of Mexican corruption that had shadowed the PRI regime for years gained full force in this context. Since corruption functioned as such a pervasive trope for Mexican politics and culture under PRI rule[3], it is no surprise that corruption—articulated as lax enforcement of Mexican environmental and labor laws—became a flashpoint in the anti-NAFTA campaign. NAFTA was touted as a cure-all, as the Bush administration maintained that "whatever defects exist will be cured by the higher economic growth that will result from NAFTA. The Bush Administration argued that the Agreement would permit more resources to be invested in effective monitoring of workplace safety and labor enforcement standards" (Levinson 1993, 225).

The debates eventuated in an assessment of the Mexican legal system that, ultimately, produced the side accords as ostensible antidote to the problem of Mexican non-enforcement of national law. They revealed that Mexico was not a lawless nation and that, in fact, the country had quite sophisticated labor and environmental laws. That revelation allowed NAFTA critics to focus on corruption and the ample lacuna between laws on the books and effective enforcement of those laws. At that point, debates among opposition groups (US opposition, in particular) focused on the issue of how to ensure that Mexican environmental and labor laws would be enforced should NAFTA pass. The following statement is representative of views that began to predominate in environmental circles: "Foreign investors, particularly American investors, were attracted to Mexico's maquiladora industry because of Mexico's lax enforcement of its environmental laws . . . The current conditions at the border are mainly attributable to Mexico's lack of environmental controls" (Ellis 1996, 622–623, 630; see also Brenner et al. 2000; Carlos Vasquez 1993; Mikulas 1999; Reblin 1996; Russell 1994, 256–257).

At this point, and unbeknownst to them, NAFTA critics had begun to pave the road that would eventually lead to NAFTA's passage. As Garvey has argued, it was not NAFTA per se "but the relatively brief side Agreements on labor and the environment that became the focus of the political debate that decided the fate of NAFTA" (Garvey 1995, 439–440).

The transnational advocacy networks, or TANs (Rodríguez-Garavito 2006), produced by grassroots NAFTA debates were as important to labor as they were to environmental interests. They had particular relevance for labor, not only in terms of the cross-border organizing that emerged in the immediate pre- and post-NAFTA days, but also for a novel awareness of the intertwined fates of both North and South labor. Independent Mexican labor unions, particularly the Authentic Labor Front[4] (Hathaway 2000), networked extensively with US unions (García Urrutia 2002; Graubart 2005, 111; Lorena Cook 1997) and drew attention to the "legal obstacle to achieving freedom of association and independent unions in Mexico" (García Urrutia 2002, 79). The oppositional stance of El Frente Auténtico del Trabajo (FAT) and other organizations within RMALC encouraged cross-border advocacy after NAFTA was signed, laying the foundation for a "new transnational political arena" (Lorena Cook 1997, 521).

US labor opposition to NAFTA was rooted initially in opposition to American jobs going to Mexican workers and, eventually, in a sense that all workers, regardless of nationality, shared a potential common destiny. A race to the bottom was a destiny to be avoided. "NAFTA was widely seen by American workers as the devil incarnate, threatening their jobs, weakening their already limited bargaining power, and lowering labor standards and living conditions" (Brooks and Fox 2002, 12; cf. García Urrutia 2002, 82; McFayden 1998, 7). As one US union representative put it, "The wages and conditions of Mexican workers are the new floor of our economy. To put it a little simplistically, either our wages and conditions are going to go down to the level of Mexico's, or we're going to figure out ways to help Mexicans raise their wages and conditions up to our levels" (quoted in La Botz 1995, 146).

As with the case of the environmental front, one of the strategies of US labor was to focus lobbying efforts on the now apparent problem of Mexican non-enforcement of labor laws (Garvey 1995, 442; Graubart 2005; MacArthur 2000, 177; Pomeroy 1996, 772). The debates had generated enough information that it became apparent that factory inspections of *maquilas* were rarely performed, due to the poorly staffed and overburdened offices of the Secretaría de Trabajo y Prevención Social (STPS) and Instituto Mexicano de Seguro Social (IMSS). A 1990 study by the US Office of Technology Assessment, "US-Mexico Trade: Pulling Together or Pulling Apart," had determined that "inspections of work places, particularly maquiladora operations, are infrequent and only in rare cases are sanctions applied by inspectors" (quoted in Fuente Muñiz 1995, 393). In a similar vein, it was also a well-known fact at the time that labor in Mexico—particularly from the 1970s onward (Middlebrook 1989)—was being widely repressed by CTM practices at the same time that the Salinista government was delivering an onslaught against many of the powerful labor leaders in the country, including the famed Don Agapito of Tamaulipas (Guerrero-Miller and Ayala 1993). The government and CTM were becoming increasingly repressive and negligent in the enforcement of labor law in order to attract foreign investment (cf. Isa 1999, 196) in a manner consistent with global first world investment and third world hosting patterns (Leopold 1988). Additionally, under the aggressively liberalizing conditions of the eighties, they sought to keep labor costs low as part of the country's "comparative advantage" (Fuentes Muñiz 1995, 384; Middlebrook and Zepeda 2003, 15), ultimately producing what Fuentes Muñiz refers to as a deformation of Mexican labor law (1995, 380).

The upshot of a changing US discourse about Mexican corruption, recombined with an increasingly united US and Mexican labor opposition, was to shift the focus of US labor away from the issue of Mexicans allegedly stealing jobs, and toward the structural conditions that encouraged the movement of capital southward. To protect its own interests, US labor recognized that it had to protect those of Mexican workers' interests, and to protect Mexican workers' interests, it had to work for greater enforcement of Mexican law. As Evans put it, "NAFTA has (inadvertently) shifted the definition of the problem from Mexican workers themselves to the political/legal barriers that stand in the way of Mexican workers' being able to organize effective unions" (Evans 2000, 235).[5]

In sum, constituencies within both the pro- and anti-NAFTA camps found common ground in their perception about the effects of lax enforcement of Mexican labor and environmental laws. This consensus was fundamental to the forging of the side accords that, in turn, were the key to NAFTA's passage (Garvey 1995).

Mexican Labor and Environmental Laws

NAFTA advocates and opponents were entirely correct in pointing to the existence of strong labor and environmental laws in Mexico. While the country's strong environmental laws were a more recent phenomenon (Mumme 1992), Mexico's labor laws were developed much earlier in the twentieth century, long before comparable laws were developed in the United States, and largely against great resistance from the latter's government and industry. As Isa notes, "Mexico's labor laws provide many of the same protections for its workers as those of the United States or other developed countries. In fact, Mexico's legal protections against employment discrimination are theoretically among the world's most comprehensive" (Isa 1999, 186). Stringent labor laws were an important legacy of the Mexican Revolution of 1910–1917 and complemented other populist ideals, such as anti-imperialism, anti-clericalism, land reform, and the creation of *ejidos* (Guerra and Torriente 1997, 512, 513; cf. Fuente Muñiz 1995, 379). Fuentes Muñiz describes this early twentieth century prescience regarding labor law as "tutelary" in nature; "that is, the principle that law must intervene on the side of the worker in order to equalize the labor-management relationship" (Fuentes Muñiz 1995, 384).

Labor rights were codified first in the 1917 Constitution and, later, in the 1931 Ley Federal de Trabajo (LFT) or Federal Labor Law. The LFT was so comprehensive that it still forms the basis of workers' rights today (Quintero Ramírez and Romo Aguilar 2001; Middlebrook and Quintero Ramírez 1998; Middlebrook 1995, 50–51). As will be discussed in Chapter 3, Rosalia marched through the *colonias* of Matamoros with a copy of the LFT under her arm in her efforts to teach workers their rights as part of her work with the Comité Fronterizo de Obreros (CFO). The LFT contains sophisticated health and safety regulations addressing details of workers' health and rights, including compensation, risk prevention, and mandatory employee training. For example, Sections XV to XVII of Article 132 maintain that the health of employees is the responsibility of employers, Section XXIV of Article 132 requires that companies allow workplace inspections, and Article 123 prohibits unhealthy or dangerous work (Quintero Ramírez and Romo Aguilar 2001). The LFT also includes the *Reglamento Federal de Seguridad, Higiene y Medio Ambiente de Trabajo* (Regulation for Safety, Hygiene and Environment in the Workplace) which provides details on the handling and storage of toxic chemicals and the obligation of employers to inform workers about the type of substances they handle. Middlebrook concisely summarizes the breadth and depth of the LFT, noting that it defines in great detail the "character of individual and collective labor contracts, including the legal obligations of workers and employers; requirements for working hours and working conditions, wages, and enterprise-level employee profit sharing; compensation for different kinds of work-related injuries and health problems; and the responsibilities of state labor authorities" (Middlebrook 1995, 63).

Although Mexican labor laws were developed long before similar protections emerged for US labor, Mexican environmental laws emerged only in the early 1970s and have largely been modeled on US regulations and institutions (Carlos Vasquez 1993, 363). For example, in 1971, the first comprehensive environmental law was passed, the Ley Federal para Prevenir y Controlar la Contaminación Ambiental (Federal Law for the Prevention and Control of Environmental Pollution), followed in 1982 by the Ley Federal de Protección del Ambiente. While the first was a fairly direct response to the environmental pollution problems that were becoming increasingly apparent in the 1970s (particularly in Mexico City), the second was more directly concerned with conservation and preservation of wilderness. In 1988, the Ley General del Equilibrio Ecologico y la Protección al Ambiente (LGEEPA) or General Law of Ecological Equilibrium and Environmental Protection was also passed. It consists of a set of regulations governing mining, forestry, and waters. There are a handful of additional national level regulations pertaining to both pollution regulation and conservation, in addition to a number of accords, initiatives, and agreements (e.g., La Paz) aimed specifically at border environment problems.

The NAFTA Side Accords

Facing formidable opposition from labor and environmental organizations, trade negotiators in Mexico and the United States spearheaded the development of two side agreements to NAFTA: the North American Agreement on Environmental Cooperation (NAAEC) and the North American Agreement on Labor Cooperation (NAALC).[6] Importantly, the push for the side accords was based on perceptions of Mexico, not the United States or Canada (Mayer 2003, 104, 108). Although Canada was released from the possibility of sanctions, Mexico was not (Fuentes

Muñiz 1995, 398, 400; Mayer 2003, 108). Trade negotiators worked on the agreements throughout 1993, eventually mollifying US labor and environmental groups (Mayer 2003, 100, 105). Renewed US demands for the trade treaty put Mexican officials in a difficult position; they had expended all of their bargaining chips, and presidential candidate Clinton's position was widely perceived in Mexico to be pandering to labor (Fuentes Muñiz 1995, 396) and environmental interests (Araya 2002, 64). Mexican negotiators interpreted the side accords as a slight to their national sovereignty, but saw no choice but to yield.[7] The principal complaint among NAFTA opponents was that both agreements lacked enforcement provisions (Evans 1995; Pomeroy 1996, 791–792; Mayer 2002; McArthur 2000, 184–185). Of the two, the environmental side agreement was more pivotal than the labor side in guaranteeing US Congressional support (Dreiling 1998, 221; MacArthur 2000), but US Congressional support for NAFTA's environmental side also sealed the fate of Mexican labor.

The agreements have a threefold purpose: (1) to continue conversations among NGOs, border populations, government institutions, and others about issues raised by the NAFTA debates; (2) to provide a transnational legal forum consisting of commissions, administrative offices, and petitioning processes that allow these conversations to continue (but in a state-sanctioned and legitimated venue); and (3) to contribute to Mexico's improved enforcement of national environmental and labor laws. The building of side protectionist measures into the letter of NAFTA law defied the very logic of economic liberalization. As Harris notes, "the most commonly proposed solution to this problem [of disparities in environmental regulation between countries] is the 'harmonization' of environmental standards—the acceptance of common standards by nations within a free-trade area. But note that this solution is not 'free trade' but something else—the creation of a supranational authority with the power to set environmental standards" (Harris 2000, 119).

As protectionist measures, the accords' passage marked the first time that "side" or "soft law" agreements (Abbott 2001) regarding health, safety, or the environment were passed in tandem with an international trade agreement (Deere and Esty 2002; Garvey 1995; Thomas and Weber 1999). Their basic purpose is to ensure that each signatory nation enforces its own actually existing environmental and labor laws. They are carefully constructed so as to prohibit legal infringement of any one or two nations on the sovereignty of the other, preserving instead a complex, pluralistic, legal web (Merry 1992) of transnational processes and soft enforcement that has, in retrospect, confirmed their toothless characterization by NAFTA critics. They have, essentially, a watchdog function in which the failure of any one nation to comply with its own laws can theoretically result in economic sanctions by the other two.[8] Sanctions have never been used.[9] Plaintiff populations must exhaust all domestic means of dispute resolution before taking their allegations to the international level.[10]

The North American Agreement on Environmental Cooperation established tri-national commissions, citizens' petitioning, and dispute resolution mechanisms (see, for example, Cho 1996; Ellis 1996; Ferretti 2002; Garvey 1995; McKinney 2000, 90–222; Mikulas 1993; Reblin 1996; Specht 1998; Yang 2005). It created the Commission on Environmental Cooperation (CEC), made up of a council, secretariat, and Joint Public Advisory Committee (JPAC). The commission receives and reviews petitions from citizens' groups and NGOs. The way in which the petition process works is as follows: A citizens' group or NGO files a petition with the CEC. If the petition is approved with respect to correctly following formal procedures, and if the substance of the petition determines it worthy of review, it is passed on to the Joint Public Advisory Committee (JPAC), which advises the Council with scientific and technical information. An investigation may ensue. If found guilty of violation of environmental laws or, as often happens, failing to perform adequate environmental assessment studies, the remaining two nations have the option of imposing sanctions against the violating or host nation.

The NAAEC has a parallel structure devoted exclusively to problems of sustainable development (particularly water, solid waste, or waste water management) along the border. This includes the Border Environment Cooperation Commission (BECC) and its lending partner, the North American Development Bank (NADBank). Together, the two are intended to (1) promote sustainable development in the region; (2) establish linkages between local, regional, and state level institutions; and (3) certify project proposals and process loan applications. In essence, the BECC reviews and certifies loan requests and, if approved, the NADBank issues the requested loans. The environmental side accord was a renewed attempt at cooperation on cross-border environmental problems where previous attempts (e.g., the 1983 La Paz Agreement, the 1992

Border Plan) had failed. Its institutions build on existing infrastructure and concerns while, at the same time, addressing new ones raised by the NAFTA debates.

The labor side accord and its corollary institutions mirror the environmental accord, with the exception of the latter's BECC and NAD-Bank. The North American Agreement on Labor Cooperation created the Commission for Labor Cooperation (CLC), composed of representatives of the relevant labor institutions and ministries, as well as dispute resolution processes (Aceves 1999; Delp et al. 2004; Garvey 1995; Graubart 2005; Guerra and Torriente 1997; Isa 1998; Mazuyer 2001; McKinney 2000, 33–89; Pomeroy 1996). The function of the agreement is to ensure that each nation complies with its own existing labor laws, which include child labor laws, unions and the right to organize, and occupational safety and health issues in the workplace. Similar to the environmental accord, the only real teeth to the agreement consists of its dispute resolution process that can ostensibly result in economic sanctions of one nation by the other two.

The labor accord is best understood through a practical explanation of how it is supposed to function with regard to citizens' complaints and petitions. The Spektra plant petition, elaborated on in subsequent chapters, provides a prototypical example.

Spektra plant workers complained first about factory health and safety violations to the Junta de Conciliación y Arbitraje, or workers' tribunal. They then traveled to the Tamaulipan state capital of Ciudad Victoria to file requests for inspections with the Secretaría del Trabajo y Previsión Social (STPS) and Instituto Mexicano de Seguro Social (IMSS). Once these requests had been submitted and reviewed, and the workers found that conditions in the plant remained unchanged, they had recourse to the labor side accord petitioning process. With the aid of a US-based NGO, a complaint was filed on their behalf with the US National Administrative Office (US NAO) in San Antonio, Texas. Upon the filing of a complaint, the appropriate labor administration office (in this case, the US NAO) requests consultations with the labor ministry office of the country in which the violations are alleged to have taken place. Ministerial level consultations are arranged to discuss the labor laws allegedly being violated, organize investigations, and resolve the complaint. If the dispute is not resolved at this ministerial level, petitioners may request the establishment of an Evaluation Committee of Experts (ECE). After investigation by the ECE, results are reported back to the

CLC. At that point, there are more deliberations and an arbitration panel may be convened. If the arbitration panel deems that some action must be taken, it seeks to find a resolution agreeable to the respective governments or, in the absence of a mutually agreeable resolution, can begin the organization of monetary sanctions. All of the above happened in the case of the Spektra workers' petition, with the exception of the organization of sanctions.

Both accords are supposed to provide oversight and accountability procedures that ostensibly deliver justice in an idealized world in which all have equal access to information and education and, thus, the opportunity to advocate for their rights as citizens (cf. Goldschmidt 2002). In reality, they represent largely Internet-mediated, labyrinthine, and cumbersome bureaucratic mazes that discourage practical participation. The ideal world scenario in which the accords were crafted is no more applicable to the border region than to any other area of the world—and conspicuously less so. Since the side accords' bureaucratic processes are mostly on-line, the digital divide makes them even more challenging to navigate than brick and mortar bureaucracies. Even were a typical *maquila* worker to have the time, energy, money, and resources to sit in a cybercafé and read the texts of the agreements and the steps required to submit a petition, they would most likely find the texts incomprehensible because they are written in legal-bureaucratic language that would typically require professional legal consulting help to decipher. Even admitting the possibility that one might successfully navigate either of the labyrinths, Garvey (1995) has pointed out that, if equity and justice had been the true goal of the accords, then an international and permanent tribunal might have been established, such as that for the European Union, so that justice could not get hijacked or thrown overboard in the course of *realpolitik*. Instead, the side accords are arbitrated through flexible processes and ad hoc committees constituted not by objective, disinterested legal professionals, but by interested parties of states and governments. The informality of the petitioning process allows for considerable politicking, stalemating, and wielding of political power when necessary, particularly since the negotiations are between government agencies.

Soft Law, Pluralism, and the Absence of Common Standards

The agreements were created with the alleged intent of providing a legitimate space for public dialogue around issues raised by NAFTA opponents so that, in the *realpolitik* rush to have the trade treaty signed and approved, it did not appear that the environmental and labor conversations were being prematurely foreclosed upon. To some degree, they may represent what Charles Hale has referred to as the shift "from protest to proposal" (Hale 2005, 18) as a technique of neoliberal governance.

Within the elaborate, tri-national legal labyrinth of the side accords, the question remains of how, precisely, were they to be enforced? The answer to this question is twofold. First, the side accords created a situation of consummate legal pluralism ensuring enforcement and discipline of any one nation by the other two. Whatever enforcement that did exist would come circuitously: first, by the grassroots or NGO level organization filing a petition; then through ministerial level consultations and investigations; and, finally, via one or both of the remaining governments pressuring the offending party to reform its ways. More direct enforcement mechanisms would have undermined the sovereignty of the participating nations.

Second, transparency and exposure of violations (guaranteed by the petitioning process itself) were presumed to undergird enforcement. Indeed, transparency was virtually a stand-in for enforcement, as the following labor accord commentary indicates: "While the NAALC process lacks traditional enforcement mechanisms, it can promote compliance by increasing the transparency of state behavior, monitoring state behavior, and ruling publicly on the lawfulness of state behavior" (Aceves 1999, 225). It is precisely the accords' alleged transparency that allows non-state actors to ensure compliance and accountability from below, completing the democratization loop: "Transparency and monitoring are facilitated by allowing these nonstate actors to submit petitions for review" (ibid.).

The accords provide a virtual prototypical situation of legal pluralism (Merry 1997, 1992a, 1992b; Rodríguez-Garavito 2006, 80–85) in a globalized world, but this is pluralism at the level of process, rather than substance. While the thorny issue of national sovereignty was of course discussed in the NAFTA debates (Deere and Esty 2002), the threat of infringement was minimized by not requiring substantive change to any one nation's national law and, second, by placing the burden of enforcement (or at least whistle blowing) on the backs of laboring or environmentally threatened populations—rather than directly into the hands of states themselves. The substantive content of each sovereign nation's laws remained untouched (with the subtext of the debates and accords suggesting that Mexico would become more legal and less corrupt through "imitation effect," while an international process ensured oversight. "Difference" between Mexico and the United States or other first world modern democratic nations was here codified in a different way; no longer a matter of type, it became a matter of degree. Moreover, in the case of Mexico, the side accords' petitioning processes were deemed an appropriate mechanism for indoctrinating seemingly unenlightened Mexican populations into the virtues of democratic political culture and providing democratic consolidation at the grassroots—a win-win if there ever was one (Simon 2007).

Due to the soft law aspect of the accords—as well as their contemporaneity with global level discourses about corruption, transparency, sustainability, accountability, and public dialogue—the language generated by the side accord institutions (evident in their announcements, email discussion lists, web pages, and self-representation) became redolent of all the above terminology. In the absence of common standards and direct enforcement possibilities, the side accords were argued by their proponents (and, to some degree, their detractors) to have the potential of nudging participant countries toward greater harmonization of labor and environmental standards.

The side accords were built on an unproblematized conception of transparency, as well as a willful neglect of the reality of the digital divide and partial vision (at best) available to Mexican border populations. Transparency undergirded their anticipated functions as combined citizens' petitioning and watchdog forums (Graubart 2005; Guerra and Torriente 1997; McFayden 1998; Pomeroy 1996), spaces for public dialogue in which citizens and policymakers alike could coordinate, share information, submit petitions, and expect full accountability. As Pomeroy notes with respect to the labor accord, "The supplemental agreement was seen as establishing a new forum in which the United States and Mexico could analyze and improve labor policies and working conditions together" (Pomeroy 1996, 789). This intent to foster cooperation is apparent, for example, in the NAALC's Article One statement of objectives:

The objectives of this agreement are to:
1. improve working conditions and living standards in each Party's territory;
2. promote, to the maximum extent possible, the labor principles set out in Annex 1;

3. encourage cooperation to promote innovation and rising levels of productivity and quality;
4. encourage publication and exchange of information, data development and coordination, and joint studies to enhance mutually beneficial understanding of the laws and institutions governing labor in each Party's territory;
5. pursue cooperative labor-related activities on the basis of mutual benefit;
6. promote compliance with, and effective enforcement by each Party's labor law; and
7. foster transparency in the administration of labor law.[11]

Both critics and proponents relied on the so-called sunshine effect for their relative optimism, that the "agreement would achieve enforcement of domestic labor laws through exposure of problems and exchange of information" (Pomeroy 1996, 789). The NAALC would "promote reform through public embarrassment" (Englehart 1997, 388) and "oversight mechanisms are aimed at enhancing the public's understanding of labor laws and the transparency of enforcement rather than punishment through trade sanctions" (ibid., 351). Becker, then president of the United Steelworkers, remarked in 1999, "This is our strongest weapon to expose the horrors facing workers who try to organize in Mexico" (cited in Graubart 2005, 99). Similarly a United States Trade Representative (USTR) report maintained the following:

> The NAALC has contributed to transparency and public debate on labor law and enforcement issues that, to a large extent, did not exist before. (. . .) Moreover, the NAALC has provided an effective channel for members of the public and interested groups to highlight their concerns that a NAFTA government may not be meeting its obligations.[12]

In spite of the accords' creators and institutions' professed commitment to accessibility, inclusion, transparency and accountability, however, the accords have been roundly criticized by the public, their target audience, for the relative absence of these intended characteristics. CEC petitioners, for example, have been frustrated by the petitioning process's operational characteristics:

- complexity and ambiguity
- lack of enforcement mechanisms and expedited timeline (three and a half years is allowed for resolution of a complaint)
- lack of opportunities for petitioner input
- heavy bureaucratization, leading to CEC rejection of petitions due to procedural errors
- lack of evidence that publicly solicited comments actually impact CEC or BECC operations
- absence of recourse for further action once a factual record is generated by the CEC and the case closed (Carlsen and Salazar 2002; Graves 1999; Thomas and Weber 1999).

Petitioning workers have had similar concerns. As Delp and others note, the labor accord process "excludes those very workers from meaningful participation" (Delp et al. 2004, ix). Delp summarizes a number of complaints that are littered across the labor accord petitioning process when she succinctly states: "Workers and their advocates were excluded from initial NAFTA negotiations, are prevented from participating in the NAALC process beyond presenting the initial submission, are not provided with results of ministerial consultations designed to resolve their own case, and have been excluded from the newly formed government-to-government health and safety working group" (ibid.). In addition to all these weaknesses, the labor side accord suffers an additional dubious reputation because of early Mexican petitioners—notably those of Han Young plant, but others as well (including Spektra workers)—being subject to union-busting, physical harassment, intimidation, and loss of employment as a result of having submitted a petition. It is these types of concerns that have encouraged perceptions of the side accord institutions as top-down affairs that merely provide a performance of participation and democracy.

Last but not least, secrecy and lack of oversight still plague both of the accords' operations. This lack of transparency is amply illustrated in a letter submitted by disappointed petitioners to then-US Labor Secretary Elaine Chao in 2002: "we were surprised to learn from you that ministerial consultations with Mexican officials are currently underway (. . .) given that we, the submitters of that petition, had not even been notified that an agreement to proceed with ministerial consultations had been reached."[13]

Sustainable Development and the Participatory Ideal

Alongside increasing pressure at the global level to reconcile trade and non-trade issues, the participatory ideal within sustainable development substantially supported policy makers' framing of the accords as tools to aid Mexico's democratic transition.

The rise of sustainable development parallels the rise of neoliberal. economics as development orthodoxy. As a development paradigm, "sustainable development" emerged in the late 1980s and early 1990s following the 1987 publication of the World Commission on Environment Development's (WCED's) report, *Our Common Future* (a.k.a., the Bruntland Commission Report). The classic and most oft-cited definition of sustainable development comes directly from the report: "development that meets the needs of the present without compromising the ability of future generations to meet their own needs" (WCED 1987, 43). The mandate of the report was deliberately broad, but with the clear intention of reconciling "two old enemies—economic growth and the preservation of the environment" (Escobar 1996, 49). Various critics (e.g., Adams 1990, 70–76; Escobar 1996; Sachs 1992; Visvanathan 1991) pointed out that the WCED approach attempted to square these divergent interests through a techno-managerial approach that simultaneously retrenched western reductionist approaches to nature as environment (or resource) and provided a blueprint for its successful management. As a model, the report failed to reconcile the irreconcilable conflict between environmental preservation and an economic orthodoxy based first and foremost on growth (Harris 2000)—nor has sustainable development succeeded in doing so since that time. The report introduced a new technico-managerial vocabulary for trade and development discussions that is now commonplace, not least because the mandate of the report was so broad that it touched virtually every domain of social life and purported to answer every challenge that had befuddled development experts until then. Concepts introduced or elaborated upon in the WCED report[14] include participation, grassroots involvement, empowerment, public dialogue, transparency, accountability, poverty eradication, efficiency and democratization, alongside environmental protections. Most of these terms are numbingly familiar today. Adams claims that *Our Common Futures'* "starting point was deliberately broad, and a move to limit its concern simply to the 'environment' was firmly resisted" (Adams 1990, 70). In other words, although introduced via a report ostensibly about the effects of development on the environment, the scope of sustainability thereafter came to include virtually all domains of social life, including a newfound valorization of participation.

While this new valorization of community and participation emerged from the terms of the sustainable development discourse, it has since been hijacked by free trade advocates. These ideas migrated unchecked from sustainability discourse to the free trade based discussions and debates about NAFTA. While classical, neo-classical, liberal and neo-liberal economics have always been fundamental to development, it is not the case that other development terms have always been part of free trade discussions. Just as participation has yet to guarantee equitable development policies, it is not clear to what degree it may guarantee the growth of democratic political culture in Mexico or elsewhere.

Neoliberalism was presumed to support the economic arm of Mexico's dual transition, and participatory development—through the side accords' petitioning processes—to support the political arm: "Heroic claims are made for participatory approaches to development. Participation of community members is assumed to contribute to enhanced efficiency and effectiveness of investment and to promote processes of democratization and empowerment" (Cleaver 2001, 36). Rajagopal argues that development's recent interest in democracy is a direct consequence of post-Cold War transition theory: "Only recently has it [development] increasingly come to rely heavily on the rhetoric of participation, empowerment, human rights, and democracy as essential aspects of supposedly authentic 'development'" (Rajagopal 2003, 146).

These ideas about the importance of participation had particular ramifications in the context of the NAFTA controversy. They informed the side accords and, equally important, led to the creation of citizens' petitioning processes of the side accord dispute resolution mechanisms. They demonstrate concretely the neoliberal conviction that greater wealth lays the foundation for greater democracy. Beyond their ostensible purpose in reconciling the two irreconcilable interests of economic growth and environmental protection (otherwise known as trade and non-trade interests), they only make sense in terms of this purported linchpin they offered as participatory linkage between democracy and development. This is because the NAFTA debates took place within the discursive terms of sustainable development already established within the international community: "In the 1990s, before the signing of the agreement, the national and international environmental community became increasingly active on the contested terrain of 'sustainable development'" (Dreilling 1998, 231). Dreilling goes on to note "NAFTA's exhortation of 'sustainable development' in the preamble" (ibid.), indicating the centrality of the sustainability ideal to the trade treaty. The promise of continued participatory possibilities after the signing of NAFTA (via the side accords' petitioning and dispute resolution procedures) was intended to quash accusations that NAFTA was a top-down affair brokered in distant capitals on the backs of border populations. The accords were to provide a state legitimated public space for ongoing dialogue about labor and environmental concerns (Graves 1999; Mumme 1999).

In conclusion, a range of actors and interests came together to produce NAFTA's environmental and labor side agreements, which ultimately secured the passage of NAFTA. These interests included sustainable development ideals as they became linked to democratization, Mexico's political and economic transformations of the twentieth century, the rise of neoliberalism as development orthodoxy, and a widely shared political conviction that transparency would lay the foundation for fair and democratic government. The side accords instantiated many of these beliefs, even as they were also a consequence of them.

Chapter 2

*Space and Place
in the Borderlands*

The border between Mexico and the United States has often been referred to as the longest boundary in the world to separate the so-called first and third worlds (cf. Alvarez 1995, 451). Gloria Anzaldúa's famous description of the border as an "open wound" where the "Third World grates up against the first and bleeds" (1987, 3) has often been summoned to drive home this empirically well-documented point. Anzaldúa's prescient words have, in recent years, been transformed from (rough) metaphor to visceral reality as border cities like Ciudad Juarez (Cd. Juarez), Reynosa, Nuevo Laredo, Matamoros, and others have been transformed into bloody battlegrounds for drug cartel turf wars. Since the relative success of US anti-drug efforts in closing off Caribbean and waterborne trafficking routes in the late 1980s (Andreas 1998) and the unfortunate drug violence that has engulfed parts of Mexico since the launching of former President Felipe Calderón's Drug War in 2006 (Castañeda 2010; Cockcroft 2010; Grayson 2010), the line has come to serve a different function. Now it helps to corral violence within Mexican border cities, as demonstrated by the especially horrific violence in Cd. Juarez since 2008 (Campbell 2011) or the massacre of seventy-two aspiring migrants just outside Matamoros in the spring of 2010.

As a productive limit to state sovereignty and territoriality (Heyman 1999), the US-Mexico border has supported the clustering of off-shore assembly plants, with all their attendant conditions, on the southern side of the US-Mexico border. As a territorial limit, the border is productive because it has historically accommodated and reinforced postmodern production regimes of flexible production and accumulation (Harvey 1989). The territorial limits of modern nation-states are essential components of the globalized capitalism that took root from the early 1970s onward. They are not incidental to, but constitutive of, contemporary global capitalist production regimes. The borders of modern nation-states—and the discordant environmental, labor, and human rights protection regimes they preserve—make present-day flexible and transnational production processes both possible and highly productive. The Mexican side of the US-Mexico border is one of the most obvious and instructive examples of this global phenomenon.

This chapter provides a sketch of borderlands history, with a focus on the lower Rio Bravo/Rio Grande region. As ethnographic setting, the border region is decidedly liminal and has been so since the first western advancing Anglo-Saxon populations encountered the northward moving Spanish conquistadores, and as each ran amuck over the indigenous populations that had previously inhabited American and Mexican territories (Truett 1999; Stern 1998; Worcester 1988). The first section briefly sketches out general borderlands history, with particular focus on the dynamics of the Lower Rio Grande/Rio Bravo region. It does not pretend to do justice to the extraordinarily rich historical literature devoted to this topic. The second portion is devoted to the border's more recent history, in which the region has been produced and reproduced by the globalizing and spatializing forces of transnational capital. Neoliberalism and the *maquila* industry stand out as particularly important non-local forces that have produced both border populations and the conditions in which they live, even as these global forces intertwine and interact with local forces. Both have come together to produce the borderlands as a marginal zone vis-à-vis its respective nation-states (cf. Das and Poole 2004).

The US-Mexico Borderlands

The term borderlands was first used by historian Herbert Bolton in his 1921 book, *The Spanish Borderlands* (cited in Truett 1999). For Bolton, the American West was but one of two equally important moving frontiers shaping the region, and it was the meeting of these two frontiers that produced the borderlands as cultural contact zone (cf. Stern 1998; Worcester 1988). Bolton was a student of the famed frontier theorist, Frederick Jackson Turner, but he also turned Turner's thesis on its head. Unlike Turner, who had theorized the American West through a largely

Anglo-Saxon conquest lens (arguing that the act of taming the West built American democratic character), Bolton drew attention to the fact that the conquered regions had previously been Spanish territory, even as he also neglected the histories of the Native American populations (Truett 1999). For him and his followers, there were multiple frontiers (cf. Weber 1988, xii) rather than a single one ordained by Manifest Destiny. "Bolton argued that the borderlands found their greatest significance not within a one way narrative of European-American colonization, but rather as the 'meeting place and fusing place of two streams of European civilization, one coming from the south, the other from the north'" (Truett 1999, 164). This border only became fixed as a permanent territorial marker with the end of the Mexican-American War in 1848 and the signing of the Treaty of Guadalupe Hidalgo.

Stern has also described the early borderlands as a "diffuse zone of acculturation" and a "complex zone of cultural, social, economic, genetic, military, political, religious and linguistic interaction between many different groups of people" (Stern 1998, 157) that made the colonial Spanish and Mexican frontier experience unlike the US frontier experience. Whereas the West functioned as both escape valve and opportunity for American pioneers, the Spanish colonial frontier was essentially an extension of colonial society. It was, therefore, a place for marginalized or the underclass: "In the Spanish Borderlands they were escaped black slaves, mestizos, and mulattos chaffing at discrimination, runaway mission Indians, Spanish presidial deserters, itinerant miners and peddlers, and assorted malcontents—horse and cattle thieves, murderers, and renegades" (Stern 1998, 158).

Many authors have described the pre-Mexican-American War period as a comparatively harmonious one in which the challenges of settler life took precedence over national politics or loyalties. There was relative interethnic harmony that mirrored the fact that all shared a common geographic space and faced similar challenges (Richardson 1999; Truett 1999). After the Texas declaration of Independence in 1836 and the Mexican-American War of 1846–1848, the region became rife with everyday violence; cattle rustling, lynching of Mexican-Americans by Anglo settlers, and raids from one side of the border to the next became the norm (Richardson 1999, 5–8). This was due partly to the ways in which the newly founded US-Mexico border mapped novel national and ethnic identities onto existing populations, and it provides an early example of how nonlocal factors have often had dire consequences for the locale of the border region. When the US-Mexico war ended, many ethnic Mexicans who had originally settled South Texas or the Rio Grande area became second-class citizens overnight vis-à-vis their Anglo neighbors. Although cross-border familial or community networks persisted then, as they do now, "the borderlands became more divided than ever, as land and life split into different worlds" (Truett 1999, 169).

Low-grade violence escalated to a new level with the onset of the Mexican Revolution in 1910 (Meed 1992; cf. Johnson 2004, 275), the use of the border for arms smuggling, United States meddling in Mexican internal politics, and cross-border skirmishes. For those of Mexican origin, the collective sense of threat was perhaps most vividly captured by the Ballad of Gregorio Cortez, and eloquently described by famed border anthropologist and folklorist Américo Paredes in *"With His Pistol in His Hand": A Border Ballad and Its Hero* (1958). This *corrido* chronicled the shooting of an American, South Texas sheriff by a Mexican farmer and the subsequent vicious hunt for Cortez by the Texas Rangers and posses. Tellingly, the initial shooting resulted from a simple miscommunication, but quickly spiraled into a heated manhunt fueled by the ethnic hatred, suspicion, and paranoia that shaped the region at the time. As Saldivar notes in his commentary on Paredes' august work, *corridos* are meant to demonstrate collective, rather than individual sensibilities. The experience of being hunted like an animal, assumed guilty without trial, and the terrors of vigilante justice were meant "to stand not as an individual but as an epic-like construction of the South Texas societies that interpellated him. As is well known, Cortez's fate, for Paredes, cannot be distinguished from communal fate" (Saldivar 1997, 40). Cortez's fate was a crystallization of the ethnic tensions that saturated the border region in the early twentieth century and which, to different degrees and through different mechanisms, continue in the contemporary era.

Lower Rio Grande History

The Lower Rio Grande Valley region sits in an alluvial plain extending outward from the river. In times past, the river would sometimes overflow its banks, naturally irrigating the flood plains that surrounded it. Also in times past, the Lower Rio Grande was lined with extensive Sabal palms, leading to its naming by Spanish explorers as the *Rio de Palmas*. The palms once extended from a fairly lush area of vegetation at the mouth of the river far up its length. However, "the centuries of clearing for farms and communities have today reduced the Sabal palms known by Cabeza de Vaca to one last stand in a small Audubon preserve outside Brownsville, and a withering drought had this summer [2002] left most of the wetlands as dry as chalk" (Reid 2004, xix). Spanish explorer, Cabeza de Vaca, found his way across the Gulf of Mexico and to the River of Palms after being shipwrecked. There he was adopted into a Native American tribe believed by many to have been Coahuiltecan.

During the early years of conquest and settlement, the Lower Rio Grande Valley remained somewhat below the Spanish Crown's radar (Zavaleta 1986). The French and English were able to settle the area heavily. The relative quiet of the early settlements came to an abrupt end after Mexico's independence in 1822, which led the decolonized state to establish area outposts. At the time, the small, relatively bucolic, and dispersed river communities were converted into a strategic military outpost and given the name Matamoros (Zavaleta 1986, 131–132, 135).

The region changed dramatically after the Texas Declaration of Independence in 1836 and the Mexican-American War of 1846–1848. Although originally located within the cultural contact zone of the Spanish Borderlands, the area was now located on the southern boundary of the United States and the northern border of Mexico. The Rio Bravo/Grande was made a permanent territorial marker between the two emergent nation-states. Although the Matamoros-Brownsville area had not moved, the region suddenly became peripheral. Later author and border native José David Saldivar described the necessary respatialization of the "native" in order to understand his or her own identity: "I tried, like Paredes, to spatialize on the map before me how this 'periphery' was once the 'center' of the imperial Spanish border province of Nuevo Santander, colonized in 1749 by José de Escandon to hold the line against English, French, and Anglo-American encroachment" (Saldivar 1997, 18).

Following the Mexican-American war, Texas and the Lower Rio Grande Valley regions became sites of continually escalating violence, due at least partially to the ways in which the redrawing of national territorial boundaries affected local social and property relations. Since the mid-eighteenth century, cattle ranching had been central to the region's economy, which also "lay at the heart of South Texas's social structure" (Johnson 2004, 276). Cattle-rustling, stealing, banditry, and the lynching of Mexicans and Mexican-Americans became more commonplace, and "Mexican-Americans living in South Texas lost much of their property to Anglo ranchers through theft, extortion, and trickery" (Richardson

1999, 7). One lifelong resident of the Lower Rio Grande Valley reported the terror of that period this way:

> If they saw you walking down the street, and one told you to come, you went. They would take a man to the outskirts of town and tell him to start running. They would shoot him in the back as he ran and report to the man in charge that they just shot another bandit. People were really afraid of them. They could do whatever they wanted, and no one ever questioned them. I still don't trust them. (quoted in Richardson 1999, 8)

In short, if the borderlands were originally imagined as a lawless region because of the allegedly unsavory characters that inhabited the lands, in the aftermath of the Mexican-American War, it became a liminal space of violence and lawlessness in which suspicion and terror increasingly reigned. Elites encouraged views of the borderlands as a marginal, uncivilized space by calling "upon images of savagery to legitimate efforts to control nature and society, the border, or la *frontera*" (Truett 1999, 167), allowing them to argue for the need to develop and so tame the region: "Many Mexican and Anglo-American power-holders claimed that smugglers and so-called 'bandits' and 'cowboys' stood in the way of 'civilized' development, and they advocated their removal from the region" (ibid.).

At the turn of the twentieth century, the South Texas border region also changed dramatically because the economy ceased to be organized predominantly around cattle-ranching and became organized around agriculture. The combination of Northern Tamaulipas and South Texas cotton farming, irrigation, agriculture, and the building of railroads all came together to make the area attractive for in-migration (Arreola 2002, 44–53). The value of farm property increased 500 percent between the years 1900 and 1920, forcing many landowners to sell their properties when they could not keep up with property taxes (Johnson 2004, 276). Later construction of the Falcon and Amistad Dams provided irrigation to otherwise arid lands and helped support the cotton boom that swept Northern Tamaulipas (and other northern Mexico regions) in the mid-twentieth century (Walsh 2008). Although in 1850 the Rio Bravo was reported to have been as "wide as the Hudson at Troy," in the current era, dams for irrigation have largely destroyed the river and caused innumerable border water skirmishes (Walsh 2004), while simultaneously drying up the area's many picturesque *resacas* (Ruiz 2000, 196).

Little remains of the original dense forest that once covered the banks of the "Great River." Most of what remains exists within protected areas and, if it is in unprotected areas, it is under continuous threat by both the development objectives of towns on both sides of the border, as well as the security measures of the border patrol agents, such as those in Brownsville where "agents of the patrol who are intent on stopping the flow of illegal migrants bulldoze virgin lands for roads, erect fences, and nightly light up the banks for the Rio Grande, thus jeopardizing the ecosystem" (Ruiz 2000, 197).

In both earlier periods and the contemporary one, the border zone has also been a region of intense connectivity, especially as it is experienced at the immediate local level among cross-border populations (Herzog 1990; Heyman 1991; Kearney and Knopp 1991; Ortiz 2001, 1999; Zavaleta 1986). Much of this connectivity emerges from local cross-border networks, such as family and social ties, civic groups and activities, and a range of economic linkages that run the gamut from the expansive macro-level connections (e.g., the *maquila* industry, drug cartels) to everyday shopping performed on both sides.[1] One can add to that list the cross-border environmental advocacy that has grown steadily in the post-NAFTA era. Local cross-border economies are also mutually interdependent. In the contemporary era, economies on the US side of the border suffer when Mexican workers fail to shop on the US side or, alternatively, *maquila* employment decreases due to contractions in the US economy, as happened in the wake of 9/11.[2]

From Space to Place: The BIP
and Maquilization of the Border Zone

Even since the US-Mexico border emerged as territorial limit at the end of the US-Mexico War, it has registered extraordinary breadth and depth due to the cultural differences, natural environment, and regional specificities that configure its length. Border cities did not emerge whole cloth from the *maquila* boom. Rather, each has its own colonial and postcolonial history, rural-urban dynamics, and cultural or regional influences not reducible to the border. As Alvarez (1995) and other border theorists have observed, there are multiple cultures within the border zone that break down not only along class and ethnic lines, but which are also heavily circumscribed geographically throughout the border's 2,000-mile length. Given the combination of contingency and consistency that has historically characterized the region, it is virtually impossible to capture a succinct border culture. Alvarez describes the latter term as a misnomer and a false starting point for analysis, due to the way in which it "either glosses over or essentializes traits and behavior" or "pigeonhole[s] this geographic region into a Wisslerian culture area type" (Alvarez 1995, 450).

Nevertheless, the sense of place in the border region has, in some ways, been overwhelmed by the spatializing forces of globalized, *maquila* production. Ruiz gives eloquence to the historical and site-specific sense of place that has steadily been eclipsed by the geographic and spatial monotony of *maquila*-based development: "Today, life on the Mexican side of the borderlands only rarely conjures up that of the 1920s. For those of us who knew the old, the dissimilarity is striking. Since the 1960s, the arrival of assembly plants, an adjunct of the global economy, has radically altered the contours of Mexican border society" (2000, 61).

The structural similarities that emerged with the mid-1960s and early 1970s *maquilization* of the border zone give external observers the impression of a seamless and distinct border culture that exists throughout its length but which, in fact, is a function of this relatively recent imposition of spatializing forces on local places and peoples. Many of the structural similarities that repeat themselves throughout the length of the border zone can be traced more or less directly to two separate, but intertwined, phenomena: first, the creation of the Border Industrialization Program (BIP) in 1965 and the lesser known Programa Nacional Fronterizo (PRONAF) in 1961; and, second, global outsourcing trends that took root from the early 1970s onward.

The ostensible primary purpose of the BIP was to provide employment to former Bracero workers (suddenly unemployed with an end to that program) and to attempt to stem the tide of illegal immigration to the United States through the creation of an economic fence (Rivera-Batiz 1986, 263). With the closing of the Bracero program, many guest workers and their families became stranded on the Mexican side of the border with few resources. Many Bracero workers had relocated their families to cities and towns on the immediate Mexican side of the border so that they could be close by when the workers crossed back into Mexico. "Indeed, the BIP was established in the aftermath of the Bracero program (that ended in 1965) and its main purpose was to absorb the former Braceros into the Mexican labor force so as to prevent their illegal immigration to the United States" (Rivera-Batiz 1986, 263; cf. Baerresen 1971; Fernandez-Kelly 1983, 209–210; Seligson and Williams 1981).

The program aimed to attract foreign investment to the area with the promise of cheap labor and an absence of import and export tariffs on imported raw materials and exported goods (taxes were and are applied only to the "value added" in the production process; Heyman 1991, 41). An additional attraction for investors was the non- or poorly-unionized character of the *maquiladora* labor force (Kopinak 1995, 30; Rivera-Batiz 1986, 263). The BIP allowed the construction of *maquila* factories and free trade zones by foreign-owned corporations, mostly from the United States, but also from Asian countries as well, particularly in the western portion of the border (Quintero Ramírez 1997). The off-shore assembly plant industry grew exponentially from the time of its founding: In 1967, there were fifty-seven *maquilas* in border cities; by 1976 there were 552, and in 1981 there were more than 600—over 90 percent of which were in the border zone (Seligson and Williams 1981, 1). The growth of assembly plants also produced enormous growth in the rates of employment associated within them; from 1969 until 1985 the number of employees jumped from an initial 15,000 to more than 240,000 (Rivera-Batiz 1986, 264).

Although *maquilas* were originally developed to cure anticipated Bracero unemployment problems, the exponential population growth throughout the region that started with the BIP era indicates that the industry simultaneously encouraged ongoing migration to the border zone, even if, as Seligson and Williams argue, the BIP was merely one of several factors exerting a "pull" during that period (Seligson and Williams 1981, esp. pp. 59, 71–74). While NAFTA was supposed to decrease migration, Cornelius and others maintain that migration has increased in the post-NAFTA period, with *maquiladoras* and border cities still functioning as "powerful magnets" (Cornelius 2002, 295) and migrating populations providing a reliable labor pool. The only Mexican resource that makes a direct contribution to the *maquila* production process is labor (Delgado Wise 2007), as Heyman's succinct description of the border assembly process also suggests: "In the maquiladoras, parts and items are put together by Mexican workers, by hand or with machinery that is usually fairly simple. (. . .) The purpose of the maquiladora is to obtain inexpensive effort at the labor-intensive steps of manufacturing" (Heyman 1991, 41).

An additional contradiction between the stated mission of the BIP and its consequent results is that the labor force has historically been predominantly female. Rather than target unemployed men, *maquilas* virtually immediately targeted women, and young women in particular (Fernandez-Kelly 1983; Kopinak 1995, 31) in a manner consistent with the outsourcing trends of multinationals seeking "docile" and young female labor (Mies 1986; Nash and Fernandez-Kelly 1983; Ong 1987). Young women were particularly favored in the largely Asian-dominated electronics or microchip industries of the western border region (which also had weak "ghost" unions, as noted in Quintero Ramírez 1997) for their small fingers and excellent eyesight (cf. Ong 1987), but they have historically represented the majority of the *maquila* labor force, even as more men began to be brought in during the 1980s and 1990s (Richardson 1999, 98). In the *maquila* industry's preference for young, female labor, it exhibited patterns consistent with manufacturing outsourcing practices beginning in the 1960s and 1970s, based on an "ideology that justifies the employment of women (preferably young women) in low-paying assembly operations by referring to presumed biological and emotional differences between the sexes" (Fernandez-Kelly 1983, 181).

In their early preference for female labor, the *maquilas* were simply regional manifestations of globalization outsourcing trends. As a legal, national and territorial marker, the US-Mexico border performed the function of providing a safe haven for predominantly US or multinational corporations searching for cheap labor (Fatemi 1990) or a "pollution haven" (Leonard 1988; Reed 1998, 3) for the production of commodities ranging from microchips to automobiles. Global economic dynamics that have produced the northern Mexico frontier are remarkably consistent with other core-periphery outsourcing trends that emerged at that time. However, the Mexican side of the US-Mexico border provided an exceptionally generous stretch of territory "in the margins of the state" (Das and Poole 2004) in which the negative externalities of intentionally under-regulated and overproduced production wastes could be housed (to be discussed in Chapter 3). It is precisely such less stringent pollution controls with which developing economies sometimes barter, laying waste to vast swaths of land and peoples, so that "nations with the lowest environmental standards and the least resource-conserving policies will acquire a comparative cost advantage over those with high standards and conservation-oriented policies" (Harris 2000, 119).

Within this broader border context, the more recent four-decade history of Matamoros has been both similar to and different from that of other border cities. The Matamoros-Brownsville area has historically been connected by the Mexican and Mexican-American populations that predominate in both cities, the fact that South Texas originally belonged to Mexico, and the extensive legal and illegal networks that bind the two (Arreola 2002; Kearney and Knopp 1991; Richardson 1999; Zavaleta 1986). The experience of Matamoros has been similar to that of other border cities like Nuevo Laredo, Cd. Juarez, Nogales, and Tijuana in the sense that city industry is now dominated by the *maquila* sector and the majority of the city's occupants are poor migrants from other regions of Mexico. As Richardson notes, "Campesinos have been pushed off their *ejidos* (communal farms) by a combination of government edicts, overpopulation, and drought. Massive migrations bring them to the cities and to the border. For example, Reynosa and Matamoros, the border cities facing McAllen and Brownsville, have grown by 600% since 1950" (Richardson 1999, 98). The Matamoros-Reynosa area saw a 74 percent population increase between 1970 and 1990 (Russell 1994, 254).

Matamoros' population explosion and geographic expansion has followed a pattern common to other border cities. In-migrating and squatting populations settle in *colonias* in the city's peripheries, gradually becoming incorporated into the city's neighborhoods. The city is heavily contaminated with organic and chemical wastes due to the lack of sanitary and public health infrastructure. Like most border cities, the populations of both Matamoros and Brownsville evidence higher than average rates of respiratory disorders, hepatitis, tuberculosis, and other air- or water-borne diseases traceable alternately to air, water, or ground water contaminants. Unlike other border cities, however, the Matamoros-Brownsville region gained a certain amount of notoriety because of a neural tube defect (NTD) cluster that occurred in the area in the early 1990s, resulting in a numerous cases of anencephaly and spina bifida. This cluster, as well as local reactions to it, is discussed in Chapter 3.

Social scientists have been studying the *maquiladora* phenomenon in relation to development, globalization, labor, gender, migration, environment, public health, and a host of other related issues for decades now (e.g., Brenner et al. 2000; Carrillo 1986; Denman 1992, 1991; Peña 1997; Fernandez-Kelly 1983; Heyman 1994, 1991; Nash and Fernandez-Kelly 1983; Quintero Ramírez 1997; Moure-Eraso et al. 1997, 1994). Originally demonized as sweatshops or satanic mills, the literature on *maquiladoras* has become more sophisticated with time. It now incorporates studies of *maquilas* in relation to both national and global economies and the effect of the industries on border environment and ecology, as well as the differences in individual or regional *maquila* practices (Quintero Ramírez 1997).

Mexican Environmental Law and the Border as Pollution Haven

The *maquila* industry and the hardships of life in border cities garnered significant public attention during the course of the NAFTA debates of the early 1990s. For both Mexican and US labor and environmental constituencies, the US-Mexico borderlands came to function as a symbol of the hazards of globalization and free trade worldwide, with many maintaining that all of Mexico would be transformed into a free trade zone under NAFTA conditions. During this period, certain iconic images came to function as "establishing shots of the border" (Fox 1999, 41–67), including images of chain link fences, the river (Rio Grande), waste water canals or *aguas negros*, or "stock shots of the 'poor but dignified people'" (Fox 1999, 61). These images came to symbolize the border at the same time that NAFTA and free trade suddenly became common household terms in the United States.

Unlike its prescience with regard to labor law (in which Mexico anticipated US labor protections by decades), Mexico did not begin to develop environmental regulations until the 1970s (Janetti-Díaz et al. 1994; Mumme 1992; Mumme, Bath, and Assetto 1988; Najera 1999). Historically, there has been strong private and indigenous interest in the protection of the natural environment in Mexico (Simonian 1995), but the federal government lagged far behind. Mexican environmental laws were modeled to a degree on US environmental laws (Carlos Vasquez 1993, 363), as were its environmental institutions. In 1971, the Ley Federal para Prevenir y Controlar la Contaminación Ambiental (Federal Law for the Prevention and Control of Environmental Pollution), the country's first comprehensive environmental law, was passed. In 1982, the Mexican Congress initiated the Ley Federal de Protección del Ambiente, which was directed specifically to the conservation and preservation of the natural environment. Also, the Ley General del Equilibrio Ecologico y la Protección al Ambiente (LGEEPA) was passed in 1988, which addressed the exploitation of natural resources through mining and forestry, as well as the protection of waters and issues related to occupational and environmental health. The current primary environmental agency is the Secretaría de Medio Ambiente y Recursos Naturales, (SEMARNAT).

Several reasons have been put forth for the well-known and historic lack of enforcement of environmental law in Mexico that provided the rationale for the environmental side accord. The first reason typically cited pertains to the oft-noted tendency of "global south" nations to function as pollution havens for globalized first world manufacturing activities (Leonard 1988; Stebbins 1992), even as NAFTA was intended to obviate this tendency through a salutary first world imitation effect (Garcia-Johnson 2000). As Leonard notes, "Although not fundamentally responsible for Mexico's rising position as an exporter of manufactured goods, the relative dearth of effective environmental and health controls has enhanced Mexico's attractiveness to some US firms participating in the *maquiladora* program, in the mineral processing sector, and in certain types of chemical manufacturing" (Leonard 1988, 154). Mexico's situation has been similar to that of other so-called developing nations in that the need to attract foreign capital has discouraged effective enforcement of environmental policies (Mumme, Bath, and Assetto 1988). Second, the PRI's decades-long one-party rule and authoritarianism proved a hindrance to environmental policy making, especially when the exploitation of natural resources was tied to aggressive Import Substitution Industrialization (ISI) policies (ibid.). Third, Mexican environmental laws were historically framed in language that was largely symbolic and rhetorical. As Mumme notes with respect to the 1971 Federal Law for the Prevention and Control of Environmental Pollution, the basic law was so "general in content and wanting in force that it remained little more than a symbolic document" (Mumme 1992, 126). The government's approach to environmental regulation reflected a general preference for regulatory methods based on award, incentives, and abatement, rather than punishment (Mumme, Bath, and Assetto 1988, 18–19).

With regard to the border environment, both the Mexican and US governments have historically demonstrated some level of concern. Largely ineffectual efforts have periodically been hashed out in an effort to cooperate and manage the border environmental problems. The first binational effort at border management produced the 1889 International Boundary Commission, which eventually led to the creation in 1944 of the Water Utilization Treaty and the creation of the International Boundary and Water Commission (IBWC), a treaty and organization still in effect today (Barry 1994, 31; Mikulas 1999, 3). Following a lapse of almost forty years, the next international accord signed into place was the 1983 La Paz Agreement between the United States and Mexico, otherwise known as the Agreement for the Cooperation for the Protection and Improvement of the Environment of the Border Area. The La Paz Agreement specifically addressed border pollution problems with fairly explicit acknowledgement of the fact that border pollution was largely attributable to *maquila* forces (Ellis 1996, 640–641). The agreement also addressed the problems of toxic waste dumping throughout the region that had become publicly acknowledged by the early 1980s (Barry 1994, 47–68; Simon 1997, 205–235).

The 1992 Border Plan was an attempt to remedy La Paz's ineffectiveness, meanwhile simultaneously increasing the tracking and repatriation of *maquila* wastes to the United States and ending the practice of illegal dumping (Reed 1998). The Border Plan purported to encourage the monitoring and collection of information concerning border pollution, increase enforcement of actually existing laws, introduce new initiatives for pollution reduction, and increase cross-border environmental cooperation. In particular, it aimed to increase cooperation between the EPA and the Secretaría de Desarrollo Urbano y Ecologia (SEDUE; SEMARNAT's name at the time), as well as public participation in monitoring and information gathering. As Ellis points out, the Border Plan failed due to lack of funding and enforcement provisions (Ellis 1996, 649–653). NAFTA's environmental side accord was intended to replace all of these previous bi-national accords and successfully address the environmental pollution problems that had failed to be remedied by previous accords (Eaton 1996, 741–743).

Environmental Destruction in the Borderlands

The border's two thousand mile stretch begins on the Pacific Coast between Tijuana and San Diego, then continues across the sometimes treacherous and often soaring Arizona and New Mexico deserts, climbing high into the Sierra Madre and Big Bend corridors, finally plunging into the long flatlands of the lower Rio Grande Valley to meet the Gulf of Mexico. While the frequently barren landscape might not meet the tastes of certain middle class American preservationists who have historically preferred green and moist landscapes as symbols of pristine, untouched nature (Cronon 1996), the border's rugged barrenness holds a special appeal for those with more Spartan tastes. The desert and arid,

scrappy, scrubby environments are a part of Nature too, as much as soaring mountains and plunging waterfalls. The entire border region remains
home to rich bio-diversity of plant and animal life, including such rare
and protected animals as the jacuarundi, oncelot and javalina. At least
two books, *Two Eagles/Dos Aguilas: The Natural World of the United
States, Mexico Borderlands* (Steinhart 1994) and *Mountain Islands and
Desert Seas: A Natural History of the US-Mexican Borderlands* (Gehlbach 1993) are devoted explicitly to describing the enormous and richly
textured natural landscape of the borderlands region. Gehlbach, in particular, provides a virtually encyclopedic account of the flora and fauna
that inhabit the region, as well as the ongoing desertification that threat-
ens both human and non-human inhabitants. Both authors emphasize the
role that man-made destruction has played in transforming border
ecology. Gehlbach, for example, devotes an entire chapter to the discussion of DDT and its presence in jackrabbits, whiptail lizards, Merriam
Kangaroo rats, "silky and desert pocket mice" (ibid., 44), and people.
He notes that bat populations—which reproduce at a much lower rate
than rodents—are particularly susceptible to DDT toxicity and claims
that "bat populations are declining in the Borderlands, and I believe it
legitimate to suspect pesticide poisoning along with natural factors"
(ibid., 47). He goes on to note that the "once spectacular evening flight
of eight million Brazilian free-tailed bats from Carlsbad Caverns, New
Mexico, has all but ceased" (ibid.).

Much of the environmental destruction of the Lower Rio Grande
Valley region began with the introduction of cattle and accelerated with
the early twentieth century shift from ranching to agriculture. For many
decades, the region of northern Tamaulipas ranging through southern
Texas has been dominated by industrialized agriculture with all that
implies: dams, irrigation, pesticides, and fertilizers. In southern Texas
farmers have historically grown peaches, lettuce, melons, and any variety
of fresh produce; in northern Tamaulipas, the agricultural preference has
been for cotton, sorghum, and wheat.

Nevertheless, environmental destruction of the borderlands took a
sharp and distinctive turn with the introduction of the *maquila* industry.
Since that time, the border region has become massively, and perhaps
irreparably, contaminated with chemical and organic wastes. The contamination is so rampant that the authors of one study have suggested
that "there is a Bhopal taking place in the border zone; it is merely taking
place over months and years, rather than seconds and minutes" (Brenner

et al. 2000, 280; cf. Peña 1997, 279). Saldivar has provided a firsthand account of this transformation in the Lower Rio Grande Valley. It merits quoting at length:

> In my childhood in Cameron County in South Texas, I saw the Texas-Mexico borderlands turn into an ecological wasteland, with more than ninety-three maquiladoras pouring out toxic waste and endangering life chances and life experiences on both sides of the border. As a result of these unregulated factories (of General Motors, Quimica Fluor, PEMEX, among others), there have been in the last decade what the border journalist Ana Arana calls "a disturbingly high number of anencephalic births" (a rare disorder that leaves infants without a complete brain) in the Rio Grande Valley. (Saldivar 1997, 19)

In both the pre- and post-NAFTA era, numerous toxicological, public health, and environmental studies have been done, demonstrating beyond dispute the high levels of toxic chemicals that saturate the border environment. In 1990, the June 26 *El Paso Herald Post* reported that the American Medical Association referred to the US-Mexico border as "a virtual cesspool and breeding ground for infectious disease" (quoted in Moure-Eraso et al. 1994, 315). Border cities in which *maquilas* thrive are particularly toxic, but many of the wastes are carried downstream via the Rio Grande and other estuaries. These same waterways, soils, and ground waters are often contaminated with the pesticide and fertilizer run-off from agriculture as well, even as they are used for irrigation. Extremely high levels of mercury, nickel, lead, chromium, arsenic, DDT, phthalate, zinc, copper, xylene, toluene, benzene, ammonia, battery acids, among other chemicals, have been found (Brenner et al. 2000, 278–279; Moure-Eraso et al. 1994, 1997). A 1991 report of the National Toxic Campaign Fund, "Border Trouble: Rivers in Peril," (Lewis, Kaltofen, and Ormsby 1991) tested three different sites along the Rio Grande and found multiple toxins at between twenty and 215,000 times the levels permissible under US laws (Simon 1997, 211). Additionally, there have been ongoing problems with gas leaks, explosions, fires, and other dangerous incidents in the Lower Rio Grande Valley (Moure-Eraso et al. 1994).

In addition to chemical contamination, there is the organic waste problem. The presence of dangerously high levels of organic wastes in the border environment is directly related to the fact that most border cities experienced exponential population growth within a few short years. Not only do border cities burden local ecologies and water resources, but explosive growth has systematically outpaced the capacity of city planners and municipal resources to keep pace with the construction of sufficient infrastructure for the appropriate management of human wastes. Most poor *colonias* have limited plumbing, if any. Ditches typically drain *aguas negras* (sewage) from indoor plumbing, dumping the wastes into human dug canals, estuaries, and larger rivers, such as the Rio Bravo. In the Matamoros area, these wastes travel directly to the Laguna Madre and Gulf of Mexico. The following sketch is typical, and more than just a "stock shot":

> Two of Matamoros' *colonias* (or squatters' camps), where
> *maquiladora* workers live, are next to open drainage ditches.
> Residents of one *colonia* obtain water from shallow wells (less
> than 20 feet deep) made by improvised hand-drilling methods,
> within approximately 100 feet of the drainage ditches of FINSA, an
> industrial park. The canal collecting the effluent of one *maquiladora*
> plant in the park has such a high level of volatile organics in the
> drainage ditch that the stream itself would be classified in the United
> States as hazardous waste. (Moure-Eraso et al. 1994, 316)

Aguas negras, one of the "main vehicle[s] for disease transmission" (Barry 1994, 30), are clearly a public health threat, but one that is numbingly familiar in Mexican border cities. Barry puts it bluntly: "As border cities expand, so do the massive quantities of sewage. In the absence of industrial waste treatment facilities, mixed in with fecal matter are the chemical wastes from industrial manufacturers, mostly *maquiladoras*" (ibid., 30). The handling and management of wastewaters has been one of the most challenging issues for border cities, as noted as late (or early) as 1992 in Cd. Juarez: "Sixty percent of Cd. Juarez is served by sewage lines, but there are no sewage treatment facilities in this city. Sewage mains discard into ditches, and the unlined ditches carry the sewage out of the city to agricultural fields, where this wastewater is used for crop irrigation" (Cech and Essman 1992, 1056–1057).

Stebbins has put a political economy slant (similar to the approach of critical medical anthropology) on the problems of hazardous and toxic waste dumping in so-called third world countries by industrialized nations. He argues that systematic toxic waste transfers play a causal role in exacerbating health risks for underdeveloped nations' populations. Debt-ridden nations find it difficult to resist monetary incentives to accept hazardous wastes. Stebbins describes this first world/third world relation as a form of "garbage imperialism": "Because of environmental regulations, landfill closings, and citizen opposition to local waste disposal facilities, industrialized countries are increasingly disposing of their dangerous waste by shipping it to the third world, where people are often poorly informed about the threats that such wastes pose to human health and the environment" (Stebbins 1992, 82).

This form of garbage imperialism has been a persistent feature of *maquila* dumping on the Mexican side of the US-Mexico border since the creation of this marginalized sector. It is a well-documented fact that *maquilas* have historically dumped into surrounding rivers, ground waters, surrounding desert, or municipal dumps (Reed 1998; Simon 1997), sowing wanton destruction for future generations to clean up. One of the most important accomplishments of environmental organizing in the immediate pre- and post-NAFTA days was the achievement of an agreement similar to the 1992 Border Plan whereby all hazardous by-products generated by *maquilas* during the production process were to be repatriated to the United States. Monitoring and accounting of repatriated wastes was performed by the US Environmental Protection Agency (EPA) until October of 2003, when the EPA hazmat tracking system was dissolved due to lack of funding.[3]

Space, Place and Back Again

Given the border region's tumultuous and conflicted history, it is impossible to overstate the importance of the border, as a territorial marker designating sovereign limits and possibilities, to the production and reproduction of the borderlands as a culturally, economically, and environmentally marginal region. As Philip Abrams argued many years ago, the state is not a monolithic affair, but an assemblage of sometimes disaggregated practices (Abrams 1988). The demarcation and policing of territorial limits is a hallmark practice of modern nation-states, alongside control over legitimate uses of force, taxation, citizenship requirements, birth and death registries, and so forth. Buchanan has remarked on the importance of spatializing non-local actors, including the state and globalized capitalism, to the production and reproduction of the place of the border region:

> If 'place' is constructed in and through social processes,
> differentiation between places becomes as much an artifact of uneven
> capitalist development as the differences between classes. [. . .]
> There is an important distinction between the notion of a border
> as the legal and spatial delimitation of the State, as a boundary or
> defining line, and the border as a geographic and cultural zone or
> space, the borderlands. Instead of having a stable identity, economy
> or geography, the border region is defined and redefined in different
> contexts. (Buchanan 2001, 286)

Ortiz has similarly argued that the interests of non-local actors, such as the state, business, and immigration laws continually cross-cut local border interests and capacities (1999, 2001). At the same time, local actors are hardly united because class, ethnic, national, and nationalistic interests cross-cut border lives. As he puts it in reference to Cd. Juarez-El Paso: "In the overlapping of the 'no man's land' space and the living places of local residents, most border dwellers conduct, or try to conduct, their everyday lives beyond, along, or in spite of the dislocating impacts and overriding presence of the non-local" (Ortiz 2001, 105). He goes on to note that, "what distinguishes the border situation is the pervasiveness of non-local actors and agendas" (ibid., 105), a point this chapter has also attempted to demonstrate.

The NAFTA side accords were ultimately a pragmatic, neoliberal response to a recurring quandary: How can seemingly underdeveloped nations enforce their national environmental and labor laws in a manner similar to their developed counterparts, but without the corresponding resources of developed nations? At the same time that the accords fell back on neoliberal truisms, they also articulated a future vision in which citizens and activists would cooperate in the immediate cross-border environment and participate in transparent and problem-solving public debates. The success of this novel vision, however, hinged on the anticipated success of neoliberal economic development policies. New wealth and resources created by NAFTA-inspired free trade was supposed to trickle down to the downtrodden and poor of the Mexican side of the border. This newfound wealth was then supposed to be channeled into enhanced oversight and enforcement by national regulatory agencies, ostensibly raising labor and environmental law enforcement to a level that would satisfy the treaty's critics, flush corruption from the Mexican political system, and ultimately bring Mexican political culture up to (imaginary) US standards. The environmental side accord, in particular, ignored the fractious history and place-based social identities of border populations, preferring instead to cast border residents as a homogenous population henceforth charged with an environmental stewardship model incubated by the accord itself.

Regardless of the aspirations of both accords, the fact remains that the Mexican side of the US-Mexico border was profligately saturated with environmental and workplace wastes before and after the signing of NAFTA. The saturation of the border region with wastes in proportions that would be considered unthinkable elsewhere is both product and function of the border region's characterization as a marginal, frontier zone. The assiduous and painstaking investigation of these wastes by Matamoros border actors will be explored in the next chapter.

Chapter 3

Investigating Waste

Ciudad Juarez has recently gained notoriety as the so-called murder capital of the world due to its drug-related violence. The city has had a reputation for extraordinary gender violence dating back at least two decades, however. Since 1993, hundreds of young women have been murdered there, their carcasses deposited in the surrounding desert, often after having been partially dismembered. The majority have been young *maquila* workers captured while traveling late at night to or from the factories at which they were employed. The combination of the Juarez femicide with skyrocketing and increasingly rapacious narco-violence has produced an increasing impression of Cd. Juarez as part of a post-human, post-apocalyptic landscape, as suggested by Bowden's *Ciudad Juarez: Laboratory of the Future.*

Melissa Wright (2001, 2006) has provided a compelling analysis of the Juarez murders. She argues that the murder of female *maquila* workers in Cd. Juarez persists and receives less public scrutiny than it should because it is intrinsically supported by a labor "turnover narrative" that condones the wasting of women's bodies by underscoring *maquila* workers' limited labor years. This narrative represents the working life course of female *maquila* laborers as one in which there is a steady accumulation of waste, the inevitable conclusion of which is death. The managerial view of women's bodies as accumulating waste as their laboring "shelf life" expends in turn supports a highly gendered cultural narrative that questions the morality and societal value of women alleged to be "loose" because out late at night. "Mexican women represent the workers of declining value since their intrinsic value never appreciates into skill but instead dissipates over time. Their value is used up, not enhanced.

Consequently, the Mexican woman represents waste in the making, as (. . .) untrainable, unskillable, and always a temporary worker" (Wright 2001, 127). Both their gender and *maquila* labor conditions guarantee that they are quickly replaced if disappeared, regardless of the conditions of their disappearance.

The difference between male and female *maquila* laborers is that male *maquila* workers are not saddled with the same sexualized moral and cultural investments as women; for this reason, their bodies are not raped or left in a desert. Wright's analysis of the labor turnover narrative can also be applied, to some degree, to male laborers and *maquila* workers in general—particularly those deemed non-trainable or non-managerial (e.g., those who will never move up within a given factory and will perform the same assembly line tasks throughout their employment in *maquilas*). This is the case for the majority of *maquila* workers so all, in a sense, have a limited work shelf life, and most represent "waste in the making" from the first day of hire because of *maquila* turnover practices.

Wright's insights speak directly to the main argument of this chapter—namely, that *maquila* labor and environmental conditions on the US–Mexico border are implicitly designed as wasting practices. This generalized wasting might not be as dramatic (for observers) or as accelerated as the wasting processes experienced by the Juarez murder victims, but it is part and parcel of the *maquila* sector's function as an enclave of "disembodied labor" (Delgado Wise and Cypher 2007) located at the margins of both the Mexican state and the United States. By disembodied labor, Delgado Wise and Cypher refer to the fact that the only linkage between the *maquila* sector and the Mexican economy is the former's access to cheap labor and the embodiment of this labor in exported products (ibid., 121) which gets exported along with those products as "value-added." The NAFTA side accords were supposed to halt the damaging aspects of the *maquila* industry that had ritually wasted both bodies and local ecologies for years before NAFTA.

This chapter first discusses the problem of the *maquila* industry's lack of backward and forward linkages within the Mexican national economy (Wilson 1992). Second, it argues that the absence of such linkages reinforces cultural, political, and economic conceptions of the border region as a "marginal space" (Das and Poole 2004), suitable for the production of various forms of waste or what ecological economics refers to as "negative externalities." The third portion briefly describes two critical events in the Matamoros-Brownsville area that galvanized public attention and drew attention to public health risks in the workplace and environment. Section four uses interviews with Spektra workers to demonstrate the musculoskeletal and chemical injuries that workers there endured. The fifth and final section describes the ways in which Spektra workers began organizing locally with the Comité Fronterizo de Obreros (CFO) following the former's experiences of a neural tube defect cluster among workers' newborns and spontaneous abortions.

Maquilas and the Absence of Backward and Forward Linkages

The *maquila* industry took root in the northern frontier partly under the auspices of Mexico's Border Industrialization Program. The BIP was created partly as a consequence of the closing of the Bracero program, which left thousands of former migrant workers and their families stranded on the border without work.

The industry has historically been founded on a number of contradictions. One contradiction is that, although it is and was supposed to help develop the Mexican economy, the sector functions largely as an enclave with few backward and forward linkages: "[M]aquiladoras continue to function as an enclave with few connections to the broader economy. Over ninety-seven percent of their non-labor inputs are imported from outside Mexico" (Hart-Landsberg 2002, 21). Operating semi-autonomously or with stronger connections with the sending country or company than with Mexico, they have not developed strong backward and forward linkages which would encourage economic growth or sectoral development within Mexico's overall economy.[1] Indeed, this absence of substantive linkages with the local economy is suggested in the roots of the word *maquila*, which historically referred to the portion of corn kept by millers as payment for their grinding of a client's corn (Ruiz 2000, 61).

Since all of the resources (raw materials, technology, etc.) for offshore assembly plant production are imported, the only local resources used are labor. As noted by Cooney, "[*maquiladoras*] imported parts and semi-finished products from the United States and, after assembly, exported the finished goods back to the United States, with import duties being paid only on the value added by the Mexican workers" (Cooney 2001, 62). As early as 1993, the Banco de Mexico reported that imports for *maquila* production were rising, rather than falling, "indicating that the Mexican hope that *maquilas* would stimulate co-production with national firms remained unrealized" (Kopinak 1995, 30–31). Mattar, Moreno-Brid, and Peres also commented on the low level of integration between national primary material input and export processing, noting that "by the beginning of the 1990s Mexico was exporting automobiles, computers, and electrical and electronic equipment, although in many cases national content was rather low" (Mattar, Moreno-Brid, and Peres 2003, 153). According to these authors, the "central problem with this development is the sophisticated exports' low level of integration with the rest of the national economy and the reduced linkage effect on other activities and non-exporting agents" (ibid.).[2] Cooney has corroborated this account on the limited increase in backward and forward linkages since *maquiladoras* have taken root in the northern Mexican frontier: "Despite encouraging claims of increased forward and backward linkages between the *maquiladoras* and the rest of Mexican manufacturing, there are evidently minimal gains for the latter, and the threat of competition from the *maquiladoras* means that further decline is to be expected if the current trends continue" (Cooney 2001, 75, 76). The Mexican government has done little to interfere with this production strategy; instead it has given foreign-owned enterprises "maximum freedom to organize production as they see fit" (Hart-Landsberg 2002, 23). Delgado Wise and Cypher summarize the issue succinctly when they state that the *maquila* sector is "a cheap-labor assembly operation with virtually no backward or forward linkages to Mexico's economy" (Delgado Wise and Cypher 2007, 126)

To depend on *maquila*-generated wages to stimulate economic growth seems disingenuous at best. The returns on labor input were meager at the outset, and they seem to have declined with time. In 1995, Kopinak reported that the average monthly real wage per worker in Nogales was US$108.25, 59 percent of the nominal US$184 wage and 4 percent of 1982 real wages. Beginning with the 1982 peso devaluation (which itself produced IMF-imposed structural adjustment measures and popular protests), the Mexican government has used the minimum wage to reduce wages generally, even as real wages in general have plummeted since the late 1970s as a "direct result of state policy opening Mexico economically" (Kopinak 1995, 36). In 1994, Russell reported wages in border cities remained low and that "these wages permit survival, but do not allow for spending on amenities or provide an alternative tax base to municipalities trying to cope with mushrooming growth" (Russell 1994, 255).

Others report the continuing decline of wages since NAFTA. According to Bensusan, wages declined "particularly in the second half of the 1990s" (Bensusan 2002, 246). The real minimum wage fell by 28.4 percent between 1994 and 1999, and the "wage gap between Mexico and the United States widened rather than closed between 1993 and 1999" (Bensusan 2002, 247).[3] Cooney also claims that between 1994 and 1996, "the population experienced a decline of real wages, which dropped by 27 percent" (Cooney 2001, 55), following "a continued decline of real wages by 50 percent through the 1980s" (ibid., 59). "The late 1980s and early 1990s witnessed a brief respite for real wages in manufacturing and a one-year increase in 1994 for *maquiladora* wages, but no increase in the minimum real wage. During the depression of 1995, Mexico lost a total of 1.85 million jobs and real wages declined by over 40 percent as a result of the peso devaluation" (ibid., 59). Maquila owners benefited from peso devaluations in 1994 and 1996 which, in turn, increased wage differentials between US and Mexican workers (ibid., 60). Cornelius supports the thesis of declining real wages by pointing out that the wage divergence between Mexico and the United States has remained the same or increased since NAFTA. Also, the alleged benefits of free trade in encouraging economic growth—and discouraging migration— have failed to materialize in a post-NAFTA era (Cornelius 2002). Indeed, Mexican migration to the United States increased steadily in the years after NAFTA. In other words, NAFTA has not necessarily been good for Mexican workers, particularly *maquila* laborers.

Negative Externalities in the Margins of the State

The *maquila* sector as enclave economy reinforces the cultural and historical conceptions of the northern Mexican frontier, and US-Mexico border, as areas marginal to both nation-states. Das and Poole (2004) have critiqued the center–periphery model that underpins modern anthropological, historical, political, and cultural understandings of the contemporary nation-state, its center and its margins. They and contributors to their volume suggest that anthropologists should problematize how centers and peripheries are constantly being reworked, subverted, or re-inscribed through everyday cultural, practical, and economic practices, rather than accept the center–margins model as natural background against which anthropological investigations take place.In modern political thought, marginal areas are often considered of less central importance to the nation-state, that is, largely as frontiers that must be conquered or territories that must be defended. Yet, as Das and Poole note, "Margins are not simply peripheral spaces. Sometimes, as in the case of the borders of a nation's state, they determine what lies inside and what lies outside" (ibid., 19). As a line, the border between Mexico and the United States has been extraordinarily productive; it determines that offshore assembly plants sit on the southern side of the border, in the so-called third world, and not in the first world to the immediate north.

The ecological economics concept of negative externalities (Daly and Cobb 1989; Harris 2000; Speth 2008) is helpful for understanding the reification of border marginality. The term has historically been used to describe pollution problems (cf. Tybout 1967). Externalities refer to the environmental pre-conditions of production conventionally considered external to production costs in both the primary and final product output phase. The primary stage includes public goods that come to producers free of charge: air, water, land, and so forth. The final output or throughput phase can include the waste generated alongside a finished product. "In a standard economic perspective, [the remedy for this] is appropriate government policies such as pollution or resource depletion taxes, public management of common property resources, and public funding or subsidies for environmental preservation" (Harris 2000, 119). As Speth puts it, these externalities are "all the indirect costs of the environmental damage imposed on those downstream of polluters and on the public at large, costs that the unaided market does not require the polluter to pay" (Speth 2008, 92). While the ecological economics model typically focuses on the environment, the model can usefully be extended to working bodies as well—particularly when those bodies end up damaged in the final output phase.

Ecological economics' negative externalities critique of orthodox economics is that the latter's economic models are constructed in such a way as to occlude the cost of public goods. These models are artifices and, as artifices, some things are included within their frames while others are not. Negative externalities are called externalities because their (public or social) cost is not calculated into production costs (Daly and Cobb 1989, 51–54). Negative externalities, additionally, are also hidden sources of value. When companies pollute or fail to provide adequate protections to workers, they do so with the intention of making money by not spending it. Proponents of ecological economics typically argue that human and environmental costs should be calculated into production costs, thereby producing economic models more faithful to reality, rather than artifactual distortions of it. The goal is to move the negative externalities inward "to a system whereby the marginal environmental cost of an activity is incorporated into the price of the product being produced" (Speth 2008, 96).

Negative Externalities as Public Health Risks

The *maquila* boom on the northern Mexico border is characterized by such externalities and damages to public environmental goods for which border communities now pay when they take out certain NADBank loans. While populations and ecology on both sides of the border may clearly suffer contamination through water or air emissions, it is the populations on the Mexican side of the border who suffer disproportionately. It is there that untreated toxic and chemical wastes have historically been dumped directly into waterways or onto the sides of shallowly dug canals: "It is an open secret that companies simply take the route which insures the lowest cost, laws and social consequences notwithstanding" (Russell 1994, 256).

Mexican border residents suffer higher levels of environmental health risks than their North American counterparts because of the concentration of toxins deposited into the immediate environment, whether it is the by-products of the lead smelting plant Alco Pacifico of Tijuana or the calcium sulfate donated by Quimica Fluor to pave Matamoros roads and keep the dust down, as commented upon by an elderly Texan at a joint Semarnat–EPA meeting.[4] He wanted to know the environmental effects for both sides of the border of Quimica Fluor's practice of paving Matamoros roads with calcium sulfate, and noted that whenever he drove through Matamoros, his eyes would burn furiously until he got off the Matamoros roads again.

Two public health scares in the Matamoros-Brownsville area helped to catalyze public awareness of the public health threats from factories' possible damaging of both environmental goods and workers. These scares inspired public discussion of toxins possibly lurking in the air, water, and workplace. The first was cross-border, while the second was specific to Matamoros. It was also because of these two critical events that Las Caracaras was founded, for they inspired Rosalia and Felipa, a Matamoros-based nurse, to begin investigating the possibility that the

Dren Cinco de Marzo was the source of health problems in the neighbor-hoods that surrounded it.

The first public health scare was an anencephaly[5] cluster that oc-curred between 1986 and 1992.[6] A graphic illustration from the Browns-ville side of the border merits quoting here:

> The nurses at Valley Regional Medical Center in Brownsville sensed something more than a horrible coincidence. Two babies born the same day in April 1991 had brains that were stunted or missing, a rare defect that usually strikes only three or four births in 10,000. Stunned, nurse Connie Riczenman called the Texas Department of Health. Before state officials could respond hours later, doctors had delivered a third, tragically malformed infant.[7]

A similar story emerged from the Matamoros side of the border, and it also deserves to be quoted at length:

> Maria del Socorro understands life's hardships better than most people her age. In 1992, at the age of seventeen, she gave birth to a stillborn child at a hospital in Matamoros, a city located at the northern border of Mexico. The child died from a rare birth defect called anencephaly, a condition that causes a fetus to develop without a brain.
>
> Maria del Socorro's story is tragic; unfortunately she is not alone. Dozens of other mothers in Matamoros, as well as in the neighboring city of Brownsville, Texas, have given birth to children with the same condition. In Matamoros, medical researchers have documented forty-two cases of anencephalic babies. (Ellis 1996, 621)

The cluster drew national media attention. There were disparate and conflicting reports on both the numbers and the time span of the clus-ter: Some reported fifteen cases within a five-mile radius of Matamoros-Brownsville from 1991–1992 (Peña 1997, 280). Earlier reports stated that between 1989 and 1991, "thirty women in this town of 130,000 [Brownsville] carried anencephalic babies."[8] Still others have reported ninety cases in a five-year time span from 1986–1991 within an extended Texas–Mexico border range (Ellis 1996). In short, the precise number of anencephaly cases was unclear at the time, and remains unclear after-ward, just as the cause of the outbreak (*maquila* pollution, pesticide runoff, inadequate sewage treatment, genetic inheritances, and corn toxins) were all up for debate.

Along the border and in Mexico, anencephaly has been linked with parental occupation, agricultural work requiring exposure to pesticides (Stemp-Morlock 2007) and corn (tortilla) consumption. At the time of the outbreak, the Matamoros president of the *maquila* trade association and the Brownville mayor both blamed malnutrition and genetic inheritances among Mexican-born populations (Peña 1997, 280). Public debates ensued as to whether the cluster was attributable to pesticides used in local crops, emissions from Matamoros factors, and at a later date, fumonisin, a fungus that grows out of the mold on corn, particularly during drought seasons. Scientists speculated that Mexican and Mexican-born populations' high consumption of corn products was the cause since higher than average rates of neural tube defects had been correlated with fumonisin in other parts of the world, such as South Africa and China.[9] Although fumonisin is notable for having multiple mutations in different animal species, its presence and probable cause of the anencephaly outbreak was deemed by Texas Department of Health Official Dr. Hendricks to be a more likely source of sickness than man-made chemicals: "Whatever caused that [outbreak] didn't stay there forever," Dr. Hendricks said. "Man-made chemicals would not have disappeared."[10] Man-made chemicals might not have disappeared, but new man-made chemicals are constantly being introduced into production processes. As will be discussed below, Spektra workers suspected the introduction of a new glue, called by the workers "Modelo CK," to have been the cause of the anencephaly cluster that occurred within the plant.

The cluster also resulted in the 1993 filing of a negligence lawsuit on behalf of Brownsville families against General Motors (GM) and over forty other foreign factories located in Matamoros. The lawsuit alleged that the anencephaly clusters had been caused by air emissions that drifted from the Matamoros plants to the US side. An out of court settlement was reached in August of 1995.[11] At the same time, the Ministry of Social Development (SEDESOL) initiated a crackdown on Matamoros and other border *maquilas,* and found violations in almost 90 percent of the factories. In Matamoros, four plants were singled out for inspections and fines, two of which were owned and operated by GM (Peña 1997, 280–281).

The rates of anencephaly on the Mexican side were purported to have been much higher than on the North American side, leading the

South Texas lawyers in charge of the case to originally seek to include Mexican plaintiffs under the favorable legal conditions created in 1990 by the *Dow Chemical Co. v. Castro Alfaro* case. In that case, the Texas Supreme Court had decided that foreign plaintiffs were allowed to bring civil actions against corporations located on Texas soil. At the time, it was a landmark case because it overturned (at least in the case of Texas) one of the primary obstacles foreign plaintiffs face when trying to bring legal action against a US agent: standing in a US court. The Supreme Court decision was later modified to say that a case could be tried only if a Texas court was willing to accept jurisdiction over a case. When it looked as though having Mexican plaintiffs included in the lawsuit would create additional obstacles for the case, the Mexicans were excluded from the lawsuit.

As noted above, there was ample documentation of elevated anencephaly rates on the US side. What remains less known—due to less extensive data collection and storage by Mexican state and public health institutions—is the extent of anencephaly and other NTDs on the Mexican side of the border. This is part of the problem of a generally underdeveloped statistical gathering regime when it comes to public or environmental health issues. As Peña has observed, "On the Mexican side, the undeveloped state of these fields is even more striking, as Carrillo suggests. This means that the entire debate over the public health effects of *maquila*-induced environmental degradation is as yet based only on scattered empirical evidence" (Peña 1997, 303).

A study was later generated by a group of South Texas physicians[12] concerned with understanding possible causal relations between NTDs and nutritional influences or environmental exposure to possible air emissions, agricultural chemicals, or other compounds. The report indicated the possibility of a correlation between Brownsville NTD rates and *maquila* activity on the Mexican side, even if a direct causal chain could not be proven. Also, although carefully worded, the report did suggest the possibility that Cameron County clusters were related to industrial air emissions by *maquilas*: "We find that the prevalence of anencephaly is associated with the number of *maquiladora* plants in Matamoros. This association seems to exist only with anencephaly" (ibid., 59). The report also noted that there was a weaker correlation between *maquiladora* activity and other neural tube defects and that they did not, at that time, "have evidence of a direct link between maternal or prenatal exposure to *maquila* emissions and the occurrence of anencephaly" (ibid.).

The second local public health scare and lawsuit was specific to Matamoros. A foreign-owned factory, Mallory Capacitor, was accused of being responsible for the birth defects of children of women workers from the late 1960s through the 1970s.[13] The children were referred as "los niños Mallory."[14] In January of 1995, Mallory Capacitor settled for $15 million dollars with eighty families of Matamoros based on allegations that the plant's activities had caused a rash of birth defects. The lawsuit filed by the affected families alleged that the children were born with a set of health effects allegedly caused by their mothers' work in the plant and their exposure to toxic chemicals there.

The case of the Mallory Syndrome came to public attention in the early 1980s when a special education teacher in Matamoros began investigating the high number of children with similar learning disabilities in her classes. She discovered that they all had in common mothers who worked at Mallory. According to both lay accounts and documented records, "Dr. Isabel de la O" became involved and followed through with professional medical investigations (cited in Moure-Eraso et al. 1994, 315). A woman who was living in Brownsville by the time her one-year-old daughter became ill recounted taking her daughter to a hospital in Corpus Christi in the mid-1970s, where the infant girl died shortly afterward: "'I was surrounded by four or five doctors,' she said in Spanish. 'They called it a phenomenon. Her body was wider than it should be. Her heart was thick on the right side, and one of her lungs didn't function.'"[15] The Mallory case was so famous in Matamoros that in February of 2002 a local monthly news magazine called *Hora Cero* ran a long story giving an update on "los niños Mallory" twenty years later.[16]

These two local public health scares put Matamoros and Brownsville populations on alert regarding the possible toxicities of the externalities that had been and were continuing to be injected into their local environments and workplaces. The concerns of Spektra workers, discussed in the next section, were also rooted in an anencephaly cluster, but this was an anencephaly cluster that occurred specifically within Spektra, the factory in which they worked. The cluster inspired some of them to undertake the initial investigations that eventually resulted in a labor side accord petition, but it also allowed them to voice concerns about the ongoing and chronic health problems that many of them faced as a consequence of working in the Spektra *maquila*.

"Los Jonkeados": Wasting Bodies in the Production Process

Jonkeado is a hybrid English–Spanish term combining "junk" and "ado" (Spanish past tense) to literally mean "junked." Spektra workers were regularly referred to as *jonkeados* within the plant once they had become musculoskeletally damaged, as many of them became. Spektra was a steering wheel and gear-shift assembly factory. This meant that workers had to cut thick leather and sew it onto one of these car parts, depending on which section of the factory they worked in. Additionally, they were constantly exposed to large vats of glues and solvents. The quotas required them to cut and sew quickly, while the heat often discouraged workers from wearing masks. As a consequence, there was a range of chronic conditions from which Spektra workers typically suffered, including carpal tunnel syndrome, shoulders that had become useless and fatigued, glue addiction, or incessant sinusitis. Then, in the early 1990s, there was an anencephaly cluster that occurred among the female counterparts of male factory workers and spontaneous abortions among female workers.

Investigations into the anencephaly cluster were initiated by Guillermo, a worker whose child had been born (and died) with anencephaly. These investigations and the conversations between workers soon grew to include informational sessions about Mexican labor and occupational health laws more broadly. This occurred with the assistance of the Comité Fronterizo de Obreros, for which Rosalia was then a trainer. That is how Guillermo and Rosalia met, and how Rosalia introduced me to Guillermo. Later, in conjunction with the Justice for Border Workers and the petition filed on behalf of the workers (discussed in Chapter 6), it became clear that the Spektra plant had regularly violated workers' rights, but the mystery of the anencephaly cluster remained unresolved.

Musculoskeletal Injuries

Spektra had a reputation in Matamoros. Many Spektra workers reported that it was difficult to find work in other plants after being at Spektra for any length of time. They were considered to be damaged, and managers seemed to think that if they hired any of these workers at their plant, a latent old injury could easily manifest itself. This would make the new plant at which the former Spektra worker was currently employed liable for the damages. This put former Spektra workers who had been damaged in a difficult position. It meant that, once let go and pensioned, they were no longer employable and would be forced to live on a monthly income that was a fraction of which they were accustomed. For example, one pensioned worker, Catalina, explained to me that when she left Spektra she received a pension from the plant that was 40 percent of her former pay due to the damage that had been done to her arm.[17] At 40 percent, her current pension was Mex$900 per month, the equivalent of approximately US$90 at the time.[18] "If I cannot work in another company, how am I supposed to survive off of nine hundred pesos per month? What am I supposed to do?" she asked. She explained to me why it was impossible to go to work for another company.

> Because, the other companies, when they find out that you are pensioned and that you have worked in Spektra plant, they do not want you—they know that you are damaged in the arms. ("So, they never hire anybody who has worked inside of Spektra?" I asked.) It is very difficult for them to give work to someone from Spektra. For example, other people who have worked there, and who are not pensioned the way I am, they do not put down where they have worked before. But for those of us who are injured and who have pensions, because there is the insurance and pension for the evaluation which they gave to us, and they know because the information is there to show that you are pensioned, and you came from Spektra. They don't want you and, aside from that, they will not even give you a medical exam.

I asked her if this problem was unique to Spektra, and if there were a lot of injured workers in Matamoros in general. She responded, "The majority are from Spektra. There are very few which are injured from other plants, people who have suffered some injury. But for the arms, and for the damage from inhaling solvents, it is definitely Spektra." Later she exclaimed, "Spektra is very famous for this!"

Most of the injuries experienced by workers can be divided up into repetitive motion or toxic exposure injuries. Among the repetitive motion injuries, carpal tunnel syndrome figured most prominently and became apparent in workers' complaints of loss of movement or strength in a particular limb.

Carpal tunnel syndrome occurred mostly among those who worked in sewing, although the sewing department also included working with glues and solvents or, at the very least, large vats of glues and solvents remained open next to workers at their stations. In the sewing department, people were responsible for sewing the leather onto either steering wheels or gearshift assemblies. In the glues and solvent area, people were responsible for dipping the existing steering wheels into glues, then wrapping the leather around the steering wheel itself. Sometimes multiple attempts were necessary in order to get a tight wrap, in which case the assembly people would be subjected to both glues and solvents.

Sewing the leather required a fair amount of endurance and strength in the shoulders, arms, and hands. Spektra plant was unique in that—unlike the rest of the *maquila* industry that originally recruited women, but then began incorporating more men as time went on—it had historically employed a predominantly male labor force into which women workers were gradually incorporated.[19] One man, Jose Ruiz, quit working at the Spektra plant because he was afraid that his shoulders would be damaged by the work. He quit and began work as a watch repairman. He lived and worked in a single room added to a larger house with plywood and corrugated tin. When we spoke, a pile of watches lay on the floor, the television was on, and ants scurried across the floor. Jose has been partially crippled since he was eight and had to use crutches to walk. He quit Spektra for this reason:

> I was laying in bed one night staring at the ceiling. It occurred to me
> that if I lost the use of my shoulders and arms, that this would be
> all that I would ever be able to do. Without my arms and shoulders,
> I am immobilized. It was then that I decided to leave the work at
> Spektra plant.[20]

Marta, who worked at Spektra for ten years (from the time she was 22 until she was 32) was assigned to the sewing department for the first four months, then she was reassigned to the final inspection area, where she stayed for the remainder of her employment. She demonstrated how the sewing took place. A steering wheel would be placed on an assembly before the worker. They would make three tight stitches in the leather, then pull back tightly until both arms were fully extended. This kept the lacing tight. Marta eventually ended up developing wrist problems that were originally diagnosed as carpal tunnel syndrome; later, however, she was told that her problem was merely psychological.

The work that Marta performed in inspections was slightly less strenuous than that in sewing. It consisted of the following:

> In inspection, we cut the leather of the steering wheel then we stick it like this with our fingers—with a small tool as well—we adhere it. One part with the fingers, another part with the tool. I had to cut off the leather that was extra, so we cut it, then we stick it with our fingers and the glue, like this. We used the white glue for this, and it smelled a lot.

Another woman, Luiza, had a different perspective on why people got injured during the sewing.[21] She said that she had suffered no known health problems from her work there, but that it was common knowledge that many workers had wrist problems. They complained, were sent to the Seguro[22], or were sent to work in personnel or the cafeteria, or they were fired. She guessed that 30 percent of the people working in the *cosecha* department had wrist problems; all of the workers believed that it was due to the sewing of steering wheels. Luiza believed that people developed wrist injuries because they hurried in order to fill their quotas. When she worked at the plant, the quota was nineteen steering wheels per day. If people could fulfill their quota by 1:30 or 2:00, she said, they could get overtime until the end of the workday or they could go home early. She did not seem to think that people who worked at a slower space had similar wrist or arm injuries.

Many of the injuries about which workers complained were thus related to the hard work of sewing and the debilitating effects of repetitive motions that required enormous upper body strength. Some of those stories shared here include both men and women, including people who participated or did not participate in the NAALC petition.

Ava was a twenty-eight year old woman who lived in an *Infonavit* neighborhood on the southern outskirts of Matamoros.[23] She had worked at Spektra for eight years. While we talked, she pulled out a pile of medical records, and said that she had been diagnosed with neuropraxia radial.[24] She explained that the diagnosis referred to a problem with her right elbow and the fact that she had lost strength in her right arm. She had worked in sewing and was only fired the year before. She did not receive any severance pay or pension; she did not know why she was fired.

She later went to look for work in two other factories. In one, she was rejected because she had previously worked at Spektra. In the second, her elbow became immediately swollen when she began to work. At the time of our interview, she was unemployed and, because she could not work nor did she have a pension, she and her family were in danger of losing their house. They could not keep up with the Mex$1600 monthly payment, which was then the equivalent of about US$160.

Juan had worked at Spektra for ten years when he was diagnosed with carpal tunnel syndrome.[25] According to his affidavit, he worked for two years in the area where the leather was prepared and suffered no injuries. Later he was transferred to sewing and it was there that he developed problems.

> As part of the sewing process, I sewed steering wheel covers onto the steering wheel. I would use my left arm and hand to sew. I used the same method for eight years every day of work. I always fulfilled my production requirements until 1998. In July of 1998, I started to have severe pain in my sewing arm. In July of 1998, I was sent to receive treatment for my arm and shoulder. I saw Dr. X. I received an injection to stop the pain. I received some electrical treatment on my arms. However, these injections and treatment only stopped the pain for a little while. That is the only treatment I received. I could not work at sewing anymore. I then worked in the office filing papers until December 17, 1999.
>
> I now have permanent damages and injury in my sewing arm. I still have constant pain in my arm and shoulder. It also hurts when I lift objects with my arm. It hurts so much that I am unable to lift my child or a bag of groceries. I also have limited movement in this arm. For instance, I cannot open a door. I never received compensation or treatment that would allow me to use my arm normally again or to ease the pain.

Also, according to the interview, after his original diagnosis, he was sent to work with the workers management referred to as the *jonkeados*. That term, when combined with these workers' stories, provides a significant window into how externalities—as physical bodily damage is calculated—got housed in workers' bodies as part of the commodity production process. It also demonstrates management's knowledge of that particular price and the routinized view of workers as mere commodities.

Juan continued to work at Spektra for another year on the assembly line with other *jonkeados*. There, they continued to sew, but were given a lower daily quota. He said that the company had been looking for a pretext to fire him, just as they were for the other injured workers. They took this when, one day, he took the day off to take his son to the doctor. He had received verbal permission for the absence, but when he returned to work the next day, he was accused of a delinquent absence. Since he only had a verbal agreement, he claimed that it was his word against that of his supervisor. He was fired immediately. At the time of our meeting, he worked in the records department at a local Soriana store.

Gilla was diagnosed with tendonitis while working at the plant.[26] The misinformation that she received regarding her rights, as well as the fact that she had to search for work immediately after leaving Spektra, severely compromised her possibility of gaining a pension.

Gilla was about forty and had three children—two teenaged daughters and a ten-year-old son. She had worked at Spektra for nine years, from 1992 to 2001. She had developed two health problems that she attributed to her work there: a bronchial disorder, eventually diagnosed as asthma, and tendonitis. She also worked in sewing. In January of 2001, she was given leave to recover from a breathing problem and when she returned to work in March, she developed a severe inflammation in her right hand. Both doctors and supervisors were flippant about her concerns, saying that it could not be because of the work or it would have emerged before. They did not want to give her physical therapy. Her right hand was constantly going to sleep, she was unable to grip things firmly because of its lack of strength, and she had lost full range of motion in her ring finger. At its worse, her finger would bend completely and she was unable to straighten it. In July of 2001 she was operated on at the Seguro in Matamoros, but it did not solve the problem. She was still pursuing more medical treatment.

When the plant fired her and three hundred other workers in October of 2001, she received only a severance check and no pension. Many of those fired with her were also injured, she claimed. Since the company claimed that she and others were fired merely because of downsizing, she could not pursue medical or pension benefits. She remained unemployed for a few weeks until she found work in an Italian-owned company that also produced steering wheels. This time she lasted only a week and a half in the sewing department until her hand became inflamed again, and she was transferred to a different department. She now works in the glue department.

Gilla had the additional problem of not being able to pursue compensation because she had to go to work in a different plant. Rosalia, who was with us during the interview, told her that she should have been compensated at 50 percent of her pay since she had lost full use of one hand. She had thus lost 50 percent of her manual capacity which, according to the Ley Federal del Trabajo (LFT), would require the same amount in compensation. The *delegado* in the Spektra plant additionally was ill-informed on the requirements of the LFT, for he informed Gilla that if she wanted to take her complaint to the Junta de Conciliación y Arbitraje she had four and a half years to do so. According to Rosalia, the time limit on complaints for former employment complaints is only two years. In either case, similar to Catalina, Gilla was unable to pursue compensation from Spektra plant since expediency had required that she return to work immediately—with or without a damaged limb.

Ana was another woman in her mid-forties who believed herself to have been injured at the plant. She had also participated in the workers' petition.[27] She had been working in *maquilas* since she was fifteen. The last factory in which she had worked was Spektra.

Ana had begun in sewing in 1993; by 1994 she had developed problems with her right hand. She went to the plant doctors, then to the union, and to the Seguro. The Seguro finally approved her as *incapacitada* and she was given workers' compensation for eight months. At the time that she began her paid leave, she was already two months pregnant with her youngest son. When she was eight months pregnant, the company sent her to Tampico to have her wrist evaluated. When I asked why in the world they would send her all the way to Tampico, she said that, "I think that they did it because they thought that I would not go since I was only a few weeks away from delivering. But I went anyway with an older son of mine." She was evaluated and given only a 10 percent pension, since they declared only her wrist was injured. Ana, like Guillermo (see below), blamed the injury on the new type of leather that had been introduced into the plant at that time:

> At one point there arrived a type of steering wheel which required a lot of strength, and that made us sicker and sicker. It was because of this sickness that they wanted to let me go, fire me. My production had gone down because of the problem with my hand. They gave me a low productivity report to sign [*un informe de baja eficiencia*], but I refused to sign it. This report was in February of 1995 and they told

me to sign this report but I told them "no," that this leather [Modelo CK Truck] was extremely hard. My arm hurt very badly. They told me to go to the union and the union told me that they were going to have me checked out by a doctor and, if I was not sick, they were going to fire me without even a cent. But for this, I was already damaged in the arm and I was already on file at the Seguro. So they sent me to see the doctor that the company had sent and, yes, I was diagnosed as injured.[28]

As her eight-month rehabilitation leave was coming to an end, she began her maternity leave, which was scheduled for forty-two days both before and after her delivery date. When she had finished both the maternity and the rehabilitation leave, she returned to the factory in November of 1995. From the time of her return, she was treated very badly in the hope that she would quit, in which case she would receive no compensation. She refused to quit and in September of 1996, they fired her. At the time, she still refused the package they offered her because the pension had been at only 10 percent of her pay. She sent letters to Ciudad Victoria (Tamaulipas) complaining, but finally gave up and accepted the 10 percent pension. She was told that, if she wanted more, she would have to pay more into the Seguro, and she did not want to pay more.

Pablo was another worker who believed he had been injured while working at the Spektra plant.[29] He had worked at Spektra for a few years up until the previous year, when he finally just quit because he could not stand the pain in his wrists any longer. He thought that the company had treated him more or less well. When he or other people complained, they would put them to work in other departments. He said that while some people were given humiliating tasks, he was simply put to work in personnel, which he did not mind. After working in personnel for six months, he was sent back to work on the steering wheels. He stayed in sewing for only a few more months, then he quit.

Another Spektra ex-worker, Alejo, provided the following statement:

I am a manual operator. I assemble and sew the leather on the steering wheels. The sewing is done manually and it is very difficult. The leather that we use is very hard, it requires a lot of force and movement by the hands. They asked of me twenty steering wheels per day—the production standard varied by the type of steering

wheel. The steering wheel most difficult to sew is the Modelo
CK Truck.

After eight years of work I have a damaged left hand. I started my
shift more or less well, but after three hours, I would feel pins and
needles in my fingers and I could not grip well the steering wheel.
They pressured me a lot to fulfill 100 percent of the production
quota, but I could only get up to 70 percent. These damages began
to appear more than a year ago. I am not the only one who is hurt;
there are more than 200 workers with damaged hands. Some of
them have lost movement in their hands and arms. They have fired
more than 150 people in the last year and they have fired them for
low productivity, and others they have forced to quit and they have
not given them any form of severance pay. Lately the plant has been
negotiating with the damaged workers—it is taking advantage of
the fact that workers are desperate and will accept anything, people
have been negotiating at the level of two thousand pesos—but these
people are stuck not being able to serve for anything and they cannot
get any other kind of work.

The workers who are damaged and who continue working—they
ask of us a production level as if we were completely healthy, they
only take into consideration the workers who have received some
kind of paperwork from a doctor from the Seguro—those who are
the most *fregados*[30] and who should not be working at all.[31]

Catalina was an especially interesting case for the medical treatment
that she received as a result of her injuries. The injury which she suffered
at the Spektra plant—an infection—was different from that of many
others and when she was treated with nerve blocks, her injury became
worse, instead of better. When we spoke, she looked for her medical
records and could not remember the exact diagnosis she had originally
received, just the nerve block and related treatments.

Catalina had worked at the factory for two years when she was injured.[32] She pricked a finger on her left hand with a sewing needle and
unexpectedly developed a bad infection. As she put it,

Well, I am an ex-worker of Spektra and I worked there for no
more than two years, and then I was on rehabilitation leave [*estuve
incapacitada*] for one year and two months as a consequence of a
work-related injury. My injury was not in the right arm, as it is for

the majority of workers, mine was in the left. On the one hand, I was injured by the work that they gave me, and on the other hand, I was further injured by the nerve blocks which they gave me in the *Seguro*.

When I ask Catalina to tell me more about the treatment, she says:

> Yes, they gave me twelve or fifteen nerve block treatments in order to desensitize me to the nerve because the pain that I had was partly because this finger was immobilized. At Spektra, I was in sewing, and I pricked myself with a needle and by the following day, I had this very damaged finger . . . in the clinic they lanced it and drained all of the pus that was inside, and from here [pointing at her finger] the damage began to run all the way up here [pointing to her shoulder] and I was incapacitated for more than one year.[33]

In a later interview, she explained that she had to make repeated trips to the "Clinica 25" in Monterrey, which was about a four-hour drive to the southwest, in order to receive the treatment and therapy.

> During this time, they gave me the worker's disability because it was a work injury. So while I was incapacitated, they paid me a complete salary, as if I was working. But when I went for too long on worker's comp, and I did not respond well to the treatment—because that is what the medical examiner's report said, that I was not responding well to the treatment: "There is not a favorable response to the treatment." So they sent me here to the IMSS and the social security decided to pension me at 40 percent which at that time was 335 pesos per month, or about thirty-two dollars. Well, thirty-two dollars a month . . . this is what they started paying me. However, each year the pension has gone up a little bit [with inflation] and now I am getting 900 pesos per month, which is about ninety dollars. So tell me what you can do with thirty dollars per month, or even ninety??! And with the disadvantage that you cannot work in another factory—you can't make it. Another thing, once the time of the illness has passed, plus the age, but when I still could do something, perhaps, they [the factories] would not accept me. I was going to various companies and they did not hire me because I was not of complete capability [*no estaba de toda habilidad*], because I am half-slow with this arm. So, for example, I cannot even grab this mop

well, I don't have strength in this arm. And from here [pointing to her hand] up to here [pointing at the back of her neck] it causes me so much pain that I cannot stand it. And this is where they first gave me the nerve blocks, here in the back of the neck.[34]

When I asked her if she only got nerve blocks in her neck, she said:

No, they gave them to me all over. Here in the neck, then they gave them to me here [pointing to front shoulder area] later they stuck in needles, because in carpal tunnel syndrome and, well, I don't remember the rest, but they gave me twelve nerve blocks in the neck, shoulder and in my back. Two times I was hospitalized for eight days so that they could hook me up to a machine which, every few hours, would inject a liquid. This liquid was supposed to numb my nerves so that they would no longer produce pain. For this reason they sent me to the pain clinic at the Clinica 25 of the Seguro in Monterrey.[35]

Catalina had to make the trip to Monterrey once per month for ten months, and occasionally, twice in a single month. The *Seguro* paid for her bus trip back and forth. But it appears that the nerve blocks only caused more problems and pain, for which she received further treatment.

Well, at the beginning when they sent me to the Clinica 25 in order to do the blocks, I returned and the pain just continued. They sent me again several times, then sent me to a neurologist, and then decided that it was a psychological problem. [. . .] Then they did several studies of me, they did psychological studies and I don't remember the rest. They gave me medication—Carbamazepina and Dizepam. These are tranquilizers.[36]

I asked whether she knew that they were tranquilizers.

No, they told me that they were for the pain. Well, yes, obviously if I was sleeping I could not feel any pain! (Laughs.) It wasn't until later that I found out what they were. A friend of mine was at my house and she said to me, "Hey, what pills are these?" I said that they were mine. She asked, "Who is taking them?" "Me!" They had told me to take half the pill and, if I was in a lot of pain, to take the whole thing. And well, in this period I took the whole pill because in this period I could not move my hand.[37]

Catalina went on to explain that her friend explained to her that the pills were tranquilizers (diazepam), and that their proper use was for insomnia, not pain. She had not received directions that were appropriate to tranquilizers. Although she had received the medicine through the *Seguro,* no one told her to be cautious if drinking or driving. The other medication—the Carbamazepina—she learned about while she was once in the waiting room of the *Seguro* itself. Chatting with another patient, the woman told her that it was also a tranquilizer. She had been taking the tranquilizers for one year and she stopped taking them when she learned through chance and hearsay that they were tranquilizers. She did not want to be an addict so, even though her arm hurt very badly, she switched to over-the-counter pain medication.

Were it not for the fact that Catalina experienced pain only in her left arm, her condition might be blamed on arthritis. In the first interview, she pointed out to me that she does have arthritis throughout her body, but she is clear on the fact that the pain in her left arm is more extreme and different from the rest of the arthritis:

> Whenever it is hot, the air conditioning causes me a lot of pain, my bones hurt . . . this arm hurts me more in the air conditioning, and this one [pointing to the right arm] does not. Arthritis, yes, all of my bones hurt, but this arm hurts me so much more than the other that I can barely stand it—it is very painful.[38]

Finally, Catalina was unequivocal about the fact that the cause of the pain in her left arm was the nerve blocks (*bloqueos*) she had received, not the original injury nor her arthritis. When I ask when the pain in her arm started, she said, "After the nerve blocks. Once they started the nerve blocks I have this pain that I can barely stand."[39]

Environmental Toxins in the Workplace

Environmental toxins caused a different set of problems among Spektra workers. Chemicals to which they were regularly exposed in Spektra included glues and solvents: Varsol™, trichloroethane, Loctite, Baltol, toluene, the white glue SICOMET, and Yellow Glue 5000 (often referred to as just *el cinco mil*).[40] Although most of the workers with whom I spoke suffered from repetitive motion injuries, there was also the anencephaly cluster, which is discussed in the next chapter. Here I relay what workers had to say about chronic and routinized exposure to these chemicals.

Proper labeling in Spanish of industrial chemicals used in *maquilas* has been a contentious issue for decades. There are often conflicting reports from NGOs, *maquila* workers' activist groups and others on whether substances are labeled properly and transparently, or not. Therefore, it was no surprise that there was some mixed reports among workers regarding the question of whether or not the chemicals with which they worked were properly labeled. The labeling was clearly uneven in Spektra plant, with some chemicals clearly marked in Spanish at some times, only in English at other times, and others still, not marked at all. This was consistent with the generally uneven enforcement of labor laws or individual company policies throughout *maquilas* on the border.

In an interview with Marta, I asked whether the substances came with labeling or if the workers received instruction during training of possible health hazards.

> Well, they did not tell us that it was dangerous to work with these chemicals, the only one which came with instructions was the white glue, because the white glue came in large boxes and there it came with labels, because we saw the boxes. The labels were in both Spanish and English. But the other ones, no, because the other chemicals came in large tanks.

When I asked if, throughout her time there, they ever explained possible hazards of these substances, she said, "At first, no. They only began to explain later, near the end, when they were already beginning to have problems and all this."[41]

The glue that workers complained most consistently about was the Yellow Glue 5000, or *el cinco mil*. Martin worked mostly with the steering wheels and with the Yellow Glue 5000. "This was the strongest glue which we used and it was changing, but it was never being absorbed sufficiently. We also used the 'tricloro' [tricloretano, or trichloroethane], and Varsol™ and different ones of water, but the Yellow Glue 5000 was the strongest."[42] As Ana put it:

> In the factory where I worked [Spektra], we used Varsol, which feels a little bit like petroleum—it is used to stick the leather to the wooden steering wheel, then with a heat gun we applied heat to attach the leather to the wheel, which came like a bone, or a rib. With the heat the leather could be ironed to get the wrinkles out. We also used tricloretano and yellow glue. I would say that the yellow glue was the one that affected us the most because it was so strong.[43]

The question of whether chemicals are properly or improperly labeled was something of a moot point when there were large open barrels full of these substances in the work area. The problem then becomes one of air circulation and exhaust systems.

Martin, who worked both on the regular assembly line and in maintenance, said that when he began working at Spektra in the early 1990s, there was only one air conditioner for a building the size of a city block. "When I started to work for this company, it was on 14th Street, it was right here in Matamoros . . . there was a lot of heat, too much heat, why? Because there was only one air conditioner for the entire factory."[44] The air conditioner was supposed to both cool the factory and clean the air. When I ask for clarification, whether there was some type of exhaust system ("extractor") in addition to the air conditioner, Martin's wife, Adelia, intervened, and said that that they, the workers, would experiment with the exhaust system behind the management's back. As she put it, the extractors absorbed when there was an official visit, and on the other 353 days of the year, they did not absorb anything.

> The exhaust system in reality did not work. They only put in "extractors" about five or six years ago. But, in practical terms, they only put them in as an optical illusion [*no mas para trampear el ojo*] because in reality they did not work. When there was a visit, that is when the extractors were running—you could put some little thing in front of it and there it would go! But when no one was visiting, you could put any tiny little thing in front of the extractor, and it would not be sucked away! This is what we saw ourselves. When there was no visit, the extractors were not turned on. A

visitor arrives and then the extractors are running and they absorb everything.[45]

Martin corroborated this account:

Look, it was maintenance. I had many friends and acquaintances who worked in maintenance and, as friends trust each other, they told me that the company said that there was no money to keep the extractors running on a regular basis. There was not sufficient money to keep the machines running efficiently.[46]

Martin's comment above can be rephrased to draw attention to the choices that company managers and owners made. They chose not to run the ventilators to keep the air clean because doing so cost money. The benefits of not spending that money accrued to the factory, while the disadvantages of not spending that money and properly ventilating the plant accrued to workers.

In addition to tendonitis, Gilla also developed a respiratory disorder that was eventually diagnosed as asthma. Her bronchial problems began two years after she started working at Spektra and continued throughout the nine years she spent there. From January until March 2001 she was sent home to rehabilitate because of her breathing problems; for part of this time she was also hospitalized. She blamed these problems mostly on the chemical vapors and the odor of the leather with which they were always working.

Ana, in addition to the problem with her right arm discussed above, also had a problem with her breathing. She was constantly sniffling— with or without a cold—and she said that she always felt congested, as though her nasal passages did not function correctly:

This problem with my nose began when I returned from my rehabilitation and maternity leaves and they had me counting the leather, splitting it up between the other workers who mounted it on the steering wheels. A lot of threads came out of the leather and I started to notice that I was having problems with my nose. It was always dirty and I went to the doctor and asked him why I was having this problem because it was going on every day.[47]

They never gave her a precise diagnosis: "I just feel my nose all the time, it feels full of phlegm. It seems to me that it must be a respiratory problem, and I always have phlegm in my nose and mouth." The topic of nose problems or respiratory disorders was also a constant discussion with Katerina, Rosalia's daughter-in-law. Her nose always seemed to be stuffed up and congested, and she always sounded as though she had a cold. Both Rosalia and Katerina blamed it on her work inside of a textile plant where she did sewing. The air was always full of threads and filaments. Katerina sometimes joked about the irony of the fact that, during the brief period that she spent working in California, part of it was in a Burger King. Later, working in a *maquila* in Matamoros, she found herself sewing Burger King uniforms.

Martin added more detail to the ways in which the leather, thread, and filaments can be irritating:

> The glue, that is one thing, but then there is the leather. I worked in many departments of Spektra plant, but when the leather arrived, I worked with the leather as well. The leather when it first arrives affects you dramatically. It is not just the leather, but the paint, because it comes painted and in many colors, and the odor can intoxicate you—you can hardly stand the smell. Plus there are the threads that emerge when you are cutting, which makes it even worse.

I asked whether or not workers ever got sick from this, or if it was just a nuisance everyone tolerated.

> No, it bothered everybody. But some of them had reactions and others, well, one does not know if one is having reactions to the leather, the smell, the threads, or to something else. If someone were to go to the clinic, they might tell you just to put on a face mask. Sometimes people went to the clinic and most of the time, they gave us masks, but to put on a mask with the heat?! It was so hot.[48]

Martin went on to say that the masks were difficult and cumbersome to wear; the heat inside was extraordinary, and the masks themselves weighed a pound or more. "If you can imagine carrying it like this on your face," he demonstrated with his hands, "and besides, they were made of plastic. Try to imagine how to put up with that while working . . . so you can see that the workers needed to use them, but it was virtually impossible."

In short, Spektra workers were regularly exposed to a range of chemicals and the factory was not properly ventilated unless it was being inspected. The damages from these circumstances eventually got housed in workers' bodies in the form of respiratory problems, chronic sinusitis, glue addiction, and, most dramatically, spontaneous abortions and neural tube defects among workers' newborns. These throughput or output types damages should be accounted for more frequently in the negative externalities arguments made with respect to ecological economics because they are just as injurious as environmental damages.

Popular Epidemiology among Spektra Workers

While all of the work and health conditions described above were chronic and ongoing within Spektra plant, it was the anencephaly cluster of 1995 that catalyzed workers to investigate. These investigations started within the factory, then proceeded through the efforts of Rosalia and the Comité Fronterizo de Obreros (CFO), which continues to advocate for maquila workers' rights today. The "popular epidemiological" (Brown 1987, 1997) data-gathering activities undertaken by workers and the CFO did not become the basis for a labor side accord petition until cross-border actors became involved. These actors, principally in the form of a US-based NGO, Justice for Border Workers, and its local level subsidiary organization, Jóvenes Pro Justicia[49] (Youth for Justice), were aware of the NAALC dispute resolution process because, as respectively North American and Mexican actors and activists with largely middle class backgrounds, they had access to the Internet and other information resources that kept them abreast of developments (laws, agreements, institutions) resulting from the NAFTA debates. This privileged position allowed them to forge a relationship with the CFO and Spektra workers, even as access to the grassroots workers and their complaints gave them material for the petition. As Brown and Fox note, "The legitimacy of Northern advocates without close ties to credible grassroots representatives is increasingly subject to question, so the value of grassroots participants in a project coalition is increasingly obvious" (Brown and Fox 1998, 457).

This access to knowledge and information stands in stark contrast to the lack of access to knowledge and information resources that characterized Spektra workers. Throughout my encounters and conversations with various former workers, I encountered none who were familiar with the North American Agreement on Labor Cooperation. As a corollary of this, few, if any, seemed to understand the nature of the petitioning process in which they had participated: a sticking point throughout the fieldwork and a topic to which I return in Chapter 6.

Rosalia was well-acquainted with the Spektra workers' petition; she was heavily involved in the original investigations into the operations of Spektra plant as a *promotora* with the local CFO. She eventually showed me many of the notes that she had taken in her interviews with workers. Her investigations epitomized the type of popular epidemiological and environmental justice activities discussed in different venues in which lay people take upon themselves the role of investigator, talking with people and attempting to construct theories and hypotheses about possible contamination or illness sources based on a steady compilation of empirical and anecdotal evidence.

Rosalia began working with the CFO in the early 1990s. As an advocacy network, the principal goal of the organization is to have representatives in each of the major border cities. The *promotoras* from this organization monitor workers' problems with the *maquilas*, spend a good deal of time talking with workers, and organize regular workshops in people's homes in which they teach laborers their rights according to the vast and comprehensive LFT. Armed with this information, workers are believed to better advocate for themselves in the workplace. This is very much a grassroots organization in which organizers and many of the participants historically have been women.[50]

When talking about her life history, Rosalia always referred to the early period of her work with the CFO as her period of consciousness-raising, political awakening, and training as an activist. Although she had always been acutely aware of injustices in life, she had not yet articulated that sense through a political project. This was the period when she acquired the voice and confidence to denounce the many injustices to which she felt she had been subjected during the course of her life, not least during the eight years she spent working in a Matamoros *maquila*. At the time, Ava was the leader of the local chapter and Rosalia received her training through her. Together, they would set off at eight o'clock in the morning to visit people in the colonias, take a break in the mid-afternoon heat, then arrange meetings for the evening.[51] Rosalia had given up this work only the year before because, as a full-time job, it did not pay enough to meet her needs. It paid Mex$200 per week, around US$20.

Investigations into Spektra work conditions began through the joint efforts of Rosalia, Ava, and a Spektra worker named Guillermo. Guillermo had lost a daughter to anencephaly, as noted in this affidavit.

> The majority of the workers complain about the chemicals and have almost all of the same problems, but the supervisors keep us pressured, so that to even begin to talk and defend yourself, you get fired. In 1993, the factory was closed by SEDESOL for one day. Prior to this the company asked us to hide the glues and toxic substances in order to put on a good face for the officials, but afterwards we returned to work and there was no change within the plant. The company lasted more than six years without extractors, until just two years ago they got some, but those that are there are not sufficient.
>
> Before, I was not entirely aware about what was going on in the plant. But one year ago, my second child was born with anencephaly and she died. I asked myself, "What is going on?" Fifteen days later another girl was born with anencephaly. In the past year [1995] there have been six cases—two of anencephaly, one of hydrocephaly and three born with respiratory disorders. Additionally, there have been ten other cases of spontaneous abortions.
>
> Since this happened, I have been talking more with my friends, talking with them about what is going on . . . in order to open their eyes. Two months ago I began to study the Ley Federal del Trabajo, to learn my rights, I began to participate in meetings with the CFO and I have learned a lot. I have believed in my friends and they have believed in me.[52]

When I met Guillermo, it was still extremely difficult for him to speak about the lost child. [53] At the time, he was driving a night-shift taxi that typically parked outside the local Soriana. When their child was born with anencephaly, Guillermo did not immediately blame the plant or initiate work-related investigations. Instead, as he and his wife grieved, he began to notice that an emergency collection box that typically passed among Spektra workers increasingly seemed to circulate for an infant-related emergency—either for a funeral or treatment for a birth defect. His final estimate based on these observations of the circulating collection box was that between fifteen and twenty infants may have died within a six-month period.

He began questioning other workers and collected a list of names.

He also began to speculate on possible causes of the cluster: Modelo CK Truck leather had been introduced around the same time, but they were also exposed to more trichloroethane at the time. He thought the latter was more likely to blame, partly because workers would dip their arms into the chemical.

He also heard a rumor around this time that Ana was meeting with a group of people from outside of the plant that talked about workers' rights. This group ended up being the CFO and the meetings about which he had heard were the evening training sessions that Rosalia and Ava offered. He and others from Spektra began going to the meetings to learn about federal labor laws. When he was fired from Spektra in 1996, it was because he had cited his federal labor rights to a manager, who immediately labeled him an agitator.

Catalina also remembered these early meetings. In the context of a conversation about Spektra's work conditions and whether they diverged from or were the norm among other Matamoros factories, she referred directly to the birth defects and spontaneous abortions, and emphasized that Spektra was the only plant that constantly produced workers with injured bodies:

> With regard to the spontaneous abortions, they said that it was just a "casualidad" but, well, three or four people, that is too much "causalidad," to come to this work and not have any problems, and this problem of working with the tricloretano, yellow glue, blue glue, and there is white glue as well. So I think that, yes, there is this problem. There was one person within the group who—I did not meet this person within the plant—they have a child with an enormous head. I don't know if they are still in the same group, but I met them in that group.[54]

I asked whether or not this was Down syndrome and she was un-equivocal: "No. It is not Down syndrome. I met them there with the people who had joined together because of the problems. There are people who in reality, I don't really know well and I don't know them from the plant. Many people, often times, they just put up with this because they need to work." She returned to the subject of her own damaged left arm, and then she got more specific about the early CFO-Spektra workers' meetings:

When we began to organize this, I found out about it through Rosalia. Rosalia contacted us, she got us into a group, and she talked with us. I don't know which organization she belonged to, but she contacted people. . . . Now I remember because Ava, also of the CFO, did an interview with me, and Rosalia was also with the CFO at that time and they began with the workers of Spektra. This is why Pedro and the JPJ became involved. Rosalia came looking for us, for workers who were injured, not just from Spektra, but from various factories. They began the meetings, and we did these meetings for two or three months and they would come back to invite us as well. I would sometimes go, and other times, I couldn't. I went for a long time without knowing exactly what they were doing because at times I could not go, I had to work or something, but they invited me and sometimes I could go and sometimes I could not. And then later, it was about two years after that, I think, that we went to San Antonio. No, it was more time. . . . We went in December of 2000.[55]

I ask when they started to organize for the petition, and who was involved at the time.

Well, a long time ago—it was probably about six years ago. The person who invited us was Rosalia, when I began to realize that they were really forming a group in reality, so that they were really trying to organize the affected workers, all this, and later, well a lot of time passed, more than a year I think, and then they started to invite me to another group. . . . I'm not sure which person came to visit us here, but we met in Rosalia's home and I don't know where this person was from.[56]

This chapter has argued that there is an organic connection between the maquila industry's lack of backward and forward linkages, the function of the *maquila* sector as an enclave economy, and the cultural and economic reification of the border zone as a marginal space. As a marginal, enclave space, both the environment and laborers that work within it have been subjected to gross environmental and labor injustices. The ecological economics concept of negative externalities has been used to argue that the creation of waste is an economically productive strategy that benefits *maquila* owners, not local residents or *maquila* laborers.

This waste production as a profit-generating economic strategy is often overlooked simply because waste does not typically factor into classical, neo-classical, or neoliberal economic formulae, but ecological economics proposes that it is essential to understanding the true costs of production. The chapter ended with a discussion of how the anencephaly and spontaneous abortion cluster within Spektra factory galvanized workers to begin information sharing, then to consult and begin a grassroots working relationship with the local CFO. The story of how the workers became organized to file a petition under NAFTA's labor side accord will resume in Chapter 6.

Chapter 4

Environmental Justice as Place-Making

I first learned about Las Caracaras while visiting one night with Rosalia in her kitchen. Throughout the time that we had spent together, she had made passing references to the range of environmental threats in the community and an organization with which she was associated but which had temporarily disbanded. This evening she introduced me to the current status of Las Caracaras. Briefly, the organization had been in an incipient stage and had been functioning smoothly for a while with a range of small activities. Around the time that Rosalia fell ill (over six months before), it had more or less fallen apart. She thought that now (2002) was a good time to try and get it organized again. "Tomas is part of it," she said, nodding toward the seventeen-year-old sitting quietly with us. When her daughter-in-law, Rosana, came into the kitchen she pointed toward her and said, "She is part of it as well." Rosana smiled agreeably and continued hunting through the refrigerator. She went on to tell me about other members of the organization and, during subsequent months of heavily participatory fieldwork, I was to learn all about it and come to know many of the members well.

The evening was pleasantly cool. It was fall and occasionally a soft breeze would waft through the window. We were sitting in the white plastic chairs of her kitchen next to an open window, which looked directly into the house on the next lot, about one-and-half feet away. Every now and then Rosalia would reach over to pull the narrow strip of curtain to one side and tip the ash from her cigarette onto the ground below. A serious young man, Tomas, was sitting with us. The story that would later be told to me by both a local priest and Rosalia about Tomas was that he came from the poorest of the *colonia*s and his mother was a prostitute. When they had visited his house to proselytize, they had found him trying to dig a tunnel out of the house with a stick. Tomas was young and extremely bright; he would later go on to study at the Autonomous University of Tamaulipas. For now, he sat listening intently as he always did when Rosalia spoke, absorbing every word of her experience and insight. It was clear that he admired her for her political savvy and her long years of work as an activist with the CFO and Las Caracaras, and had put himself in something of an apprenticeship role to her. As time went on, it became clear that he spent more time in Rosalia's house than in his own, and that the family had semi-adopted him.

Rosalia was telling us about the seven years she worked in a *maquila*. This was the turn in the *maquila* that almost everyone on the border seemed to take at some point. Within her household, three people (one son, a son-in-law and a daughter-in-law) were currently working in *maquila*s while another, Katerina. had recently stopped in order to pursue her certification as an English teacher. Rosalia said that life was difficult then; she rose at five o'clock in the morning to prepare a morning meal for her family (which then consisted of three children and her husband) and then, while it was still dark, she went to catch the bus to the industrial park on the other side of the city. She worked the day shift, but with the long bus rides across the city, she normally did not get home until about seven in the evening. Then she would cook and clean until midnight, when she was finally able to go to bed, only to rise again five hours later. She worked in a US-owned factory assembling children's toys, most of which would be exported back to the United States for American children.

Knowing that it was primarily my interest in the Spektra workers' petition that had drawn me to the border, Rosalia had told me bits and pieces of this story before. Perhaps because we were sitting inside the kitchen next to an open window and the *Dren Cinco de Marzo* made its noxious presence felt even here that she asked suddenly, "Suzanne, haven't you noticed the horrible odors that come from the canal next to our house?" I answered that I had noticed; I noticed when I drove over the canal to get to their neighborhood, when I was anywhere in its vicinity, and I also noted that the smells seemed difficult to identify. I had never smelled anything quite like it, and it made my nose sting when I was very close by. I asked whether or not it always stunk so badly or whether it was just at certain times of the year.

"Always—the smell never goes away, even in the winter months," Rosalia declared resolutely. She added that it was infested with all kinds of vermin and toxic wastes from the *maquilas*. The vapors were so strong in the summer months that they had to keep their windows closed at night—even with the heat—or else they would wake up with horrible headaches. The *Dren Cinco de Marzo* was a drainage ditch like hundreds of others in border cities. It sat just one block from Rosalia's house and functioned as a dividing line between the *colonias* that abutted it on either side. Throughout its length, dilapidated bridges connected one side of the canal with the other. In other places, precariously constructed and twisted footbridges connected the two sides. The canal was an open, festering wound, to borrow from Anzaldua's characterization of the borderlands more broadly (1987), sunk about ten feet in the ground and laden with organic and toxic wastes.

Many months after this initial conversation, Rosalia, her husband Arturo, Tomas, and I drove out through the privately owned lands and fields south of Matamoros in order to identify the precise location at which the canal spilled into the Laguna Madre.[1] Notably, we were able to smell the canal long before we saw it. It was only by following our noses that we were able to locate the mouth of what, at that point of the dry season, was a wide but shallow stream. A horse stood picturesquely at the bank dipping its nose into the water, but all we were able to see at the time were the iridescent gleam and frothy borders of what seemed a toxic, if somewhat dried up, stream.

The Founding of Las Caracaras

As a consequence of the widely reported border public health scares of neural tube defects and "los niños Mallory," Las Caracaras was founded through the joint efforts of two women, Nurse Felipa and Rosalia, in the late 1990s.[2] Nurse Felipa was a nurse who worked in a neighborhood close to Rosalia's that also bordered on the *Dren Cinco de Marzo*. Nurse Felipa had a number of concerns about the health of the residents in the neighborhood in which she worked, and Rosalia had similar concerns about her own neighborhood. As explained by Rosalia, the two considered themselves collaborators, but there was a clearly a status difference between the two: Nurse Felipa was a professionally trained nurse "with light skin and glasses" who worked in a poor and allegedly contaminated neighborhood, while living in a nicer and cleaner one. Rosalia, in contrast, was of lesser status and lived within the same community that she (or they) believed to be contaminated.

An early observation of the two was that many of the children that lived at the border of the canal had splotchy and miscolored skin, and they took this as an indication of possible environmental pollutants. Their center of activities was a nearby clinic in a poor neighborhood in which Nurse Felipa dispensed medicines donated to her by a US faith-based organization. Although Felipa was clearly the person spearheading the operation, Rosalia worked closely with her and learned a great deal from her. She was also, at the time, pursuing her labor advocacy with the CFO, a job that brought her into constant and close contact with various community members. She publicized the local clinic and its services, and talked with community members about possible environmental public health threats. Las Caracaras members provided the following written profile of their organization as part of one of their two grant proposals to the Sierra Club:

> Las Caracaras is concerned with ecological problems caused by the *maquiladoras* and Quimica Fluor, because through the years several illnesses have emerged among workers and their children. This is not the only problem; also the subsoil and agricultural products in and around Matamoros have been affected. When we had the good fortune to meet people from the Sierra Club, there arose a hope in us that there might be someone else who concerned themselves as much as us for our situation here, and we believed that together we could move ahead with projects concerning the environment.
>
> Our initial concern began when we noticed that if one traveled the area around the *Dren Cinco de Marzo*, we found children that had been bitten on the hands, feet, or face by rats, whose hair was falling out, and who had spots on their skin—all of which we attributed to living so close to the *Dren Cinco de Marzo*. We began investigating this and discovered discharged "aguas negras contaminadas" and drainage pipes which came straight from the *maquilas* and emptied this water into the *Dren*. The drain itself smelled as horribly as these usual *maquila* discharges. Also, we found clandestine dumps, as well as mud and debris left over after the treatment of water from the *maquiladoras*.

The *Dren Cinco de Marzo* was originally constructed to flush the city of water during the rainy seasons, but it had come to function as a repository for *aguas negras*[3] and *maquila* wastes, as even a city engineer readily admitted[4]. Beginning in the city center, it snakes through thirteen *colonias,* past the municipal dump, and eventually arrives at the Laguna Madre, approximately twenty kilometers to the south of Matamoros. As Tomas put it,

> The *Dren Cinco de Marzo* is supposed to be a clean water drain for the city, but it is also being used to get rid of sewage . . . and people throw a lot of garbage around the canal. The water, when it isn't flowing or when there aren't any rains, the water becomes a source of mosquitoes and infection. It is also the home of rats, snakes, and cockroaches—all sorts of animals that really are like plagues. They are plagues for the people who live next to the canal.[5]

Whether or not these inner city ditches are contaminated with organic wastes is not in question by state, municipal, or state authorities. It is widely known that they function as sewage canals for the poorer *colonias* on the outskirts of the city, and that this exposed waste encourages high rates of TB, hepatitis, and even dengue fever. The question of toxic waste is more hotly debated: non-industry observers mostly claim that the *maquilas* continue to dump as they did in the pre-NAFTA era. Meanwhile, Mexican and American state environmental agencies like to believe that the wastes were repatriated. Municipal authorities have historically tacitly acknowledged that the possibility of illegal dumping continues to exist. As for Rosalia, their family, and the communities that lived next to canals such as this or the municipal dump, there was no doubt. Not only were the smells definitely chemical and odd in nature, but Rosalia's husband Arturo, who had worked for many years as a trash collector, had himself dumped the toxic chemicals either at the municipal dump or directly into these smelly canals.

Members of Las Caracaras are largely residents of Colonias Rojas, Verdes, y Blancas—all poor and expanding neighborhoods (or camps of *paracaidistas*) located in the southeastern portion of the city. They attempt to represent the interests of the thirteen *colonias* that line the canal throughout the city. The core membership of the group consists of between fifteen and twenty people who were constantly attending meetings or held positions within the *mesa directiva*.[6] The number of people attending meetings often fluctuated, as Rosalia and others were constantly trying to recruit new members, so there were often new faces which one would see once, twice, perhaps on a regular basis, or maybe never again. On the other hand, it was relatively easy for the group to mobilize large groups of people for specific one-day projects, such as a cleanup or tree-planting endeavor. This mobilization was often achieved through the informal networks of family, friendships, neighbors, and, especially in the case of Rosalia, her ongoing community-based religious work.

These neighborhoods are among many that surround Matamoros in its outskirts. They are composed predominantly of migrants from the interior regions of Mexico. Like most of the other squatter camps-cum-*colonias,* services are poor: Many people have only outhouses, roads are unpaved and pocked with treacherous potholes, and telephone and electricity services are incomplete. In Colonia Roja, for example, where Tomas lived and many of the inhabitants were from the state of Veracruz, there was only one common water faucet, no electricity, and completely unpaved roads.

The *Dren Cinco de Marzo* and Area Beautification

The most pressing goal of Las Caracaras was to have the *Dren Cinco de Marzo* cleaned up and enclosed or *entubado.* An equally important and, in some ways, more attainable goal was to keep the canal's banks, if not the canal itself, clean. Along with the environmental and public health risks the canal was believed to represent, the *Dren* was also a horrible eyesore: Its banks were littered with garbage; plastic bags clung to leafless plants, dangling in the wind; when it overflowed during the rainy season, rats could be seen scurrying along its banks and sometimes invading people's houses. Members were thus equally concerned with simply having the garbage removed and the banks cleared on a regular basis. They would sometimes organize volunteer cleanup teams that would go out for a morning or afternoon to collect litter; in the past this had included some volunteers from a loosely organized Brownsville environmental group. These cleanup efforts were usually accompanied by educational efforts to discourage people from throwing their garbage into the canal or onto its precipitous edges. Rosalia targeted special effort toward the meat vendors who would throw the remains of barbecued meat—bones, gristle and all—on the canal's edges. The latter days of Rosalia's work with the CFO overlapped with the initial organization of Las Caracaras.

Thus, when Rosalia had the opportunity to speak with workers about labor rights, she would also promote the goals of Las Caracaras and environmental justice. For her, the two were always inextricably intertwined.

None of these efforts would have been necessary had the Matamoros Limpieza Pública (LP) stayed on top of its tasks in these neighborhoods. So, along with picking up garbage, organizing neighborhood watch committees, and engaging in general educational campaigns on the importance of urban cleanliness to good health, Las Caracaras would also regularly make the trip downtown to the LP in order to pressure municipal authorities to come and collect the garbage in their neighborhoods. They also regularly pressured the Junta de Aguas y Drenajes (JAD) to monitor discharges into the canal. They were much more successful with the LP than with the JAD. The LP would come regularly for a while to collect garbage, then collections would drop off until Las Caracaras made the trip downtown again to pester them, then the LP would come back to collect more. They were even occasionally successful in pressuring the LP into using trucks to make major sweeps of the canal's banks. After those trips, the canal did look almost presentable, and certainly much more tolerable.

While Las Caracaras was clearly an environmental justice organization, members also had aspirations for area beautification and an urban aesthetic that revealed place-making ideals. Their goals included cleaning up the *Dren* and having it restored to a fresh water canal or covered, but also making the collective space around the *Dren* more attractive, a goal reiterated though countless meetings and the occasional tree planting project. They imagined the canal's banks reforested with native plants and shrubbery (to be sustainable), having sidewalks so that people might have a pleasant place to stroll or exercise, and a playground where children of surrounding *colonias* could play. Rosalia was especially fond of eliciting this goal, waving her hands at the canal's banks to designate desirable places for park benches, playgrounds, plazas where people could gather, and trees to provide some shade. Such aesthetically pleasing gathering spots would build community pride and allow people to peripatetically traverse this part of the city with some pleasure, rather than dodging two-foot potholes and heavy rainy season mud. This vision was one of a modern and dignified urban experience, rather than the fractured, cramped and incomplete one in which they currently lived.

Appadurai has underlined the importance of imagination to contemporary social life and, in particular, to migrating or migrant populations

(1996). Ethnographic accounting of the function of imagination among deterritorialized subjects as they reterritorialize through place-making requires what he calls "thick description with a difference" (ibid., 55) as populations craft—or attempt to craft—a sense of locality (ibid., 52). There is a double accounting of imagination and local practices as they come together in the production of "place." Ethnographic recognition of the power and function of imagination is not merely an exercise in felicity but, rather, an acknowledgement of the importance of inspiration and agency in the face of seemingly over-determining structural and globalizing forces. "What is implied is that even the meanest and most hopeless of lives, the most brutal and dehumanizing of circumstances, the harshest of lived inequalities are now open to the play of the imagination. [. . .] Thus, the biographies of ordinary people are constructions (or fabrications) in which the imagination plays an important social role" (ibid., 54). Drawing attention to the place-making aspect of border environmental justice work restores an important understanding of agency, which the overwhelming structural determinants of migration, as well as mind-boggling levels of border environmental problems, tend to elide.

Migrant Journeys

The importance of place-making to Las Caracaras members becomes evident when one listens to their stories of migration, commentaries on their homes of elsewhere, and assessments of the problem of Matamoros as a "city of strangers." Memories of home or places of origin played an important role in their place-making activities in Matamoros. These stories help to paint an ethnographic portrait that is true to the extended life trajectory of migrants, rather than the limited time frame typically captured in portraits of border activists. Since Rosalia was the elected president of the organization and some of her immediate and extended family participated consistently in the group, I begin with their history. I also know this history well, given the amount of time that I spent Rosalia and her extended family.[7]

Rosalia's family was originally from Jalisco. Her grandparents had moved to northeastern Mexico during the southern Texas and Tamaulipas cotton boom of the 1940s. The cotton boom was part of the "Mexican Miracle," a period that lasted roughly from the 1940s to 1970s, during which the Mexican government pursued a development strategy of Import Substitution Industrialization (ISI) that included a rapid expansion of the agribusiness sector. Her family moved for opportunities in the cotton fields. Rosalia was born and grew up in a small town called San Fernando about ninety miles southwest of Matamoros. Although the parceling up of *ejido* lands into individual plots which could then be sold was achieved with President Salinas de Gortari's reform of Article 27 of the Mexican Constitution,[8] Rosalia and her husband, Arturo Grande, still retained a plot in San Fernando. In this way, they were unlike many rural to urban or international immigrants who sold their original land-holdings, often in order to pay for the journey and new start elsewhere. As she told me on many occasions—particularly those when the family did not have enough food to eat and she was considering selling tacos on the street or used clothes in the fishing communities of Laguna Madre—they could have used the money gained by selling the land, but they also felt as though they needed a safety net in case their *colonia* in Matamoros was ever displaced in the way that residents of Colonia Cuauhtémoc had been.[9]

Coming from a relatively small family of three children, Rosalia described her childhood and early adult years as fairly uneventful. Shy and timid, she had left school after finishing the elementary years in order to work in the fields with her family. Later, she worked in a jewelry store in town and, when she was nineteen, she took a nursing course and became a nurse in the town's clinic. During this period, she also met and married her husband, Arturo (whom she called Arturo Grande to distinguish him from her eldest son, Arturo Chico[10]), and they had three children together, all of whom were born in the US.

While they were still young, the couple migrated to Stockton, California where they lived in the seasonal workers' shacks that were then familiar sights in the rural California landscape. They worked as undocumented agricultural laborers for seven years, harvesting primarily strawberries, lettuce, and tomatoes. Rosalia told me the story once of how, during an Immigration and Naturalization Service raid in the fields, Arturo Grande was arrested and deported to Mexico. The family was reunited only when he walked back on foot from Tijuana, spending eight days walking through the desert to get back to his wife and their two small children. This was before Operation Gatekeeper (Nevins 2002) and the progressive militarization of the Mexico-California border, which would eventually force undocumented immigrants into the even more hazardous Arizona and New Mexico border regions. This resulted in increased migrant deaths from heat and dehydration, as well as the frontier "justice" efforts of border Minutemen. When I later asked Arturo about this unwanted trek through the desert, he only grimaced in acknowledgement, clearly not wanting to revisit the memory further. In a world in which hardship was the norm, there was no need to split hairs over dates or revisit the worst of difficult memories.

As time wore on, Rosalia and Arturo Grande tired of the hardship of living as undocumented workers in the United States and missed their home in Tamaulipas. By then they had a third child, a three-month-old infant named Maria. They took her and the two boys and moved back to their *ejido* landholdings in San Fernando. Unfortunately, it proved impossible to scratch out a living there so they moved again—this time to Matamoros. They stayed with Arturo Grande's brother for their first two-and-a-half years in the city before moving to the Colonia Verde. Like their neighbors, they had initially squatted the plot of land where they lived. They were eventually able to purchase the lot from the city for Mex$2000. Since its initial establishment through squatting activities, the community had grown and become partially incorporated as a *colonia*. Most of the homes in the neighborhood were two-story cement structures with fences around small yards. Many homes, though not all, had indoor plumbing and electricity. Showers were typically one-temperature (cold) spigots and toilets met the bare necessities. The main road had recently been paved. This was considered a blessing since all of the surrounding unpaved roads turned into hazardous, cavernous, pothole-ridden mazes in the rainy season.

Although relatively well-developed and serviced, Colonia Verde did not have telephone poles or wires. When Las Caracaras would later apply to the Sierra Club for a seed grant through the Beyond the Border program, one of the group's top priorities was simply to establish an office in a neighboring *colonia* that was equipped with telephone wires and Internet connectivity. This goal complemented nicely the objectives of the Sierra Club's program to help border environmental groups overcome the quotidian obstacles of poverty, lack of resources, and infrastructure in order to network and accomplish their environmental goals. The fact that Rosalia (as President of Las Caracaras) lived in a neighborhood without even the most rudimentary communication technology would prove to be a sticking point in the organization's ongoing development. Although I witnessed the everyday challenges with which Rosalia's family continually lived, I did not understand the depth of the family's long struggles until I formally interviewed with Maria, who provided emotional and nuanced detail to conditions from an earlier period.[11]

When I first met Maria, she was sixteen years old and had recently dropped out of a Brownsville high school at tenth grade. She was mature, smart, articulate, and dedicated to her mother, family, and the cause of Las Caracaras. "After all," she told me once, "I am going to have a child here and I don't want him or her to grow up with the same contamination we have suffered." Maria had attended elementary school in Matamoros and later transferred to the Brownsville side. There had been two principle reasons for this. One, Maria was a US citizen and schooling on the Brownsville side was free, in comparison with the daunting costs for registration, uniforms, and books that she or her family would have to pay for her to attend secondary school in Matamoros. Second, her mother wanted her to learn to speak English and was certain that Maria would do so if forced to speak up in the American classroom. Maria claimed to understand English perfectly and, in fact, she did. On the rare occasions in which we might drive to Brownsville together or when the Sierra Club representatives were present and I might be speaking English with them, she understood it all. Nevertheless, I never heard her utter a word in English. She claimed that she refused to speak the language because it caused her too much *verguenza*, or shame, but I suspected that there was an element of well-deserved defiance in her refusal as well.

Maria lived with her young, hard-working, and adoring fiancé, Armando, in a bedroom on the second story of the house. Rosalia's oldest son, his wife, and child lived in the other bedroom. They were unmarried because either a civil or religious ceremony would have been too expensive. Although Maria was a regular and important contributing member to Las Caracaras' work (in fact, her mother demanded it since she was not going to school), Armando did not because he always seemed to be working sixty to seventy hours per week at the *maquila*.

At the time of our interview, Maria was seventeen years old and had recently given birth to her own seven-month-old son, Marco. Since I had heard her mother make frequent reference to the shack that they had cobbled together when they first moved to this lot, I asked Maria to describe the house to me as well as she could when they first moved in. Her response was moving. Normally calm, cool, and collected, she broke into uncontrollable tears. The tears were not for her, but for her mother and father and the horrible poverty they had endured in order to have what they had now. She told me the history of the house and the comfortably furnished living room in which we then sat:

> First it was made of cardboard, and then it was made of wood. My mother maintained the house here and my father worked as a trash collector. Later my mother worked in a *maquiladora* and that was how we began picking ourselves up, little by little, trying to move ahead. This house [she points around the room] the way it is now, this is how it was before with four rooms. My mother drew it on a page in a notebook, and there she kept her dream of having a house like this. That is how she wanted to build it, and that is how it is now.[12]

Rosalia had often told me about how they had "picked themselves up" little by little, but Maria's tears made the pain of that long process more apparent. The story of families making the transition from cardboard walls and tin roofs to furnished (and more secure) cement dwellings is a familiar one throughout sprawling border cities. As migrating populations move to border cities, they often construct their initial dwellings from the pallets or from the cardboard boxes tossed off by the *maquilas*. These packing materials are used to import duty-free the materials that will then be assembled and exported. This duty-free importation of building materials combined with the additional duty-free export of finished products (except the value added by *maquila* workers' labor) is yet one more example of how the *maquila* industry fails to develop backward and forward linkages with the Mexican economy in general, and thus does not generate industrial or economic development at a scale that would benefit diverse economic and social sectors. Mexican border residents' resourceful recycling of these toss-offs into homes represents in material form the absence of these linkages. It also exemplifies another aspect of the ecological economics throughput model that accounts for the waste produced alongside commodities and peoples. The waste of *maquilas* is creatively and necessarily used to build homes.

Maria went on to say that one of the things that kept her and Armando together was the fact that "he has the same dream that my mother once had" of owning his own home. Drawing a correlation between the poverty in which Armando's family currently lived, and the poverty in which her family once lived, she asked if I remembered visiting his home. I said I did. At the time, I was surprised to realize that there were differentiations between poverty at this level, and that Armando's home and neighborhood was clearly much more poor than that of Rosalia and Arturo's home in Colonia Verde. I had gone to Armando's family home with all female members of Rosalia's family one day. We spent the day conducting a lottery to help Rosalia collect enough money to make the return trip to Monterrey for follow up on her surgery and blood tests. The neighborhood itself had been virtually inaccessible due to the bad roads and rainy season muds, and we had hoofed part of the way in by foot. It was to these poor living conditions that Maria referred in order to highlight the common dream of her, her mother, and Armando, while at the same time drawing attention to the fact that her family had moved up in the world and, in fact, Armando felt that his own living situation and status had improved since moving in with them. She also mentioned the fact that both of their fathers had been garbage collectors and, although her father was now a guard in a bar, Armando's father continued with the other vocation. Armando had begun working in a *maquila* again (his second time) six months before since they had a child to support. He did the same type of steering wheel assembly work as the Spektra workers. His take-home pay was between Mex$480 and Mex$500 per week, roughly the equivalent of US$50 at the time.

Rosalia's two sons each lived nearby or in the same house. Arturo Chico lived upstairs with his wife Katerina, their daughter, and a newborn baby. Octavio, the oldest, lived one block away with his wife, Rosana, their daughter, and another newborn, Octavio Chico.[13] Octavio did not really participate in Las Caracaras activities; a weight problem kept him from working regularly. Instead, he did odd jobs and Rosana usually kept a *maquila* job, meanwhile participating occasionally in Las Caracaras.

Arturo Chico currently worked in a *maquila,* meanwhile his wife struggled to get through an English language course that would prepare her to become an elementary school English teacher. The course was offered at the local Universidad Autonoma de Tamaulipas[14] and was part of a Mexican government-sponsored program to produce more certified primary school English language teachers. The program paid students during the period of their enrollment. Katerina regularly spent an hour or two per day going over her English lessons and by the end of 2002, she was teaching her own classes at a local school.

Katerina was very active with Las Caracaras. Since we spent so much time together, I had heard bits and pieces of the story of how she arrived in Matamoros, usually interspersed with jokes and commentary about the time that she had spent in the US. Katerina was born and grew up in a small town about two hours south of Ciudad Victoria, the capital of Tamaulipas. [15] She claimed that her mother, who had moved to Matamoros from Tampico a few years before and with whom she had only tense relations, had eight brothers and sisters. Four of them were now in Matamoros, three were on "the other side," and one remained on the ranch where they had all grown up. When Katerina was born, she lived with her mother as an infant only for the first two weeks of her life, at which time her grandmother came to get her. Katerina considered her mother irresponsible, overly emotional, and inclined to play the helpless woman role. It was clear that Katerina—ambitious, self-sufficient, and a newlywed in a stable marriage and family—intended to live her life in a way she considered more respectable than her mother's. She lived with her grandmother until she was ten.

In a remarkable story laced with her ability to see the humor in the absurd, Katerina also told me how she had come to meet her father a couple of years prior, when she was in her early twenties. She met him by accident when she went to Cd. Victoria to register as *regidora* for the local Partido Revolucionario Democratico. The civil servant who received her registration within the labyrinthine bureaucracy of the state capital remarkably had the same highly unusual last name as Katerina. Logically, she asked if he knew her father. Of course he did; he was her father. That was how they met. Katerina had two half-brothers. One was already in the United States—Indianapolis—and the other, Gustavo, was currently living with them. He was seventeen, had arrived only a few short months before from Ciudad Mante and, although he wanted to cross illegally to the United States, she had convinced him to stay, work, and wait until he got papers.

Katerina first came to Matamoros when she was ten. One of her aunts came to their farm in Cd. Mante and asked if Katerina would like to come to Matamoros and take care of her children. Katerina had already finished primary school, but she would have to move in order to go to secondary school. So she moved in with the Matamoros aunt and was told that if she did not keep the house sufficiently clean, she would not be allowed to go to school. She stayed with this aunt for a couple of years and attended secondary school. While in Matamoros, she would return to Cd. Mante for vacations.

Another aunt who lived in Santa Ana, California came to their Cd. Mante farm for a visit. She also wanted someone to care for her children. She said that since Katerina was single and "without a future" there in Cd. Mante, she would take her to California with her. She could go to school there and take care of the children. Out of financial necessity, the first aunt agreed. At thirteen years of age, Katerina crossed the border with a coyote as an illegal immigrant. Her California aunt and uncle arranged her crossing with a coyote to whom they paid US$500.

On the path where we crossed [near Tijuana] the coyotes eventually abandoned us. On the hill, we met other coyotes that we did not know. And these were the ones who took us to California to the other coyotes. The others who had originally contracted with my aunt did not follow through. They left us on the hill. We had to cross on foot, running, and drop to the ground every time the *migra* came by. Once on the ground a tarantula crawled up on my face, I was so afraid—but I could not scream—and I held down the scream until I got rid of the tarantula!! We slept on the hill for one night—on the ground, with branches, dirt, and everything.[16]

She finally made it to her aunt's home. "When I arrived, she told me that I could not go to school, but only care for the children. I signed up for high school anyway. I went as an undocumented and it served me well, since with all the ups and downs I learned some English anyway which has helped me become a teacher." Katerina stayed in California for two years, although she had a miserable existence. She says that this aunt hated her, and made her cook and clean constantly for room and board. She also worked at a Burger King through a vocational program at the school and to make some money. In the classroom, she was punished if she ever spoke in Spanish, so she became best friends with a young Japanese woman who was also a non-English speaker. When I asked how in the world they talked, she said "through sign language, of course." They became best friends.

Meanwhile, the situation at her aunt's house continued to deteriorate. The aunt was jealous of Katerina's increasing English language skills; she was also afraid that the teenager was becoming attractive to her husband. When Katerina was fifteen, the aunt ran her out of the house. She went to live with a nun and began cleaning houses on Saturdays and Sundays in order to earn a living while she continued to go to school.

Finally, she could not take it anymore. Earlier, she had purchased false papers for employment purposes, but now her aunt was threatening to report her to the US Immigration and Naturalization Service (INS). She caught a bus to Tijuana and eventually made her way back to Matamoros. In Matamoros, she stayed with the first aunt, finished high school, met and married Arturo Chico. About her California experience, she said, "I had a lot of desire to learn, but it was a terrible experience. I tried to take advantage of the experience since I like English a lot, and so I learned a lot. Then, when I returned, I continued to study and now I am an English teacher."[17]

Among other Las Caracaras members, the stories of migration and the search for opportunity were similar. Gabriela, for example, was a woman in her mid-thirties who was also one of the few middle or lower middle class members of the group. She had worked in a *maquila* for seventeen years in an administrative position and was the owner of a child-care center in Matamoros. Gabriela's experience was exceptional because she had defied the turnover narrative and practices of the industry. She had been singled out early on as someone who was trainable that could work in an administrative position. "Distinguishing between the trainable and the untrainable—the 'quitters' and the 'continuers' (Lucker and Alvarez 1985)—requires an evaluation of employees early in their careers in order to put them on the right track, either the unskilled or the skilled one" (Wright 2001, 134). As Cooney notes, "There appear to be limited possibilities for advancement beyond a certain level of management in many *maquiladoras*, and the possibilities are even fewer for women" (Cooney 2001, 72). Even though she was extremely bright and educated, however, Gabriela had never made it past administrative positions into management. At the time that I met her she was also a single mother with a twelve-year-old child whose father had left many years earlier to live in the United States.

Gabriela was born in and grew up in a small town called Ciudad Ocampo, which was about two hours south of Ciudad Victoria. Her family had a farm there and she had three brothers. She was only fifteen when she came to Matamoros. She came with an uncle and his family, mostly in an attempt to better her own lot in life, but also to separate herself from her father's alcoholism. Her parents eventually followed and, at the time of our meeting, had been living with her for three or four years. She had migrated primarily to continue her education, both in secondary school and *preparatoria.*

> I came when I was fifteen because our economic situation, well, it seemed better to find some work and be able to continue studying at the same time. We did not have an economic situation there that would support any of us going to school. And two of my brothers were already here. [. . .] So it was mostly my decision. My parents were not doing well, I needed to separate myself from them, and they also saw that they could not support me while I went to school, and I had only studied through the second year of high school at that point. So, going to school and studying as well, that is, going to work from seven until five then making time to go to school and study at night.[18]

She goes on to say that she continued to work and study at night until she finished her education. Then she went to work in a *maquila.*

Don Luis was another very active member within Las Caracaras. He and his wife, Virginia, lived in Colonia Roja and had four children together.[19] They had previously lived on an *ejido* in Panuco, in the State of Veracruz. They had migrated almost twelve years before in 1991. They came to Matamoros primarily in order to improve their children's opportunity to receive an education. In Panuco, they did not have the money to send their children to high school. Matamoros was chosen because it seemed like a good place to find work as a mason, which is what Don Luis did, although he had also studied in a seminary for several years. "We all want to give a little more to our children," he said. They said that, in those days, for high school you had to pay for registration and, for primary school, you had to pay for both registration and books. Just the books cost Mex$50, but "now, thank God" they gave them the books, and before they did not. "If we went to buy books, we were stuck without food, and if we paid the rent, we were stuck without food, and later to pay the water and electricity for where we were renting." Their eldest daughter was working in a *maquila,* but she had made it at least part of the way through secondary school.

Don Luis and Virginia's transition to Matamoros had been difficult, even though they had friends here and contacts who were masons. Don Luis came first and stayed with friends for six months while looking for work, which he eventually found. Later he was able to go back for the rest of the family. When they came, someone lent them a house in exchange for Virginia's working in the homeowners' restaurant. This same homeowner helped them to pay for one year of school for their children. Virginia went on to say,

> I also went to work for a man doing cleaning and received Mex$30 a day for that—US$3 per day which helped a lot. Later the oldest girl began to do housework and that also helped. Then I was pregnant again, and I gave birth and we kept working on and off in the restaurants and in people's houses. This is how we continued until later we were able to rent. We rented for six years over on Avenida del Niño, until we came to live here [in Colonia Roja]. But yes, we struggled a little. Well, in the first place, he [Don Luis] did not earn much in his work, and then with the older girl in high school and working, I had to stay at home with the kids.[20]

Felipe was an educated young man who worked in Matamoros in the wholesale food distribution business.[21] He came to Matamoros during his third year of high school, about five years before. At the time, members of his family were going separate ways—his mother to the United States, and a brother and sister came to Matamoros. He followed his siblings and came to live with them and his grandmother here.

He came to Matamoros for both economic and health reasons. Since he was thin and relatively weak, he said he felt as though he needed to be in a place where he could make more money in order to support his nutrition, as well as be in a place where he would be supported morally by family. His mother's departure to the United States in pursuit of a romantic relationship had not been well accepted by the children; his father had died in a car accident only a few years before. "I had a grandmother here whom I had seen before on trips with my mother. So, mostly I came for the development of my body. But I was aware that the northern border had economic advantages as well":

> The salaries in Michoacan are the lowest salaries in Mexico. Every region has its own minimum wage, and in Michoacan it was much lower than on the border. The work situation there is also not very good. There are only some very small factories and they are all Mexican-owned with very low salaries. The salary in Michoacan is very low compared to the border; right now the salary—at the utmost—is about 500 pesos per week, or fifty dollars at current exchange rates. But the salaries there are generally between 350 and 500 pesos.[22]

His grandparents were the last to live in the countryside of Michoacan, rather than directly in the city of Morelia, and he claimed that his grandmother still owned her *ejido* lands there. His father had been from the city. His parents had met when his mother migrated there from the *ejido* in order to look for work. His paternal grandparents had also had some land and money, but his grandfather was an alcoholic, so all was more or less lost on that side of the family. In Matamoros he married a woman who had been born in the city. Her parents had moved here from an *ejido* nearby, and they all lived together in a small rented house on the southwestern side of the city.

One of the younger members of Las Caracaras, Tomas, had another interesting story of migration which, similar to Rosalia, he traced back to his grandparents. His grandparents were originally from Tula, Tamaulipas, which was near the border of San Luis Potosí. "They came here to Valle Hermoso [a city about sixty miles to the southeast] originally for the cotton harvest and they lived here for a while, then returned to Tula. My mother first went back with them, but she had family here in Valle Hermoso and they had a farm, so she came to stay with them." He was born there in Valle Hermoso, though he does not know his father, who lived in Reynosa. He was brought to Matamoros right after he was born and lived with someone here until he was six, when he was returned to his mother who then lived on an *ejido* close to San Fernando. His mother was a seamstress, so she later came to Matamoros looking for work.

This story of migration and struggle was repeated in different forms at different times: Alejandra and her husband were from San Luis Potosí; Rosana, Rosalia's other daughter-in-law, was from Monterrey; Father Gonzalez was from a small town near Ciudad Victoria; Rosalia's nephew, Laro, who sometimes participated with Las Caracaras, had also come with his family from an *ejido* in San Fernando.

Similar to Las Caracaras members, Spektra workers were also migrants from other regions of Mexico. The majority were from San Luis Potosí, although others were from Veracruz. The migrant trail—even within Mexico itself—often moves directly northward, so many people of Matamoros were from states directly to the south—San Luis Potosí, Veracruz, or perhaps even Mexico City. Meanwhile the migrant community of a city like Tijuana—or the migrant laborers on the US side of the western portion of the border—come more often from states like Michoacan, Jalisco, and Oaxaca. As has often been noted, the NAFTA had disastrous effects on the Mexican countryside as the country was flooded with grain imports, transforming a once maize-based, self-sufficient rural population into a dependent one. As rural populations have moved off their lands and *ejidos* have been parceled up and sold, the migration has been in the direction of major cities like Mexico City or steadily northward—if not to the United States then certainly to the border cities and the promise and opportunity which they are perceived to hold in terms of employment and educational possibilities.

Former Spektra workers Martin and Adelia lived in a neighborhood close to Rosalia's, but they also had a home on the US side. They spent the week over there so that their two daughters could learn English in a Brownsville school, then return to Matamoros on weekends. They had each worked at Spektra for more than a decade.[23] They had both grown up in the state of San Luis Potosí, and she in Ciudad Valle, near the capital. She came to Matamoros when she was eighteen with one sister. The rest remained in San Luis. When I asked what type of work her family did when she was growing up, she said, "They were farmers, they worked in agriculture and the rest of my family is still there, doing more or less the same thing." I asked why she and her sister left, and she said, "To work." At that point her husband intervened,

> Work in the fields is much more difficult than working in factories. . . . With all of the sun and the difficulties, life is just harder than in the city. And you don't make much money. We had a ranch there, part of an ejido, but it was too much work. Here, you don't make much money, but you make a little bit more.

Now Adelia no longer works outside of the home, and her husband does some other kind of work in the US side.

One forty-two-year-old woman, Luiza, who declined to be tape recorded, said that she moved with her husband and two children to Matamoros in the early 1980s.[24] She worked at Spektra for seven years, from 1993 to 2000 and did not have any complaints. She and her family had come from San Luis Potosí, where they had grown up on a farm. She had six brothers and sisters. One other sister had since moved to Matamoros, while the rest remained in San Luis Potosí.

She and her husband had moved to Matamoros to find work and found it very quickly. He worked as a street vendor, while she worked in the *maquilas*. First she worked in Fisher Price for seven years, then she stayed at home for a couple of years, then went to work at the Spektra plant until 2000. She gave up the work for the simple reason that her husband thought someone should be at home during the day so that the house would not be robbed.

In another case, Marta, a thirty-two-year-old woman explained to me that she was also from San Luis Potosí.[25] There had been nine children in her family; of the nine, four had come to Matamoros. She said that when she was growing up, "My father worked on a farm. Taking care of animals, so we, well, I worked in the fields too, planting and harvesting, all of that. My father worked on another farm with my little brother." I asked her when she began to work and she told me at age thirteen, right after elementary school. When I asked how she came to Matamoros looking for work, she responded:

> I came when I was sixteen in order to work in the *maquiladoras* . . . I came because my brother, he had come here already with my sister-in-law and after he came back home and told me that I should come here to work with him. So I came here with him. He got me some work and so I stayed here to work.

"Did you go to work directly in a *maquila?*" I asked. "No, when I was sixteen I worked in a cafeteria, later I went to care for an elderly and invalid woman, and later I worked in a factory called 'Tente,' later called 'Lucir.'" Marta stayed at Tente/Lucir for four years where workers were treated well. Later, she worked in another plant where they manufactured small plastic flowers and there the workers were also treated well, but this factory closed. In the next factory she lasted only one month because she did not like it. Then she finally went to work for Spektra, where she stayed for almost ten years—she was twenty-two when she began working there.

In these cases, as in the case of Las Caracaras members, the decision to migrate was cast as a choice to better one's own and one's children's life opportunities. The past—past places and past times—was cast as a barren land in which opportunities were nonexistent and one could hope only to repeat the same cycle as one's ancestors. The border cities, in contrast, represented change: an opportunity to leapfrog ahead in terms of one's class location and social status. In this sense, they appeared to represent a democratic and liberating potential not present in the erstwhile rural homelands.

Luiza made this point poignantly when she said that, in San Luis Potosí, her children would have simply continued life the way that she and others had for many generations. She herself had only a sixth-grade education. She said that by moving to Matamoros and working in the *maquilas,* she and her husband were able to give their children opportunities that they would not have been able to give them otherwise. And the reason they were able to send them to school was simply that they were now able to purchase school supplies, uniforms and books, the cost of which was otherwise prohibitive. The financial obstacles to purchasing these supplies were always challenging; Katerina, Rosalia's daughter in law, had wanted to send her own four-year-old daughter to preschool the year before, but had been unable to afford it. Luiza told me proudly that her sons—ages eighteen, seventeen, and thirteen—had all done well. The oldest was currently at the Instituto Tecnologico de Matamoros, the second was in a local college, and the youngest was in his second year of high school.

"Life was better there"

When I asked, as I often did, for Caracaras members to tell me about their places of origin, responses were typically enthusiastic, loquacious, and often tinged with what seemed to be nostalgia for a more innocent place and time. Although many had made the voyage to the border for educational or economic opportunities, the price for that voyage had become more visible as they passed the years in a crowded and unkempt border city. Many maintained that returning to their *ejido* homelands was not an option; not only had many sold their parcels to finance their fresh starts on the border, but many also articulated— sometimes directly, other times indirectly—the sense that the days of pristine country life or rural autonomy were coming to an end, if they had not already. It was not simply the case that they could not return to the countryside, a slower pace of life, and cleaner environments; rather, these possibilities were drying up for all Mexicans. Lands lay arid and fallow or were dedicated to agribusiness. What corn or grains one might grow could never add up to economic self-sufficiency again, because the Mexican grain market had been saturated by cheaper US corn imports. In other words, the geography of migration seemed to have been undergirded by a temporal narrative that placed country life beyond the pale and firmly in the past, and urban life firmly in both the present and impending future.

Tomas, who lived in Matamoros until he was six and then moved out to an *ejido* with his mother, said that he found the environment outside of Matamoro much healthier:

> There it is very quiet, and all of the people are good people. When I lived there, everything was good, there were plenty of harvests (corn, beans, sorghum) and there was just a lot of life there. There you could sustain a family just by working the harvest and selling it. The ejiditarios were united as a community. Afterward, this all disappeared, people began to sell their lands and some people went to the US—that was around 1994. [. . .] Life there was better. I wasn't really much healthier because I was sick a lot, but all of the food was healthy and nutritious. Meat, eggs, vegetables, fruit—all types of vegetables. The air was fresh, not like here, it was surrounded by mountains—there wasn't any contamination in that air.[26]

Tomas said that he had no plans for returning to the countryside because he needed to work. When I asked him what would have to change about the area in which he had previously lived for him to go back, he stated the following:

> What I would like to change there are the people. . . . Or that the government might give more support to the farmers who work on the land, yes. There, you live well, but, well this is what is affecting the farmers—that they are not supported by their own government. On the other hand, there's the United States, China. . . . and the farmers here cannot sell their products. So what I would like is that the government supports more the farmers here than in other countries, so that farming would be stable. All over Mexico there have been protests around this theme.[27]

When I asked Gabriela to tell me about her childhood in Ciudad Ocampo, she reminded me that she did not leave because she did not like the place, but because of her father's drinking problems. She seemed aware that her memories of the country might also be shaped by the innocence of childhood. The place itself, she said,

was very pretty. To me it seemed very pretty but perhaps that
was because I was the only girl and I was very spoiled and loved!
As the only girl, I do not remember ever lacking anything. It is
countryside there, it was something beautiful because you can enjoy
the countryside, the air, the night with the stars and the moon in its
full splendor, not like here that sometimes with the contamination
you cannot enjoy the same things. And the food—well, we did not
eat much meat, but the food that we did eat was very nutritious.
Whatever came from milk we ate a lot, we grew fresh vegetables, and
we ate very well! I'm not sure how to make a comparison between
then and now in terms of food. . . . Here, if you have money you can
eat more or less well, right? But with regard to the environment, for
me it was much healthier there, definitely. Here no, here you pass by
the canal in the morning and you have to cover your nose because of
the horrible odors. You go to work in a *maquiladora* and you enter
into the *maquiladora* and your eyes burn, you feel horrible. There
[Ocampo] the morning was fresh, right? It was pleasant, rich, and the
nighttime as well. There you could go chasing butterflies, little birds
and everything. And here, where are the butterflies? I have never seen
a butterfly here.[28]

Katerina was always happy to talk about her childhood on the ranch
in Ciudad Mante. She said that they never had any money and she had
no idea how her grandmother raised nine of her own children there,
plus three grandchildren.

But on the ranch we had everything: mangos, oranges, limes,
squash, cows, milk, everything! When we did not have coffee, my
grandmother made tea from the leaves of avocado trees, also fried
plantains. We ate very well—roosters, chickens, eggs, nopales. Thank
God, we never lacked good food to eat. My grandfather also grew
corn, sugarcane, beans, wheat—we had everything there! Now things
are falling apart little by little. But my grandmother made cheese
from the milk and we used to sell the cheese. She also prepared
snacks with chile and we sold these things as well. My grandmother
sold used clothes and I helped her. Sometimes they paid us with
roosters rather than money. The corn that my grandfather grew we
sold occasionally, but this was very rare since we used it to prepare
everything. We made tamales and tortillas. There was a well to get

water, a river, mangos, everything. We had no money, but we were not lacking in anything.[29]

I ask Katerina how she would compare the quality of life between the farm and her life in Matamoros.

Life was so much better then! It was all natural, nothing was contaminated, we cut everything from the root and since we grew the corn ourselves, of course we knew that it too was not contaminated. We planted it ourselves, we shucked the corn ourselves. We lived on a ranch, nothing was contaminated. Well, there were not any cars or anything. They say that the environment gets contaminated with cars and fumes, but we had none of that. In terms of the quality of life, food and all, my opinion is that it was much better before than it is now. Sure I was a child and childhood is the most beautiful period of your life because you have no worries—you just ask for things— which I understand now that I am a mother.

Later on she said that, although there were still fresh vegetables, fruits, and water, it was not the same. "It is not the same because my grandfather does not grow the corn anymore. He is too old to plow the land for planting, and we never had machinery or horses. And if we don't have corn, if we cannot make tortillas, what are we going to do? And with what are we going to buy tortillas?"

Unlike the others, Felipe's basis of comparison was not with a rural area but, rather, with another major city. He said he was surprised by many things when he moved to Matamoros—the slower pace of life, the fact that it seemed to be a city with a rural mentality, and so forth—but that he had always thought about this:

How is it possible that a city like Matamoros, with so many resources for work, so many factories, and with some of the higher salaries, with this superior source of income because of all the factories that are here. [...] How is it possible that there are so many streets full of trash, rivers full of water—it rains just a little and it begins flooding immediately! How is it possible that with so many resources, this city could be like this? In contrast, how is it possible that in Michoacan, where the salaries are so much lower and you do not have the same resources with the factories, that it is so much cleaner there?[30]

Felipe went on to say that, in Morelia, they did not even have the same problems with the municipal dump. There, the dump was located far away and there was no problem with people fearing that they might become contaminated by it. This was unlike Matamoros, where the dump that was located within the city limits had an inextinguishable blaze, and people lived in shacks right at its edges.

He added that even the water and solid waste drainage systems in Matamoros seemed haywire. In Morelia, the fresh water system was separate from the sewage system, as in most Mexican cities. In contrast, in Matamoros, the two were intertwined. "The drain that is used for sewage is the same as the one which is used for rain. In most parts of Mexico, the drainage systems are completely separate." He hypothesized that the constant flooding of Matamoros during the rainy season was due not only to the lack of drains, but also to the possibility that the existing water drains were being invaded by the sewage system.

For some members of Las Caracaras, comparisons between "there" and "here" were voiced clearly in terms of the superiority of Nature in their places of origin, compared with the relative lack of Nature in Matamoros. For others, the comparison was made simply with regard to other cities or places. Many believed that the very fact that Matamoros was a city of strangers was the source of its environmental problems, requiring no less than a change of consciousness before the city itself could be cleaned up. This change was also part of Las Caracaras' long-term mission—a program of consciousness-raising inspired by Paolo Freire, which would both educate and empower Matamorenses with respect to their urban and natural environments.

As Smith (1994) has noted there is among refugees, exiles, migrants and immigrants, an undeniable tendency to want to create in one's new space a sense of home or place. Speaking of "Little Havana," "Koreatown" and other ethnically defined spaces within US cities, he notes that "in these social spaces, selected elements of the past are re-captured in the place-making spatial practices of new immigrants and refugees." As members Las Caracaras gathered for late night meetings huddled in Rosalia's front yard or in a spare room of the local church, they brought these disparate histories with them as they attempted to patchwork something in common: namely, aesthetically pleasing and safe environmental futures for themselves and their children. Their actions "express[ed] the desire to reterritorialize as a collective response to displacement and deterritorialization" (Smith 1994, 19). Although it appeared certain that most Caracaras knew that they could not go back" or recreate precisely what they once had, knowledge of what they once had reminded them that what they currently had was not enough.

Throwing Out the Trash in a City of Strangers

Las Caracaras members tended to blame Matamoros' environmental problems on the city's social composition as a "city of strangers." Felipe, Gabriela, Oscar, and Tomas, in particular, articulated strong views regarding both the relationship between one urban environment and another, as well as the possible social explanations for why Matamoros suffered such dire environmental challenges. At the time of these interviews—with the onset of the rainy season and the prospect of flooded streets, homes, and garbage floating everywhere—the city was in the midst of its *cultura de basura* and *tirar la basura*[31] campaign. Some articulated their views through this prism, meanwhile remarking sardonically that the city officials only pursued city clean-up during times of crisis or elections. For example, Felipe, again comparing Morelia and Matamoros, tied the lack of a sense of community in Matamoros to the different work routines in each:

> There [Morelia], people are a little bit cleaner than here. People get up early and clean their homes. Similarly, the city has street sweepers and cleaners who get up early to keep the city clean. With regard to Matamoros, it seems as though there are more people here. But there is also a different work culture. In Morelia, there is only one work shift. In Matamoros, there are three. People here are working so much here that it is hard for them to take an interest in things outside of themselves and their routine. Perhaps if there were a park or a zoo, or something like that, it would get their attention and make them pay more attention to their immediate environment. Really, though, they tend to worry more about their personal concerns, than the general environment or other people.[32]

He went on to discuss the problems with Matamoros having largely a transient population, or a population that aspires to be elsewhere, or on "the other side":

There are many immigrants who make it Matamoros but then
cannot make it to the other side. There is a constant problem of this
"transient" population. When one comes to Matamoros—especially
after returning from a cleaner city—Matamoros looks like a city from
a movie, almost apocalyptic, but it doesn't seem to matter to most
people, plus they all ignore or mistreat each other. There is no sense
of responsibility or consciousness that, if one person throws out their
trash in the street, other people are going to throw out their trash
as well. It makes them lazy, or they do not want to worry about the
future or what might happen.[33]

He added that it was the population itself that needed to be educated and
made more self-conscious of its actions. "Perhaps if this can be done, as
new people come they will see a clean city and perhaps they will also try
to keep it clean. But if the same people who live here do not do anything
to maintain their areas clean, then who else is going to keep their home
clean?"

These sentiments were echoed by Oscar, who blamed the lack of a
cultura de basura on the population profile of Matamoros: "People come
from all over Mexico. They do not treat each other kindly. In other parts
of Mexico cities are kept cleaner because people are in their own communities and have the social relations to discipline them to respect their
own environments." He was also unequivocal in placing the blame for
the pollution squarely on the backs of the Matamorenses themselves:
"We have to learn to clean up after ourselves, we have to learn to respect our environments and offspring enough. We are ultimately responsible—and nobody else."[34]

Gabriela, who maintained that she was doing her work with Las Caracaras primarily for her daughter's future also echoed these themes.

I would say that about 80 percent of the population of Matamoros
is not from here. Different cultures, different ideas, different
everything. There is a total lack of control in everything, in not
throwing trash, in everything. Everyone just does what they want to
here. I can pass by and throw down my trash, I pass by and burn a
tire, I pass by and you pass by . . . you see?

For Tomas, it was primarily the lack of education and sense of
citizenship that kept Matamoros in chaos. He reiterated the views that

the problem was not just with the *maquilas* or municipal authorities; rather, the population of Matamoros had to develop its own sense of place, community, citizenship, and stewardship toward both the natural and built environment. The bigger problem, then, remained the fact that the social composition of Matamoros was the greatest obstacle to instilling this type of consciousness. The hope of Las Caracaras was that in accomplishing concrete tasks—like covering the canal and getting its banks cleaned, and importing some "nature" by planting native trees and shrubs, creating a space in which people could recreate—they would begin to instill a sense of pride and community in local neighborhoods, and the city would begin to pick itself up, little by little.

The Sierra Club and the Beyond the Borders Program

The goals of Las Caracaras also dovetailed nicely with a newly launched Beyond the Borders Program of the US- based Sierra Club. Over the course of more than a year, the two organizations developed a relationship that was exemplary of the type of cross-border advocacy that emerged in the NAFTA era (Evans 2000; Brooks and Fox 2002; Mancillas 2002; Smith 1994). As described by Evans, one function of such transnational advocacy networks is that they shift "power by connecting dis-privileged Third World groups and communities to political actors and arenas that can affect decisions in hegemonic global networks" (Evans 2000, 231). The Sierra Club attempted to effect such a power shift both by encouraging collaboration between resource-challenged Mexican environmental groups and themselves—a powerful US-based NGO. The purpose of the Beyond the Border program was to transfer resources from a resource rich US-based NGO to resource poor Mexican environmental groups so that the latter could have adequate resources necessary to effect environmental change from below. With transnational resources and support, they could conceivably negotiate with municipal, state, or federal authorities, and pressure the government into conformity with its own existing environmental laws—much as the environmental side accord was intended to do.

In 2002, Las Caracaras resumed a relationship with the Sierra Club begun some years before when Las Caracaras had attended a meeting in Brownsville with Sierra Club members and other border environment groups. At this meeting, Rosalia had spoken eloquently and powerfully on the topic of environmental contamination and justice, leading to her inadvertent and unintended usurpation of Nurse Felipa as head of the organization. Rosalia and others had also organized a toxic tour of Matamoros for the Sierra Club visitors. The visitors had been so impressed by Las Caracaras and Rosalia's testimony that they made a subsequent donation of US$5000 for the group. The organization had afterward experienced a number of pitfalls, including, though not limited to, Rosalia's health problems. Much of the money from this original no-strings-attached gift still sat in the bank by the year 2002, and the original impression Las Caracaras had made on the Sierra Club clearly remained.

The relationship between the two organizations resumed with a meeting initiated in 2002 by the Sierra Club in Brownsville in which it sought to sow the seeds for the Beyond the Borders Program. During this meeting, the representative of the Beyond the Borders program at the time, Oscar, announced the new program and passed out literature detailing requirements and deadlines for the grant competition. Las Caracaras was the model target organization: It was a grassroots environmental justice organization constituted primarily of economically disenfranchised Mexicans; it was clear about its organizational goals and environmental objectives; collectively, members of the group had a rich and detailed empirical knowledge about the extent and causes of contamination in their area; and the group lacked the resources necessary to establish themselves in the local community sufficient to have a lasting environmental impact.

These funds for the new Beyond the Border program were earmarked specifically for environmental rehabilitation or cleanup projects on the Mexican side of the US-Mexico border or in other areas of Mexico. For the Sierra Club, the new program signaled their own venture into the field of environmental justice and a new concern with the relationship between the environment and people's health. This initiative marked an important departure from the organization's previous profile as one concerned primarily with white, middle to upper middle class concerns exclusively with the environment, and the conservation and preservation of nature. As Oscar described it during the launch meeting, the Sierra Club was coming to the realization, like many environmental groups, that in order to protect the environment it was necessary to protect human populations living in local environments.

During the meeting, Oscar passed out a leaflet in which the Sierra Club announced that it had launched an initiative designed to support and strengthen grassroots environmental and community groups in Mexico. The goals of this new grant making Mexico project are to help these grassroots groups throughout Mexico in their fight to protect the environment, to educate Sierra Club members about Mexican environment and environmental justice issues, and to involve Sierra Club volunteers in supporting Mexican environmental activism.[35]

Additionally, the program announcement stipulated that the Sierra Club was interested in funding projects that sought to strengthen grass-roots organizing, encourage "environmental stewardship and corporate accountability," identify and attempt to resolve environmental risks, improve "public, occupational, and environmental health conditions," as well as encourage collaborative relations between the Sierra Club and Mexican entities. Organizations that it was interested in funding included grass root groups, pollution prevention and/or cleanup projects, and "land and natural resource stewardship programs." Organizations or projects with overriding political or religious goals were not eligible to receive grants. This latter stipulation would later be used by Las Caracaras to try and unseat members of the Partido de la Revolución Democrática (PRD) from the organization's executive committee. A detailed account of this meeting is provided in Chapter 5.

Over the course of the next year, Las Caracaras and the Sierra Club continued to develop a relationship that revolved largely around the latter's organizational representatives' visits to Matamoros. Oscar was eventually replaced by a new representative. Both Sierra Club representatives offered advice and capacity-building workshops to Las Caracaras. Capacity building generally refers to an attempt by one organization to develop the human resources, technical skills, and organizational management of another group, with the final goal that the second group becomes autonomous and capable of pursuing its own development independently. Through these workshops and time-intensive visits, both representatives attempted to cultivate the organization and a good working relationship with it, as well as prime Las Caracaras to submit a successful grant proposal for the Beyond the Border program. As part of my fieldwork, I helped to facilitate this relationship.

The Sierra Club program, particularly with its proposal writing element, helped Las Caracaras to define more clearly its immediate goals in relation to the *Dren Cinco de Marzo*. It also gave members additional esteem and confidence as an organization receiving organizational support from such an esteemed and influential US-based NGO. As in most transnational relations, whether involving funding or not, Las Caracaras seemed to think that its goals acquired greater legitimacy because of endorsement by a nonlocal actor. The red thread that kept the two organizations in conversation throughout the year was the goal of preparing Las Caracaras to apply for and receive a grant, which would seemingly set the group on the path to increased organizational independence.

During the year, Las Caracaras went through the process twice. The first time it was on the cusp of receiving the grant, but Rosalia withdrew its candidacy due to frictions within the group. The second time, it won the grant and kept it.

The relationship between Las Caracaras and the Sierra Club had tangible positive and negative consequences for the fledgling organization. On the one hand, this support allowed Las Caracaras to begin to establish itself as a functional entity in Matamoros. It was able to apply for *asociación civil* status, petition the municipal government to clean up the *Dren Cinco de Marzo,* attend Border 2012 Regional Workgroup meetings and, eventually, to initiate the process of being represented in the Matamoros Comité Ciudadano, or Citizens' Committee, in the city's application for a NADBank loan. Additionally, though to a much lesser degree, its level of organizational development allowed Las Caracaras to be invited into the then-developing binational Laguna Madre protection initiative. Members of Las Caracaras also set up an office, began to learn basic computer skills, developed meeting agendas, and otherwise demonstrated the effects of the Sierra Club's capacity-building efforts.

On the other hand, the relationship brought to the surface tensions that had remained latent in the loosely organized organization. These tensions revolved around class, ethnic. and gender differences principally between Rosalia, the organization's president, other members, and some of the organization's middle class PRD members. This tension was most visible (and most destructive) in the relationship between Rosalia and the PRD constituency, but it reverberated throughout other group relations as well, since the majority were of the same class status as Rosalia (largely poor, working or lower working class, of rural origins, and uneducated). The reason these latent tensions transformed into overt conflict when they did seemed to revolve around the possibility of the organization receiving funding. When there were no funding possibilities, the conflicts remained latent.

Chapter 5

Environmental Organizing and Citizenship on the Border

The previous chapter traced the footprints of migrants as they made their ways from southern and central Mexico to the border city of Matamoros. This chapter examines efforts to craft an ecological footprint or "eco-region" consciousness that transcends borders and nation-states. The drive to think in terms of bio- or eco-regions, rather than in terms of regions defined primarily by nation-state boundaries, has been present in environmental history and ecological economics for some time. This impulse has also been implicit, and sometimes explicit, in NAFTA's environmental accord and accompanying border-specific institutions. The accord and institutions were created to rehabilitate, enhance, and preserve the environment on both sides of the border.

The environmental mechanisms of NAFTA—which include the North American Agreement on Environmental Cooperation, the Commission on Environmental Cooperation, the Border Environmental Cooperation Commission, the North American Development Bank, Joint Public Advisory Council and its incumbent Citizens' Committees— were all created with the aim and scope of addressing the environmental needs of border populations. By default or pragmatic considerations, eco-region became the operative principle of the accord and cross-border allegiances it was intended to encourage.

This privileging of an eco-regional frame allowed for border communities to be imagined as sustainable building blocks upon which environmental rehabilitation, preservation, and participatory democracy could be built. However, the framing and conceptualization of the borderlands as a specific bio-region belied a fundamental paradox: namely, that the bio-region of the borderland was not untouched nature with naturally inhabiting and stewarding ecological communities but, rather, a "second space" (Brady 2002; Escobar 1996) built by and for capitalism and the nation-state itself. As a second space kind of place, it is inevitably cross cut by inequalities produced and reproduced by the dominant economic system and the border itself.

The environmental side accord was founded on a paradox. It was intended to encourage a sense of environmental citizenship and allegiance to the transnational space and place of the border, yet to operationalize the accord is to participate in a nation-building exercise from below. While the border as place encompasses both US and Mexican regions, the legal borderlands of the accords (Dudziack and Volpp 2005) support the reproduction of the respective nation-states and their laws because of their legally pluralistic structure (Merry 1992). While twin and contradictory commitments are well-recognized features of the environmental citizenship model (Dobson 2003), it is especially pronounced in the environmental side agreement.

The environmental side accord functions through participation, and participation was recognized in the founding document of sustainable development, *Our Common Future* (WCED 1987), as essential to both democracy and sustainability. In this report, the Bruntland Commission authors listed first, within their "requirements of a strategy for sustainable development" the following: "A political system that secures effective participation in decision-making" (WCED 1987, 65). Since the late 1980s, participation has been considered essential to successful sustainable development. It was offered as a corrective to top-down development practices that had existed for decades until then, and which were increasingly recognized to isolate target populations. As many participation specialists have noted (Cleaver 2001; Cooke and Kothari 2001; Desai 2002; McAslan 2002; Mosse 2001; Peters 2000; Rahnema 1992), the ideal of participation came into vogue with the recognition that development projects could only gain traction in local, nonwestern settings when native populations were given the opportunity to participate. Kothari provides a concise summary of the general goals of participatory development when he notes that they endeavor to "enable those individuals and groups previously excluded by more top-down planning processes, and who are often marginalized by their separation and isolation from the production of knowledge and the formulation of policies and practices, to be included in decisions that affect their lives" (Kothari 2001, 139). Cooke and Kothari together claim the following:

> The ostensible aim of participatory approaches to development was to make 'people' central to development by encouraging beneficiary involvement in interventions that affect them and over which they previously had limited control or influence. [...] Participatory approaches to development, then, are justified in terms of sustainability, relevance and empowerment. (Cooke and Kothari 2001, 5)

The purpose of the environmental side accord was to provide legitimate and state-sanctioned opportunities for democratic participation in environmental decision making and the resolution of environmental disputes. It was intended to replace the very public environmental protests against NAFTA that took place before the trade treaty went into effect. The structure and function of the accord relies exclusively on bottom-to-top participation and the conviction that the accord provides a win-win. Citizen pursuit of environmental rehabilitation and conservation within the transnational side accord petitioning process would supposedly strengthen democracy on the Mexican side of the border and, at the same time, encourage environmental consciousness and rehabilitation of the borderlands. In this schema, border populations were imagined as building blocks of both sustainable development and democracy: "If the ideology of the earlier aid agenda was developmentalism, the ideology of this new agenda is 'communitarianism' (a variant of classical individualism) in which local communities are to be responsible for their own development, no longer conceived as a national project organized by the state" (Robinson 2003, 227).

This first part of this chapter examines a failed attempt at local cross-border environmental organizing between the Brownsville-based Coalition of Contaminated Communities and Las Caracaras. This section provides an ethnographic snapshot of the pitfalls, opportunities, and quagmires that shape border environmental activism among seemingly equal environmental citizens. This effort was productive, however, in reproducing social aspects of local border culture that both defy and undermine ideals of seamless environmental cross-border advocacy: namely, ethnic or national group tension among and between social identity groups that inhabit the borderlands, as well as digital fault lines that confound the best efforts.

The second half of this chapter examines the mandated participation of the environmental accord as practiced by the Matamoros Junta de Aguas y Drenajes (JAD; Water and Sanitation) in its effort to build popular support for a NADBank loan application. This 2001 loan bid (eventually approved) was for a water treatment plant, as well as the repair of the city's underground pipes. These pipes regularly broke and released sewage into the ground and ground waters and were considered a significant public health threat. In accordance with the NAAEC, the JAD solicited popular support and comment on the proposed project (*Plan Integral de Aguas Potables y Saneamiento* or PIAPS) through appropriate channels of the Joint Public Advisory Council (JPAC) and Comités Ciudadanos (Citizens' Committees). In particular, the JAD sought to strengthen its ties with and support from the "popular classes" by securing the backing of Las Caracaras. In spite of the democratic pretensions and the performance of participation according to NADBank and BECC requirements, however, this effort was beleaguered by fundamental inequalities between the stakeholding parties, in a manner similar to the local cross-border coalition-building effort.

A Beleaguered Attempt at Local Cross-Border Environmental Organizing: Las Caracaras Encounters the Coalition

The failed cross-border advocacy effort between the Brownsville Coalition against Contaminated Communities (CCC) and the Matamoros Caracaras began early in the spring of 2002 with an email I received from the Brownsville CCC announcing an upcoming meeting. I was on its mailing list since I had attended a few CCC meetings in the summer and fall of 2001. Previous meetings indicated it was an ad hoc organization that, under the will and drive of a couple of members (including a lawyer whose son had been born with spina bifida), was striving to become more organized. This first email message of 2002 was a call for participation in a group meeting in which members would discuss plans to apply for an EPA grant for an environmental justice project in the Lower Rio Grande Valley.

The day after I received the email invitation, I mentioned it to Rosalia and Father Gonzalez while we were having lunch. The lunch meeting had been set up because I wanted to query Father Gonzalez about his own involvement in the Spektra workers' petition. At news of the Brownsville meeting, both Father Gonzalez and Rosalia became excited and decided at once that all Las Caracaras members who could attend should do so. The next question that came up was why they had not been informed of this meeting previously. Had the CCC been having meetings all along and this was the first time that they were invited? Was Javier working with the group on the other side and, if so, why had he not informed the Matamoros group of the meetings? Was he representing the interests of Las Caracaras, meanwhile not actually attending the Matamoros meetings? When I told them, additionally, that the CCC (according to its email) was planning on applying for an EPA grant, this only added to the general confusion and dismay that had so quickly followed their initial excitement.

That evening, Rosalia called an emergency meeting of Las Caracaras to inform other members of the invitation and to encourage all eligible members (i.e., those with paperwork) to attend. In this brief meeting, they discussed the priorities of Las Caracaras and whether or not they had an interest in working with the CCC. There had been a prior, but fleeting, collaboration between the two groups. Las Caracaras members spoke politely of the *norteamericanos'* efforts one year hence, when they had come over with garbage bags and trudged the banks of the *Dren Cinco de Marzo* with Las Caracaras, conscripts, and others, to help clean up. Since that time contact between the two had been tenuous at best, but largely nonexistent.

On the evening of the Brownsville meeting between Las Caracaras and the CCC, I met Rosalia and others at her house. In spite of the tangible excitement of the preceding days, it looked as though the sole Caracaras attendees would be Rosalia, Arturo Grande, Eduardo (a local PRD political party aspirant), and me. Father Gonzalez had a prior engagement and others did not have the required documentation. Rosalia and I traveled in my car, and Arturo Grande and Eduardo traveled in another. We agreed that if we got separated crossing the bridge, Rosalia and I would wait for them on the other side. I had received directions to the designated meeting spot in the email.

As it turned out, the house where the meeting was scheduled to take place was in one of the wealthier sections of Brownsville. We parked and approached the house. I immediately began to feel uncomfortable at the luxury that presented itself. The house had a large lawn, lush potted plants spread across a colonial style red-tiled porch, and the entrance to the house had a set of wide and welcoming glass doors. I hoped that my companions did not feel out of place and, glancing back, noticed that Arturo's shoulders had begun to slacken a bit, as they often did, while Eduardo thrust out his chin in amusement, and Rosalia trudged on defiantly and proudly—but not without a smirk on her face. Her self-education and religious training had taught her to never be ashamed of her poverty; her convictions held that the wealth of one was firmly and inextricably rooted in the impoverishment of another. She was, in effect, a walking embodiment of the principle of development and under-development, channeling Gunder Frank, made even more organic and visceral here with her head held high and the gallows humor jokes that I could tell were brewing beneath the surface. The scene was certainly laced with irony and Rosalia's smirk showed it.

We were welcomed at the door by the couple hosting the meeting and led into a spacious living room with a roaring fire. Mexican artifacts and folk paintings decorated the room; the Santa Fe design style gave it all a pleasantly rustic quality. Beyond the living room, people had already begun to gather in the dining room, while in the kitchen women fussed over proper presentation of the potluck dishes. We were all graciously received, handed a beverage, and eventually settled into our respective places around the table. During dinner, Rosalia, Arturo, and Eduardo reacquainted themselves with CCC members whom they had previously met.

After dinner, the meeting began with the announcement of the agenda. It soon became clear that, from the perspective of the CCC organizers, the purpose of this meeting was to iron out the details of the project that they hoped to propose to the EPA and to develop a plan that would allow them to have a complete proposal by the rapidly approaching deadline. In total, about twenty-five people were present. Although Las Caracaras had been formally invited, it quickly became apparent that the invitation had been more of an afterthought than anything else. The rest of the group was completely unprepared for the topics that the Matamoros contingent would later introduce to the discussion.

From the beginning, a concerted effort was made to speak in both Spanish and English, with the speaking person saying what he or she had to say first in his or her primary language, then translating, or allowing someone else more capable do the translation. The insistence on translation did not come directly from the CCC but, rather, from the Sierra Club border representative who was also present at the meeting, Oscar. Oscar had arrived in Brownsville the previous day as part of one of his regular tours to check in on Sierra Club border chapters—of which the

Brownsville CCC was one—and to inform himself of the activities of the sponsored or soon-to-be-sponsored groups of the Sierra Club's Beyond the Border program. Perhaps because of, or in addition to, his self-imposed task of ensuring that everything was equitably translated, the two groups seemed increasingly to look to him to mediate the meeting.

With the necessity of ongoing translation established and three of us tasked with that job, the discussion turned to the reason for the meeting. The CCC had decided that it wanted to submit a proposal for an EPA grant and, since the deadline was rapidly approaching, the purpose of this get-together was to decide precisely what type of project CCC wished to propose and to plan the proposal. CCC quickly decided to pursue the most popular suggestion so far—a canoe trip down the Rio Grande in which water and sediment samples would be collected for laboratory tests. Similar to the Spektra workers and Las Caracaras, what CCC members were proposing was a "popular epidemiological" type study in which the lay public undertakes the challenge of scientific or quasi-scientific tasks (Brown 1987, 1997). Although these kinds of tests had been done for years by toxicologists, biologists, and public health experts, they seemed convinced of the unique nature of this proposed study because it could result in important citizen-science alliances. These types of alliances were encouraged by the environmental accord, as well its predecessor (i.e., La Paz) and the subsequent Border XXI. As Brown, Irwin, and others have argued (Couto 1986; Fischer 2000; Irwin 1995), such alliances are unique because the lay contaminated community knows its immediate environment in a way that an external expert cannot.

Unlike many environmental justice and popular epidemiological movements, neither Las Caracaras nor the CCC had to begin their organizing efforts with the mere suspicion that their environments might be contaminated by dangerous wastes. That fact had been established at least since the early period of the NAFTA debates (Brenner et al. 2000; Moure-Eraso et al. 1994). Instead, they moved quickly to the more challenging task of trying to identify the appropriate scientific method for their proposed undertaking, made all the more urgent by the impending proposal deadline. A seasoned proposal writer and adjunct professor at the local University of Texas at Brownsville was serendipitously present and directed the discussion toward the most immediate pressing questions: Which waters should they test? Should they test the soil of the Rio Grande banks as well? And would that require different equipment and a different lab? What about the ground waters? Should they get scientific training for this undertaking and, if so, how and where could they get that? How much would laboratory tests for each of the samples cost and would different laboratories be required for the detection of chemical and organic wastes? Could they use the same lab for all the tests? What was an appropriate sample size to prove contamination? What would they do with their findings if they did get the grant?

The discussion around the mile-long dining room table was fascinating to the anthropologist in the room with an unremitting interest in environmental justice and popular epidemiology movements. However, the one-sided discussion was also circuitous because the CCC members did not know their immediate environment very well. Their speculations were based largely on abstractions, hearsay, the news or studies they had read, rather than on direct experience or observation. This is partly because they did not live directly with the most visible waste, which was reserved for Matamoros as a function of the unequal distribution of waste that the border made possible (Simon 2010; Stebbins 1992). Matamoros had the most visible and foul smelling waste: canals and open sewage drains, football fields full of garbage that took flight on windy days and sent plastic bags and whatnot through the poorer city sectors, the ever-expanding and burning municipal dump, and the two-story-high mound of bone white calcium sulfate outside of Quimica Fluor. While Brownsville was quite possibly equally contaminated by air emissions and water-borne pollutants, this contamination could only be rendered visible through scientific intervention or the occasional illness, disease, or NTD cluster. Therefore, none of the heretofore CCC-dominated discussion included details about which canals were connected with industrial parks or dumps, the fact that the Rio Grande sat in a large alluvial plain essentially connecting the twin cities at the subterranean and ground water level, the presence of pesticide or insecticide run-off, or where or how chemical and organic toxic waste canals spilled directly into the river.

Unlike CCC members, Las Caracaras knew a great deal about the contamination in its immediate environment, partly because of investigations it had already undertaken. It could have answered the questions the CCC people were speculating about, yet Las Caracaras representatives were not called upon. For the four of us who knew that Las Caracaras had been considering a similar project for itself and who had all of the first-hand knowledge necessary to launch it immediately, there was some irony in the fact that they had been, by default, excluded from the conversation. Rosalia, Eduardo, and Arturo began to exchange sardonic looks among themselves, and raised eyebrows pointed at me as if to say, "What did we tell you?" The tension mounted from the corner where they sat, indicated by deep sighs, folded arms, and the occasional eye roll, none of which seemed to catch the Americans' attention.

Finally, Eduardo intervened. His question changed the course of the evening's discussion. "How," he asked, "was Las Caracaras to be involved in this project?" More importantly, "Why were we invited to this meeting?" Not bothering to wait for a response from the now flustered group around the table, he went on to eloquently summarize and express his view of the proposed project. His overall review was very favorable and his summary succinct, because these same discussions had already occurred within Las Caracaras. He ended his comments diplomatically, noting that he felt that the role of Las Caracaras had not been adequately defined. He also wanted to know precisely what "coalition" in the name Coalition against Contaminated Communities referred to. If this organization was a coalition, of which groups was it comprised? If Las Caracaras were considered part of this coalition, why had it not been invited to previous meetings? Was the CCC claiming itself to be a coalition merely to advance its own interests (i.e., receive this grant)? Had CCC been taking advantage of Las Caracaras by claiming to represent it when, in fact, the Las Caracaras group had not been consulted at all?

These questions were put forward in a direct and non-confrontational manner. Nevertheless, the air became tense as the Americans grappled (somewhat aghast) with the questions of identity, politics, and representation that had just been placed before them by the subaltern population at the table. The discussion remained heated for the remainder of the evening, alternating back and forth between proposing a project for an EPA grant and foundational issues of adequately defining the "Coalition." The Matamoros contingent and its ally in this debate, the Sierra Club representative, felt that proper attention should be given to fundamental issues of representation and collective decision making first. Among the CCC members, some expressed no opinion, seemingly because of their discomfort, meanwhile others pressed to have the agenda of the meeting returned to the proposed EPA project.

A key figure in pushing forward discussion of the project, rather than organizational identity, was the adjunct professor who had volunteered her grant-writing skills to the CCC. Her approach to the problem was entirely pragmatic. She argued that Las Caracaras and its interests should be represented within the grant in an ancillary manner, essentially as a prop that would strengthen the overall feasibility of the proposal. The CCC project would aim primarily toward collection of water and sediment samples from the Rio Grande and Las Caracaras could help to collect samples from the Mexican side of the river. This was suggested after a discussion pointing out that hard data collection should be complemented by qualitative interviews with, and health surveys of, the residents living immediately on the banks of the river, especially as it headed out toward the Gulf of Mexico. The incorporation of Las Caracaras was to be pragmatic and strategic, according to this schema; its interests would be represented within the grant, and, in exchange, Las Caracaras would also have some say in the project as a whole. The grant writer's intervention would turn out to be the final point of debate for the evening and the axis around which further discussion of Las Caracaras–CCC collaboration would evolve. The CCC wanted to recruit Las Caracaras to gather data and lend credibility to the project as a legitimately cross-border one.

Eduardo, Rosalia, Arturo, and Oscar continued to insist on the importance of consensual decision making and collective equality within the organization, meanwhile the remainder of the CCC members pushed ahead with their deadline-inspired agenda. The insistence on full representation and collective decision-making procedures suggested that members of Las Caracaras actually had much more experience with collective actions than did the members of the CCC, many of whom appeared to be novice activists. Oscar eventually commented that it seemed as though the CCC wanted to put the cart before the horse. It was decided that the two organizations were clearly at an impasse and should meet again in a few days to decide two things: first, whether they were willing to undertake a joint project; and, second, what the nature of the coalition should be, if they were to continue to work under that name. The meeting ended late at night with considerably ruffled feathers on both sides.

"Somos Tercermundistas!"[1]

Las Caracaras met separately in Matamoros the next night. The primary purpose of this meeting was to inform those who had been unable to cross of the previous evening's events, then come to a decision about whether they wanted to participate with the Brownsville coalition and possible EPA project. Over Rosalia's protests, it had been decided that we would meet at a coffee shop downtown. Father Gonzalez had insisted that he could foot the bill. Although Eduardo arrived two hours late, we could not start without him. In the meantime, the rest of us chatted while Rosalia was interviewed by a reporter from a local *priista* radio station.

The evening's discussion revolved primarily around trying to sort out some of the confusion from the night before. The group turned frequently to me, as though I, a *gringa*, could explain the vagaries of the CCC, although I explained that I was equally baffled by the Brownsville group. When pressed, I admitted that my impression had been that they were confused, disorganized, and that they had clearly been mistaken in assuming representation of Las Caracaras, particularly since the latter had not been invited to previous meetings. It seemed as though their lack of knowledge, direction, and organizational unity could only partially be ameliorated by the temporary presence of the experienced grant writer and adjunct professor.

Once Eduardo arrived, they decided that the primary decision to make during this meeting was whether or not they wanted to be included in the proposed project or even to be associated with the Brownsville group, regardless of whether or not the CCC won the EPA grant. The discussion continued for well over two hours and at times tempers flared. Members that had been unable to attend the previous night's meeting were angry at the presumption of the Brownsville group, and at one point a particularly mercurial and educated figure remarked that they clearly saw them as *tercermundistas* who, presumably, had to be led and trained by their *yanqui* neighbors. On this point there seemed to be little disagreement. The CCC had engaged in a classic and poorly masked imperialist move. The group decided unanimously that it did not want to participate with the CCC under any circumstances, and that diplomatic attempts to clear the air and institute more democratic processes were insufficient to make amends at this point: the "*norteamericanos*" had shown their true colors and the damage had been done for the time being. Regardless of how much Las Caracaras might have benefited from the support of a grant, the following Monday meeting would be reserved for airing their complaints and advising the CCC to change its name and continue on its own.

La Parroquia

A few days later, another joint meeting was held between the CCC and Las Caracaras. This time the meeting was held on the Matamoros side in the interest of cross-border equity and for the pragmatic purpose that all members of the Matamoros group could attend. The meeting was held in Father Gonzalez' *parroquia,* and Las Caracaras packed the room out. Only three Americans came to this meeting, two women and Javier. Javier had not been at the initial meeting in Brownsville, but had caught wind of it. The Brownsville group had clearly continued discussions over the previous few days, and the two women were there to represent their interests. Also in attendance was another US-based indigenous rights NGO that had subsequently discovered that its name had also been included in the list of the groups supposedly represented by the Coalition. Throughout the meeting, one of the women from the Brownsville group leaned nervously against a doorway and chain-smoked. Both of the women looked frequently to me for help, as though enlisting the sympathy of another *gringa* in the midst of this sea of foreign faces and tongues who, as politely as possible, essentially raked them over the coals.

The discussion concerning the urgency of the proposal vis-à-vis the concerns of the equitable representation within a coalition continued. By the end of another long evening, it was clear that the CCC would not budge in its effort to move ahead with the grant proposal, and equally clear that Las Caracaras and the indigenous rights group felt that they had been unjustly misrepresented. The meeting was a fairly brutal calling to accounts. The decision was made by both Las Caracaras as well as the other indigenous rights group to not participate with the CCC in its efforts. They recommended to the CCC that they persevere in their attempts to win a grant and they wished them luck. At the same time, the Matamoros folks made it clear to the CCC representatives that if they wanted to participate with Mexican organizations in the future, they would have to pursue this goal in a more equitable, transparent, and less presumptuous manner. The CCC was never heard from again.

Blaming the "Judas" Figure

In the days, weeks, and many meetings following this failed coalition-building effort, Javier's behavior received much attention and speculation from Caracaras members. During the course of the evening-long debate in the *parroquia,* Javier, who had been apprised of events in the initial Brownsville meeting, shifted his position completely. He started out lending full support to the CCC's goal of developing an EPA grant proposal and including Las Caracaras in it. By evening's end, however, he came to support the Mexican group's emphasis on laying a strong organizational foundation first and foremost. The CCC had made a mistake in not consulting all of its members. The primary goal of the group, he claimed, should have been to build strong and collective roots for a coalition, rather than simply win a grant.

While there may have been any number of reasons for Javier to change his position, it was interpreted in the worst light possible. He was cast in subsequent commentary as being weak of character, as having had his treasonous activities discovered by the Matamoros people, and, in the worst case scenario, as evidence of his turncoat or Judas nature. At the bottom of these accusations subsequently voiced was a suspicion (now "confirmed") that he had been selling information about Las Caracaras or representing the group to the CCC for his own benefit and without their consent. The unanimous view seemed to be that he had switched sides in the long meeting in the parish for fear of losing his Mexican connection and Las Caracaras' substantial environmental knowledge. His shift of positions had not come from realizing a mistake but, rather, from a treasonous and disloyal nature which manipulated people and groups for his own benefit. Their conviction that he shifted to their side in the debate only confirmed the original belief that they and their allegedly damaged bodies and environment were an important source of capital—cultural or otherwise—for those gringos, activists, reporters, investigators, and anthropologists who could gain access to this knowledge and presume to represent them.

Local, cross-border environmental organizing contains within it all sorts of participatory challenges; the relative proximity of cross-border populations does little to ameliorate this. This recounting of events makes clear that issues of identity, time, and organizational structure were bound up together in this encounter, which led to rapid dissolution of any coalition possibilities. Although all three are at play in this set of events, the conflicts over timelines and organizational structures merely served to crystallize issues of power, identity, and representation. On the face of it, it is clear that the groups parted ways because the Matamoros organization believed that the Brownsville group was engaging in a typical form of *yanqui* imperialism, if now guised in a softer, environmental form.

BECC Participatory Requirements and the Matamoros NADBank Loan

While the encounter between Las Caracaras and the CCC was spontaneous and locally generated, the environmental side accord of NAFTA also sought to encourage greater participation of border communities in environmental issues.

NAFTA established two bilateral institutions, the NADBank and the BECC, "specifically to deal with environmental problems along the US-Mexico border" (McKinney 2000, 161). The BECC conducts most of its business in an online environment (Graves 1999) and is considered by many to exhibit extraordinarily high participatory and civil society input possibilities (Ferretti 2002; Goldschmidt 2002; Thomas and Weber 1999), even as this task of fulfillment "fell primarily to border groups" (Fox 2012, 12). As Fox notes, after the passage of NAFTA, "[M]ost independent environmental policy observers see the BECC and NADBank as setting higher standards for public participation in the policy process, at the same time as they have yet to have a significant impact on the border environment" (Fox 2000, 12).

The BECC and NADBank work together. The BECC is in charge of certifying proposed projects. An important part of that certification is that project applicants demonstrate to the BECC that they have significant public participation and support. It is only after this certification is complete that the project can receive funding from NADBank. Section 4 of the Charter of the North American Development Bank and Border Environment Cooperation Commission is titled, "Relationship with the Public." It is worth quoting at length:

The Commission shall establish procedures in English and Spanish:
1. ensuring, to the extent possible, public availability of documentary information on all projects for which a request for assistance or an application for certification is made;
2. for giving written notice of and providing members of the public reasonable opportunity to comment on any general guidelines which may be established by the Commission for environmental infrastructure projects for which it provides assistance, and on all applications for certification received by the Commission; and

3. whereby the Board of Directors could receive complaints from
    groups affected by projects that the Commission has assisted or
    certified and could obtain independent assessments as to whether
    the terms of this Charter or the procedures established by the
    Board of Directors pursuant to this Chapter have been observed.
    (quoted in McKinney 2000, 183)

When the BECC evaluates a project, it must ensure that it meets the
minimum criteria for six distinct categories: (1) human health and environment; (2) technical feasibility; (3) financial feasibility and management; (4) community participation; (5) applicant's provision to the
affected community of a comprehensive document explaining the proposal and project, in addition to documentation of the applicant's fulfillment of participatory requirements; and (6) sustainable development
(McKinney 2000, 166–167). The criteria for community participation
include the following: the development of a comprehensive community
participation plan; the establishment of a steering committee representative of a broad range of community actors; representatives from both
sides of the border, if the project affects both Mexico and the United
States; and a requirement that the loan applicant "meet individually with
local organizations that will be affected by the project. The purpose of
such meetings is both to inform the public about the project and to develop support for it" (McKinney 2001, 167). It was precisely for this latter reason that the Matamoros JAD sought out Las Caracaras.

In 2002, the JAD began preparing an application for a loan for the rehabilitation of many of the city's collapsed underground pipes. The plan
was called *Plan Integral de Aguas Potables y Saneamiento* (PIAPS) and
it had to conform to BECC criteria. In August of that year, it organized
its first Comité Ciudadano. This is the Citizens' Committee, alternately
referred to as the Steering Committee. The Citizens' Committee is one
of the most important conduits for NADBank applicants to ensure community participation and understanding of the proposed project. The
Citizens' Committee is ideally composed of a broad cross section of the
affected community and functions as a representative of the entire city
or municipality. It receives information from and meets with the project
applicants so that it is fully informed and, vice versa, shares information with its members' constituencies and assesses their support for the
project or lack thereof. It is intended to function as an informational and
educative node within the cross-cutting and complicated requirements

of the BECC, but it is also the only requirement targeted specifically at community participation. Therefore, it must gauge popular support and communicate public concerns, discontent, comments, or complaints back to the project applicant who, if performing its job adequately, addresses and documents concerns, then forwards this information upward to the BECC.

Educating Participation: Drumming Up Popular Support

In the weeks and months following the encounter with the Brownsville CCC, Las Caracaras continued working to establish an office, make surrounding *colonias* more aware of their presence, and acquire *asociación civil* (civic association) status. Oscar returned every few weeks to train them in capacity building and, in his absence, I did. Las Caracaras went through two grant cycles with the Sierra Club and was awarded two grants. Rosalia declined the first because she thought PRD members were trying to usurp her and accepted the second (after the PRD had left the group). With funds left over from the original seed grant given two years before, Las Caracaras purchased a desk, filing cabinet, writing supplies, and other basic office furniture. An office was set up on the second floor of Father Gonzalez's church for a brief period, but Rosalia did not like working there because she felt as though the priest was trying to boss her around. Her sensitivity to the fact that she was poor and had only an elementary school education, in contrast with the more educated priest and PRD members, often made her bristle and worry that they would try to bully and intimidate her.

In May of 2002, Carlos, a PRD member who had some influence within the city, invited an engineer from the Matamoros JAD to explain the PIAPS plan to Las Caracaras.[2] On the evening of the presentation, a group of about twenty of us gathered in Las Caracaras' office, which was then located in the church. Abel, the engineer, showed up equipped with graphs, a projector, power point, and slides. At the beginning of the presentation, he said that the city was working on a fifty-year plan to provide clean and potable water for all of its citizens. Moreover, PIAPS (or *Plan Integral*, for short) was part of the larger program called Programa Fronterizo XXI as well as a project being proposed to the BECC and NADBank. As Mikulas has noted, the Programa Fronterizo XXI was an extension of both the 1983 La Paz Agreement and the environmental accord, emphasizing "public participation and strengthened cooperation with state and local agencies to achieve sustainable development along the border" and listing as its "central strategies 'public involvement, decentralization of environmental management through state and local capacity building, and improved communication and cooperation among federal, state and local government agencies'" (Mikulas 1999, 507).

According to Abel, the most important part of this plan involved repairing *caidas*, more than thirty of which plagued the city. *Caidas*, he explained, were broken and leaking pipes. The French materials used to build the original underground wastewater pipes for the city were of inferior quality; they had constricted through time, leaving thin pipes running through larger caverns which, under the weight of ever heavier traffic and trucks following the *maquila* boom and population explosion, collapsed under pressure. These are sewage pipes that then contaminate sub soils and ground waters. During the rainy season, sewage "possibly" mixed with the rain that flooded the city's streets. The *Plan Integral* being developed by the city's engineers would remedy this problem and be financed principally by the NADBank, with additional funds forthcoming from the state and municipal government.

In addition, Abel pointed out that the repair of the *caidas* was only the first step in a larger plan to develop more water treatment plants (at the time, there was only one for a city of close to a million people) and an overall improvement of health and sanitation conditions. An important impetus for the plan, he explained, were the public health problems caused by sewage draining indiscriminately. It was a public health problem and "an epidemic does not recognize a border." Echoing the concerns of Las Caracaras for the *Dren Cinco de Marzo*, he noted as well that many of the drains originally constructed to prevent flooding during the rainy season were routinely used for general dumping by the population, as well as possible clandestine dumping by *maquilas*.

Finally, the engineer provided a flowchart demonstration of how one applies for loans through the NADBank. In the process, he introduced and explained a number of acronyms and institutions relevant to the environmental side and border development. He even explained that the Comité Ciudadano was a requirement of the BECC in order for the JAD to qualify for a NADBank loan, thereby disclosing in a transparent manner his own reason for being in the *parroquia* that evening. Near the end of the highly informative presentation, he went so far as to say that a BECC committee might ask the following questions of the Comité Ciudadano, and that if Las Caracaras were willing to participate in the

Comité, representatives should be prepared to answer these questions: "Do they know which is the problem? Do they know what the solution should be?" If the JAD were to prove that it had fulfilled its requirements for participation in the BECC certification process, the proof would be a fully informed citizenry. He also said that although he did not know precisely how the Comité Ciudadano was to be constituted, nor had he any say in the matter, he hoped that Las Caracaras would be represented within the committee.

Abel then turned off the projector that had been aimed at a blank wall and opened the session to questions from the audience. It had become clear from the few questions thrown out during the presentation that Caracaras members were well aware of the fact that the JAD engineer was there that evening not merely as a gesture of good will—or even as a favor to Carlos—but because of his own vested interest. Abel had good-naturedly received the suggestive jokes and comments along those lines and did not pretend that his intentions were otherwise. In response to a question posed by Eduardo, he confirmed again that, "Yes, popular support is one of the requirements for a NADBank loan." At this there were a few guffaws and snickering, until someone else spoke up and said the obvious: "Well, it would be difficult to gain support since everyone in the city knows that the JAD has typically favored the needs of the wealthier communities. Why should we believe that things would be any different now? More importantly, why should we help to bring to fruition a project which would have no benefits for us, but only for the rich?"

Abel sheepishly admitted that, yes, it was true that the city had traditionally favored wealthier neighborhoods, but if the people would just give the city and the JAD a chance, they were ready to "democratize" and change their image and practices. He used the opportunity to throw in an anecdote about himself, reporting that he actually had never been to this *colonia,* and when he did try to travel to this and similar *colonias,* he invariably got lost on the twisting and unnamed roads. This disclosure on his part was seemingly intended to demonstrate to Las Caracaras how he was democratizing himself. He next disclosed that he actually lived in Brownsville; this disclosure, somewhat unfortunately for him, came without a hint of irony.

In a reversal of earlier patterns—as made clear by the questions put forward by the group—this engineer had a vested interest in explaining and, in a sense, selling the *Plan Integral* to this politically and largely economically marginalized group. The BECC requirement of an informed citizenry had some tangible effect on the city by coercing it into a course of action it might not have otherwise considered. As Abel put it during the meeting, "The city government is trying to be less corrupt, more democratic, more transparent, but it needs the people to give them a chance first." He guaranteed that, in addition to transparent discussions prior to the signing of a NADBank loan, the Comité Ciudadano, once comprised, would also give follow up on JAD activities to ensure that the JAD acted in accordance with its obligations to the city's citizens.

The Comité Ciudadano

In early September of 2002, the Matamoros Comité Ciudadano was announced.[3] Based on newspaper reports, the reports of two Caracaras members that were able to attend a few meetings, and events following the rollout of the Comité, the constitution of the committee resembled that of the Good Neighbor Environmental Board meeting that Rosalia, Alejandra, and I had attended in the same fall of 2002. They turned out to be predominantly representatives of business, education, industry, and civic organizations (like the socialite Rotary Club)—in short, largely middle class and professional individuals or groups. It was never revealed how these representatives of a thin slice of Matamoros' overall demographic profile were notified or invited. If the selection process was anything like that of the Good Neighbor Environmental Board meeting, they had received private email invitations. Digital, social, and class divides meant that the opportunity to participate was not open to all, and that genuine participation involving all sectors of Matamoros society was by no means a foregone conclusion. In the days and weeks leading up to the announcement of the creation of the Comité, there was not a single announcement in the local newspaper, *El Bravo,* regarding the fact that a steering committee was being formed, never mind an open call for participation.

Through the influence of Father Gonzalez and the JAD, Las Caracaras did receive an email invitation to attend the first meeting. The email invitation went to Father Gonzalez. Las Caracaras had remained in contact with the JAD because Rosalia and other members were making repeated trips to City Hall in order to request more frequent garbage pickups and cleaning sweeps of the banks of the *Dren Cinco de Marzo.* By that time, Rosalia and others had developed something of a working relation with both the head of the JAD and some sanitation workers.

Father Gonzalez and Gabriela were able to attend the first Citizens' Committee meeting and, although listed last, at least Las Caracaras appeared on the preliminary list of participants. According to the two of them, attendees were introduced to PIAPS during the first meeting in a manner similar to Las Caracaras' introduction a few months before. Members of the committee were told that the project had a time frame of twenty years for completion and would require an investment of approximately US$50 million to come in the form of a NADBank loan. The president of the Committee, who was also head of the local Canacintra,[4] said that regular public meetings would be held so that the public could remain informed about the proceedings. The Mayor of Matamoros affirmed on the following day that the BECC certification of the *Plan Integral* for Matamoros would be a national achievement, and that the city would put all of its administrative force into receiving this certification by the BECC.[5]

Also in September, Las Caracaras made a huge step forward when Father Gonzalez gained a valuable position within the Consejo de saneamiento de agua potable en Matamoros (Council on Health of Drinking Water in Matamoros), a subcommittee within the Comité Ciudadano. This subcommittee, with Father Gonzalez' input, would be working directly with the BECC as part of the latter's task of ensuring that all NADBank loans conformed with the six categories and criteria of the BECC.

Unfortunately, Las Caracaras' rising profile within Matamoros and the opportunity to participate in influential circles were short-lived. Continued friction between Father Gonzalez and others resulted in his refusing to report on the few meetings he purportedly attended. When he left the group in the fall of 2002, it was unknown whether he continued to attend the Comité or Consejo meetings and, if he did, it was unknown whether or not he claimed to represent Las Caracaras. It is unlikely that he did since, prior to his departure from Las Caracaras, the organization had been removed from the committee's email list for reasons that he claimed not to know. Father Gonzalez's departure from Las Caracaras was also bound up with internal friction within Las Caracaras about money. Money within the organization was only an issue because of Sierra Club support—without the latter they would not have had funds. When Father Gonzalez left Las Caracaras, the latter also lost its tenuous connection with the Comité.

Allegations of Corruption: The Information Void

In the weeks and months following the announcement of the Comité, there continued to be a lot of confusion at the popular level regarding why the municipal government and JAD were trying to get a loan in the first place. The confusion existed because the majority of Matamorenses are poor migrants that live in an information void without access to either newspapers or the Internet. Anderson (1983) has emphasized the importance of that seemingly most pedestrian of objects, the daily newspaper, to nation building. He argued that it was through the modern newspaper that imagined communities could be reached, binding up all communities in, if not conversation, at least common informational flows. The newspaper was so important to the sense of belonging that Anderson went so far to compare it to morning prayer, suggesting that knowledge within one household performing morning prayer that the next household was likewise performing, and the next, ad infinitum, encouraged a sense of national community (Anderson 1983, 39).

Among economically disenfranchised, *maquila*-laboring border populations, such as members of Las Caracaras and the majority of Matamoros, the cost of a newspaper at five pesos (approximately $US.50 at the time), was prohibitive. In an interview with Don Luis and his wife, both were emphatic about the fact that given the cost of electricity, food, and other bare necessities, a newspaper would have been a luxury that would break the family budget. An account simply for the purchase of the daily newspaper, El Bravo, was included in the budgets of both grant applications submitted by Las Caracaras to the Sierra Club.⁶ Since all information regarding the PIAPS proposal was contained within the local newspapers, most people simply did not know about it, except through rumor or hearsay, much less understand and participate in it. While even an informed citizenry might have had doubts and suspicions about the proposed project, the absence of information most certainly encouraged suspicions of corruption. This point was poignantly made in an encounter I had while conducting an interview with Don Luis and his wife, Virginia.

The couple was in their mid-forties and lived in Colonia Roja. I had known Don Luis for at least six months through participation in Las Caracaras, but this was the first time that I had visited him in his home. I had come to interview him regarding his role in Las Caracaras.⁷ He and his wife had four children, ranging in age from five to twenty-three. Walking into the yard, we passed the outhouse to one side and then entered the patio. There was a large stone washtub where Virginia washed clothes by hand and an open fire pit with spent coals where the family did the cooking. Their home was a ramshackle conglomeration of found pieces of plywood nailed together to provide a semblance of shelter. Inside, the house was divided evenly into two rooms—one for the children and a second that served as simultaneous kitchen and master bedroom. The windows and doors were covered with loose fabric. The floor was dirt. No sooner had I sat down than Virginia placed into my hands a large pile of photographs from the recent wedding of one son and the communion of another. We slowly made our way through another sizable stack of photographs that included pictures of weddings, *quinceañaras,* and deceased relatives. These photographs were the prize possessions of the family.

Throughout the interview, Luis and Virginia sat on their bed with a lemon yellow bedspread while I faced them from a chair turned outward from the kitchen table, the tape recorder on another chair between us. Above their heads a three-foot-high Mickey Mouse face smiled down at me, the face painted on a loose piece of plywood they had found and made part of their wall. Above the head of the matrimonial bed was a picture of Pope John Paul II. They had graciously agreed to a joint interview and set aside all of their Sunday for the occasion.

About halfway through the interview, an elderly woman in a blue housecoat and big, horn-rimmed glasses stepped through the curtain covering the back door and into the combined kitchen and bedroom. She looked surprised to see me there, but settled into a chair next to the doorway upon invitation. She sat and listened silently to the interview for a good hour, then enthusiastically jumped into the conversation when the tape recorder was shut off and we began talking about the proposed PIAPS.

They were uniformly convinced that the plan would end in corruption and utter chaos. "Chaos, because how could they go about ripping up the roads and the pipes throughout the *colonias?* Where would people get their water? It was bad enough that in this neighborhood people had to travel down the dirt road to a community faucet. And what about the people who would be displaced? Would they be treated like the *Colonia Cuauhtemoc* and have to go and live in the Plaza Hidalgo?" I agreed with them that impending chaos was always a possibility where government bureaucracies were concerned.

More important than the chaos, they maintained, was the almost certain problem of corruption. "All of the money from the loan will be lost in inflated contracts, bids made by brothers, family, friends, and who will be stuck paying the bill? Citizens of Matamoros, of course!" The older woman, whose name I had learned was Maria Guadalupe, exclaimed. She was vehement in her rejection of PIAPS. "Not only will they never finish the work so that they can continue to receive the big paycheck, but they will do the work sloppily—constructing new pipes on top of collapsing ones—in order to ensure that they can go through the same cycle of bidding, loan, and payment again. The work will never be finished, and who is to be accountable afterwards?" It seemed as though they were all in agreement that the people from the municipal government, contractors, and, most importantly, the JAD were all involved merely as a get rich quick scheme or, alternatively, in the case of the then-head of the JAD, to prepare himself to become a mayor in the city.

In short, there seemed to be considerable confusion as to the whole PIAPS agenda, as well as to the question of whether or not the city was to receive a grant or a loan. This was partly because only the week before the Tamaulipas Governor Yarrington signed an agreement with the EPA and other contributing institutions for Matamoros to receive a Mex$94 million grant; the grant was seed money in order to jumpstart the city on the BECC approval process for PIAPS. Newspapers might have been helpful in clearing up the confusion. One thing that was clear was that when they thought it was a grant, they were merely concerned. When they thought that it was a loan, they wanted no part of it. "Who is going to pay the loan back?" they asked. "How can we afford a loan when we cannot afford even water and electricity, especially with the price hikes in electricity of this past spring?" Don Luis and Virginia used candles for light in their modest home.

Although it was ostensibly the job of the JAD and Comité Ciudadano to explain both PIAPS and the certification and loan process in which the city was now embroiled, it didn't seem as though they had done their job. There had been enough parceled information—transparency coupled with opacity—to allow city government to pursue its goals while nominally conforming to BECC requirements. As the observations of Don Luis and others attest, because the Comité Ciudadano did not extend into the labyrinth of the popular classes, and information was not distributed in such a way that the poorer groups could access it, the population remained essentially uninformed. This lack of information led Don Luis, his neighbor Maria, and others to the default assumption of corruption. As a consequence the experience of participation was perceived as a top-down affair. Robinson's observations here seem apropos:

> Increasing linkage among civil societies does not necessarily prove emancipatory for popular majorities and emergent global civil society does not generate an automatic globalization-from-below representing popular aspirations. The official development discourse of 'fostering and strengthening civil society' translates in practice into the penetration of civil society downward, from the global capitalist system to the most local community and municipal level." (Robinson 2003, 224)

In late June of 2003, the BECC certified PIAPS. The NADBank and Matamoros JAD signed an initial agreement for a grant worth US$15 million and a loan for US$33 million to cover the first phase of the program. The total estimated cost at the time was US$77 million.[8]

Both scenarios described in this chapter contained elements of environmental citizenship, even if the activities and events narrated here might not have been given that label by the actors themselves. In the case of the cross-border coalition-building effort, the two organizations started out with a shared understanding of the common environmental and public health problems that plagued them both. Ecological or regional consciousness brought them together in spite of the border, even as the border—in both literal and figurative terms—also drove them apart. The North American Agreement on Environmental Cooperation banked on the capacity of border populations to put their eco-consciousness first in efforts to rehabilitate the border environment that groups on both sides of the border inhabit. However, the subterranean pull of historical and contemporary social, ethnic, and national tensions made collaboration impossible in this case. The environmental and labor side accords were laid down like grids across the border region, and presumed a homogeneity and sense of collective identity and destiny that did not necessarily exist. Existing tensions, cultural divisions, and political investments did not dissolve immediately in the face of pressing environmental threats.

The second scenario of the Matamoros application for a NADBank loan provided a glimpse into the participatory practices, educative aspirations, and public-oriented requirements of the joint BECC–NADBank endeavor. These two institutions are bilateral, rather than trilateral, in their constitution, highlighting again the importance of border environmental problems in the NAFTA debates and the subsequently developed environmental side accord. Mirroring the contemporary orthodox sustainable development valorization of participation as a means of achieving sustainable development with traction in local communities, the BECC was created with clear and explicit guidelines that participation was a condition for receiving a NADBank loan. These participatory requirements of public comment, civil society engagement, and dispute resolution procedures are currently part of the standard modus operandi of other major development funding agencies, such as the Inter-American Development Bank (IDB) and World Bank. The BECC requirements reflect both the now-orthodox emphasis on the value of participation to sustainable development, as well as practical mechanisms for participation introduced by both the environmental and labor side accords. In the setting described here, participatory requirements were part of an effort to cultivate a sense of environmental citizenship that, at the same time, would cultivate a sense of democratic political culture among the Mexican populations as part of their transition.

Chapter 6

Transnational Networks and Grassroots Splintering

This chapter discusses the effects that non-local environmental and labor organizations from the United States had on the Matamoros-based Spektra workers' organizing efforts and Las Caracaras. In particular, it describes the ways in which these emergent movements became painfully fractured once the possibility of transnational resources presented itself. In both cases, allegations of corruption and opportunism became rampant. Also in both cases, fairly cohesive and well-organized grassroots groups (based on consensus, transparency, and shared objectives) at the local level tipped over into fractious and politicized relations as latent hostilities and ancient rivalries came to the surface. Eclipsing the seemingly smooth forward movement of local organizing, once transnationalized, these same groups' meetings, plans, and organizational hierarchies became murky and rumor-laden. Since some had higher class status and greater access to communication technologies like phone and the Internet, there were increasing suspicions and accusations of deliberate opacity in these members' communications with powerful US-based NGOs. The relative local level transparency, in short, was eclipsed by experiences of opacity and allegations that some members were being less than forthcoming in their dealings with nonlocal actors.

These are common themes and experiences for each of the movements' experiences with non-local actors, even as the details are specific to each case. In the case of the Spektra workers' movement, for example, the CFO and workers within the plant had been working diligently for several months to collect information that might demonstrate possible violations of health and safety regulations within the Spektra plant.

150

These investigations were inspired by a temporary spike in the numbers of anencephalic births and spontaneous abortions, as well as the chronic problem of workers suffering repeated arm, wrist, and shoulder injuries due to the strenuous repetitive motion work. When the US-based Justice for Border Workers became involved, it aspired to use the information already gathered and collect additional data, in order to file a petition under the labor side accord of NAFTA. Once filed, and with no subsequent corrective or punitive action taken vis-à-vis Spektra plant, workers began to feel as though their compromised bodies had been doubly bartered: first, by Spektra plant; and second, by the NGO that organized the petition in an effort to "test" the side accord dispute resolution process.

The case of Las Caracaras was different, but equally laden with a sense of opacity, corruption, and opportunism that eventually seeped into the roots and relations within the organization itself. Once the possibility of Sierra Club funding became real—evident in the organization's winning seed grant money twice—the organization splintered completely along pre-existing (if somewhat latent) lines of class, ethnicity, gender, and political party affiliations that had existed all along. While the organization had been able to withstand and absorb these frictions up to that time, incoming resources—welcome as they should have been—brought these tensions to the surface in a way that the organization could no longer absorb.

The cross-border coalition efforts instantiated in the cases of both the Spektra workers and Las Caracaras are examples of the transnational advocacy that has become so ubiquitous in a globalized world. As Robinson notes, "[T]he emergence of a global economy provides the material basis for a global civil society. For many analysts of globalization, the civil societies of each country are becoming transnationalized through integration into associational networks that span numerous countries" (2003, 223).

It has been widely noted that such networks, including NGOs, INGOs, ENGOs, and grassroots groups, form a critical component of transnational advocacy and global civil society." Transnational advocacy, and the coalitions that emerge from them have a global spread that is believed by many to counteract, combat, ameliorate, or even civilize deepening global capitalism. Transnational advocacy networks, similar to new social movements (Escobar and Alvarez 1992; Slater 1995), tackle a range of issues: human, gender, and labor rights; environmental destruction and ecological preservation; an end to child soldiering; the rights of the poor to housing and health opportunities; and so forth.

Transnational advocacy has clearly grown worldwide in recent years. This growth has special relevance for cross-border organizing between Mexico and the United States. It is indicative of a general global trend, but on the border, it also stemmed directly from NAFTA negotiations, and the environmental and labor opposition that preceded the signing of the agreement. "In the South, the exploitative labor conditions and the unfulfilled promise of employment and growth have turned *maquilas* into an icon of the failure of late twentieth-century neoliberalism. In bridging the North-South divide through highly pluralistic, dynamic, and decentralized transnational advocacy networks (TANs), the anti-sweatshop movement holds out the prospect of a revamped twenty-first century labor internationalism" (Rodríguez-Garavito 2006, 64).

Much cross-border organizing has focused specifically on environmental and labor issues in Mexico revealed by the NAFTA debate, with the express goal of improving the situation of workers' rights, health, and safety, as well as remedying environmental pollution and encouraging greater conservation (Graubart 2005; Hogenboom 1996). As Hogenboom notes with reference to environmental advocacy, "NAFTA preparations were to give a strong impulse for transnational cooperation between ENGOs in the three countries" (1996, 994). However, as with transnational advocacy elsewhere, advocacy on the border has also been handicapped by the occasional lack of accountability mechanisms, coupled with national power differentials.

Brown and Fox (1998) have developed a comprehensive inventory of the opportunities for and obstacles against building accountability within transnational coalitions. They define the "struggle for accountability" "*within* transnational environment and development coalitions" as "the effort to construct balanced power relations among coalition members and particularly between grassroots groups and the international nongovernmental organizations (INGOs) that in theory represent them" (1998, 439). Much of their analysis is apropos for understanding the pitfalls and successes of coalition building for both Spektra workers and Las Caracaras. They divide coalitions into two types: "project campaign coalitions" and "policy reform campaigns." I rely primarily on their analysis of project campaign coalitions. Although both the Justice for Border Workers and the Sierra Club aimed their transnational coalition-building efforts with Matamoros groups toward policy reform, the project campaign coalition model captures more completely the dynamics and struggles involved in developing successful coalitions with grassroots groups.

There are three relevant themes that emerge from the Brown and Fox essay. First, they stress the sequence of steps that are necessary for the evolution of a coalition: "problem definition, direction setting, implementation, and revision" (1998, 451). Second, they draw attention to the different effects that power differentials, geographic distance, culture, and ideology may have on coalition-building efforts. Third, they note that many transnational coalitions are marked more by conflict than cooperation, and argue that the development of trust and mutual accountability is a lengthy process of dialogue and problem solving, embedded in the four phases of coalition evolution. Trust is essential to building long-lasting coalitions. Spektra workers' trust became corrupted under the JBW campaign, yet trust seemed to grow continually in the Sierra Club–Caracaras relationship. Analyzing these different trajectories with the tools offered by Brown and Fox might help to partially explain these disparities.

Fox and Brown also draw attention to three issues relevant to understanding the three different coalition-building efforts described in this book: (1) between Las Caracaras and the INGO Sierra Club; (2) between Las Caracaras and the Brownsville Coalition against Contaminated Communities; and (3) between Spektra Workers and the NGO Justice for Border Workers. The three issues are as follows: (1) the difference between project campaign coalitions and policy reform coalitions; (2) the importance of the development of trust, open dialogue, and conflict · resolution throughout the life cycle of a coalition; and (3) the timeline and necessarily sequential steps germane to the development of successful transnational coalitions.

In the case of the Spektra workers' petition described here, each issue is of equal weight in understanding the unfortunate consequences of the petition from the perspective of workers—namely, that they felt doubly victimized: first, by Spektra plant and, second, by the JBW. Although details of the relations between the JBW and Spektra workers follow on subsequent pages, Spektra workers' experiences with JBW, as relayed to me, demonstrated the failure of the JBW to achieve even a minimal level of trust and accountability in their relations with Spektra workers. The same was true of the coalition-building effort between Las Caracaras and the Brownsville CCC, albeit for different reasons. These two experiences contrast sharply with the mutual trust that developed between Las Caracaras and the Sierra Club.

The next section describes the transnationalization of the Spektra workers' movement as a US-based NGO became involved with the workers' movement with the express purpose of operationalizing the NAALC dispute resolution process. The involvement of the NGO was a gradual process that involved various "delocalizing" steps in which non-Spektra and nonlocal actors took an interest in the movement, eventually transforming it from a local to a cross-border advocacy effort. The second section of this chapter discusses the Sierra Club–Las Caracaras coalition building effort.

Transnationalizing the Local: JPJ and JBW Involvement with CFO and Spektra Workers

Until Pedro and the Jóvenes Pro Justicia (JPJ) and Justice for Border Workers (JBW)[1] became involved, there were essentially two aspects to Spektra workers' activities. On the one hand, some were collecting information within the plant and among fellow workers in a manner typical of popular epidemiological movements. On the other, they were receiving training and attending regular meetings of the Comité Fronterizo Obreros in order to learn more about their occupational health and safety rights according to the 1931 Ley Federal de Trabajo. CFO workers Ava and Rosalia were dedicated to understanding and eradicating the problems of Spektra plant, and Spektra workers were learning their rights in order to lobby better for themselves within the plant. At this point in the early 1990s, the efforts of both the workers and the CFO were explicitly local. Their plan was simply to document as extensively as possible the illnesses that were occurring within the plant, figure out whether or not the NTD and spontaneous abortion cluster correlated with anything new happening inside the factory, and use their information to file complaints with the local arbitration council and the STPS. At this grassroots level, relations were cohesive, cooperative, and completely transparent.

The shift from local level organizing to transnational coalition building occurred slowly and somewhat unbeknownst to Ava or Rosalia. According to both, a fiery young man came to them while they were undertaking Spektra investigations and claimed that he wanted to apprentice himself to them and learn all that they knew about workers' rights and the LFT.[2] His name was Pedro and he was passionately against *maquila* exploitation of Mexican laborers and claimed that he wanted to write an expose of the industry. Apprenticing himself to the CFO would allow him to learn the book knowledge of federal labor law, as well as give him access to the same workers with whom Ava and Rosalia were then working. Badly needing someone who could work without pay and who had a lot of energy that their own middle-aged bodies no longer generated, the two were more than happy to take him under their wings as protégé.

Pedro was earnest enough in his desire to learn the true *maquila* experience that he also went to work in several *maquilas* in order to understand organically the quotidian trials and tribulations of factory workers. However, according to Ava, after several months of apprenticeship and access to privileged CFO information, he also became more secretive about what he was learning in different factories. Both she and Rosalia resented this because they had shared extensively with him, particularly about the circumstances of Spektra workers; they had invested much energy teaching him about the LFT and grooming him to be a future, permanent CFO advocate. According to Ava, all could have benefited from what he was learning by working inside other factories since neither she nor Rosalia was young enough anymore to be hired. Pedro had not engaged in a fair exchange; the novice protégé was beginning to seem less like an earnest pupil and more like an opportunistic *arribista*.[3]

Pedro continued working with the CFO for several more months, taking special interest in the Spektra workers' case, which was the main case the CFO was working on at the time. Then, however, he began to organize separate meetings with Spektra workers—separate from the CFO. Rosalia thought that he had done this in order to "raise his own status" with the group. When he formed a local chapter of the Jóvenes Pro Justicia (hereafter JPJ)[4], he split off from the CFO completely and, allegedly, turned the workers against the CFO.

Both Ava and Rosalia were quite bitter about this turn of events (evident even in their storytelling several years hence) because they had invested so much time and energy in the Spektra workers' case. I had often heard Rosalia and others lament that Pedro and his associates with the JPJ were *mañoso*[5] and corrupt. Ava framed her frustration this way:

> I was very angry, angry with members of this other group. The work that we had been doing for several years, and the names so carefully

collected, well, it is something that happened, but I cannot defend . . .
I cannot defend *un señor* who is looking for his own benefits, who
was trying to learn about our work, to learn the Ley Federal de
Trabajo, to get to know the groups, take advantage of the groups, and
then to take this work to the Justice for Border Workers![6]

After Pedro began this splitting of the group, one set of Spektra
workers suddenly and inexplicably did not want to see the CFO workers
at all: "This hurt a lot, right? That they did not like us anymore, that they
no longer wanted to see us nor for us to go there. No more—they only
liked Pedro."[7]

When the JPJ joined forces with the JBW, they continued their investigations of Spektra working conditions. They also began organizing
meetings with workers, collected affidavits and expert testimony and,
eventually, filed a petition for the workers with the US National Administrative Offices in San Antonio, Texas, under the auspices of the labor
side agreement. Guillermo corroborated this account that Pedro had
originally become familiar with Spektra workers' case via the CFO, but
then later the group "became divided" and "Pedro began to lead them
toward the petition." This is what initiated the trajectory of the Spektra
workers' justice movement away from the CFO and in the direction of
the JBW and an NAALC petition.[8]

In the same interview, Ava went on to say that, in her opinion,
the strategic mistake that Pedro and the JBW made was to go so loud
and public with the Spektra case. "They were too inflammatory, and
this turned forces against the workers." In contrast, she noted that the
strategy of the CFO had always been to work quietly and diligently, and
that was precisely the reason that it had been so successful: "One must
keep a low profile here if one wants to do this kind of work." She stated
that Pedro chose the opposite route because he wanted fame and money
for himself. Ava, similar to Javier and Rosalia, argued very strongly
that the JBW exploited the Spektra workers' case only in order to ele-
vate its own prestige as an NGO and to bring in more donations for the
organization:

They [the JBW] are not really interested in the workers and their
problems. . . . They always stay at the "first stage," they want only to
publicize information that will grab attention. . . . but to go and really
work—this organization [the CFO] became very strong over several

years in order to accomplish this type of work. See, in Mexico we do not have the capacity for very strong movements. It cannot be done like that. It can't be done like that because of the *maquilas*—when they see a movement that is more or less strong, they try to appease, or pay off, all of that. So, Pedro does not work properly. It isn't convenient for him to work, I don't think that he knows how to work in any other manner. This requires a lot of work, giving your whole life. To date, he does not want to give that. . . . to really work with the groups, as coordinators, as *promotoras,* with groups from the *colonias,* all of this is hard work! For the JBW to come and get all of this fame for our work, and to use this "big issue" style in order to get attention and money from foundations—and a lot of money from foundations—it does not work.[9]

Clearly, this recounting of events suggests that the opportunity for creating accountability between Spektra workers, the CFO, JPJ, and JBW was missed at the outset, confirming Brown and Fox's suggestion that, "the problems of accountability may be particularly challenging within loose and fluid coalitions, such as the alliances of NGOs and social movement organizations involved in transnational campaigns" (1998, 440). Indeed, it would appear that the CFO, JPJ, Pedro, the JBW, and Spektra workers were in agreement on problem definition only—the first phase of transnational coalition building (1998, 449–451). As Pedro and the JPJ hitched the grassroots interests and problems of Spektra workers to the JBW, they set off in a different direction, the preparation of a labor side accord petition, without even clarifying with the workers themselves. This was an international route in the pursuit of justice, rather than the national route preferred by the CFO in which violations of workers' rights were to be corrected according to Mexican national traditions and institutions: the Ley Federal de Trabajo, the Junta de Conciliación y Arbitraje, the Secretaría del Trabajo y Previsión Social, and the Confederación de Trabajadores Mexicanos.

This initial divergence and subsequent accountability failure only partially fits with the concepts developed by Brown and Fox, however. The two suggest, for example, "the potential for conflict is particularly high in circumstances characterized by cultural differences, diverse ideologies, discrepancies in wealth, and power inequalities" (Brown and Fox 1998, 441). They also repeatedly emphasize the importance of geography and the challenges of accountability when transnational coalitions are far flung between the global "North" and "South." Geography cannot explain the divergence here because the CFO and JPJ were operating in the same city and the JBW was located in a Texas city only a few hours' drive away. More than geographical distance per se, the border itself would eventually become a huge obstacle to accountability.

This divergence in direction setting helps to explain the acrimonious parting between the CFO and joint JPJ-JBW. However, it still fails to explain the subsequent opacity experienced by Spektra workers with regard to the labor accord petitioning process in which they had become enmeshed under the guidance of the now-linked Mexican JPJ and US-based JBW. In interviews, the most common and persistent complaint voiced by Spektra workers was their utter lack of comprehension about what happened to their stories once they told them to the JPJ-JBW, what was the purpose of sharing those stories, why the JPJ-JBW had never returned to them with news and, more generally, the sheer opacity that saturated the process from beginning to end. By virtually all accounts, they thought that they had participated in a lawsuit and willingly gave affidavits and interviews. Those that could traveled to the National Administrative Offices in San Antonio for a hearing. After filing the petition, they claimed not to have received any follow up information from Pedro or the JPJ on its status. I spent the beginning of every interview I conducted with a former Spektra worker—often one, two, or three hours—explaining my purpose for being there and, in painstaking detail, what the labor side accord was and how it functioned. On many occasions, I had to tell them that they could never expect to receive any remuneration for their injuries.

This confusion was made amply clear in my first encounter with a former Spektra worker named Ana.

On my first visit to Rosalia's house in November of 2001, I explained to her the fieldwork project that I hoped to undertake, which was simply a study of the Spektra workers' petition through interviews with former and current factory workers. I explained all of this to her as she listened patiently, propped up on pillows in her bed as she recovered from surgery. She immediately sent her seventeen-year-old daughter, Maria, out in search of Ana, a friend and neighbor of hers who had worked at Spektra and participated in the petition. While we snacked on cookies and Nescafé that Maria had prepared before being sent on her errand, she and Javier exchanged small talk.

When Maria returned with Ana in tow, I also explained to her the goal of my fieldwork project. After the typical set of queries about my motives and with whom or what institution I was connected, she agreed to talk with me, but only because she and Rosalia were close friends. My request was never really answered, however, because among the three of them a heated discussion broke out about the petition. Although Javier had warned me of the workers' confusion, I hadn't believed it myself until I heard Ana insist vociferously to both Javier and Rosalia that the petition was really a lawsuit. In a scenario that was to repeat itself over and over again during the course of the fieldwork, it became clear that Ana had agreed to speak with me only because she hoped that I had come with news about the lawsuit. And who could blame her? While Ana insisted that it was a lawsuit, Javier tried to reason with her, and Rosalia pleaded with her as a friend, to understand that it was a different kind of petition, and there was absolutely no possibility of monetary compensation for her now or in the future for her disabled wrist or chronic sinusitis. Together they tried to tell her that it was done, finished, and she needed to stop hoping for news from *el otro lado*.

In this case, the ex-Spektra worker believed that when she submitted an affidavit to the JPJ-JBW and their likely legal counsels, she was submitting court evidence, and that when she went to San Antonio to testify at the Secretary of Labor's National Administrative Office's hearing, she had testified in a court of law. Whereas the emotional intensity of this encounter with Ana was not repeated in subsequent interviews, the confusion repeated itself with striking and disconcerting regularity.

Fault Lines in the Spektra Petition

By the time I met Rosalia and Ana, I had already been introduced to the idea that perhaps there had been something corrupt about the Spektra workers' petition. Javier had recounted to me his experiences with the JBW and Spektra workers.[10] As a cross-border organizer and one of the few border people I encountered that seemed to be completely at ease on either side of the border, Javier had been one of the founding members of the JBW. He remained with the organization until 1998 when it began, via Pedro, organizing the Spektra workers for the petition.

Javier left the organization after witnessing how the JBW was presenting the labor accord petition to Spektra workers. Specifically, disagreements between him and the JBW president emerged when the latter began bringing in lawyers from a Texas university to speak with and collect affidavits from the workers. The lawyers were brought in to develop official documentation for the petition, without which the petition would not have passed the initial vetting phase of the Commission on Labor Cooperation. According to Javier, the workers became confused at the appearance of lawyers and began to believe that the information they were providing would be used for a lawsuit. Javier became enraged about this and confronted the JBW's president in a large meeting with the workers, trying to convince him to tell the workers that they were only involved in a side accord petition, not a lawsuit. The president refused to do this. Javier claimed to have told the workers one last time that it was only a petition and that there was no possibility of monetary reward. Then he walked out. In the spring of 2001, some of the Spektra workers had come to find him in Brownsville and pleaded with him to help them organize a lawsuit. He told them that it was impossible, that they had already used up all of their public or visibility capital in the highly visible Spektra workers' petition.[11]

Ava was one of the workers. She had been diagnosed with "neuropraxia radial" and had participated with the group during the early period of information gathering by the JPJ. During this period, she said that she sometimes attended their meetings; at other times people came to her house to talk with her. She claimed that the petition, at the time, was presented as a lawsuit—a *demanda*—against the company *en el otro lado o alla,* she signaled with her head. When I questioned her again to see if there was any doubt about this, she was unequivocal; it was a lawsuit that was supposed to go directly to company headquarters. She said that the objective of the action was to become *pensionados* by the company itself. She was clear that the purpose was to receive a pension directly from the factory itself, and not from the *Seguro.*

Another person, Juan, had provided an affidavit in support of the petition and had gone to San Antonio for the hearing, although he was not called upon to testify.[12] He did not attend the JPJ meetings, but organizers came to his home and interviewed him. At the time of our interview he was still concerned about never having received any news or benefits. He also advised me that if I encountered resistance or lack of interest among workers, it was just that they had lost hope and interest with the passage of time. Juan was also under the impression that they had participated in a lawsuit, but he also readily admitted that he might not have been properly informed because he was a bit peripheral to the process. By chance, he had run into one of the organizers earlier in the spring and was told that the matter was still being discussed. That was the last he heard. Juan maintained that, more than anything, he felt disillusioned and disappointed that the people in charge had not kept the participants more informed on the status of the action.

Shortly after we met for the first time, Catalina's mother was diagnosed with cancer. For several months, she spent Monday through Friday with her mother in the neighboring border city of Reynosa, where the latter received chemotherapy. When we were able to catch up again for an interview, we talked at length again about her nerve blocks and injuries. When I began to inquire about the petition itself, she grew mum and visibly hesitant. When I told her that I had met with the JPJ people and complied with all of their requests, yet they still refused to speak to me, she finally gave in a little bit:

> Listen, as for Pedro, I don't talk with him, the ones who were working with us were like, Roberto, right? Our friends. We all agreed to go to San Antonio, and to explain the problems that we had. More than anything, explain and expose our problems, so that they would realize this. Of all the people who were damaged there, we all have our testimony, I don't need a pencil or paper to explain what I have to say, no! I did not need the written testimony because I could tell them myself about my injuries—without reading anything because I don't need to read what I live! So that is how I spoke, and that is how I explained my situation.[13]

On a return visit to Martin and Adelia's house (Adelia had earlier promised to help me find more workers), Adelia and I talked more about the petition itself.[14] Adelia and Martin had attended both the early meetings that were organized by the CFO, as well as some of the later meetings organized by Pedro and the JPJ. She was uncertain whether they were calling it a *demanda civil* or a *queja* at that point but, eventually, she and her husband had decided between themselves that the process was useless and they stopped attending. They then lost contact with the group and were not entirely sure what the trajectory had been afterwards.

Both Pablo and Marta said that they knew of the petition and organization within the plant. Marta was not directly involved and, in fact, she wondered why she was never contacted since she also had wrist problems that had been diagnosed both as carpal tunnel syndrome and as a psychological problem.[15] Pablo, for his part, said that he did not participate in the actual JPJ petition, but that he did participate in two meetings—one between workers and employers in the plant, and a second with the Junta de Conciliación de Arbitraje. He estimates that about twenty men were present at the first meeting and, although he did not want to get involved, he was trying to calm the angry men.[16]

After my initial attempt at an interview with Ana in Rosalia's home, I tried several times to schedule other interviews with her, but she repeatedly failed to show up. Rosalia hypothesized that she must have been in contact with the JPJ people and that they told her not to speak with me. That was the only explanation she could come up with for why Ana spoke so freely in the beginning, then refused to say anything more.

In a second interview performed in Guillermo's home, I asked him to iterate the events surrounding the petition and, specifically, to clarify what his perception was since he had been involved in organizing Spektra workers since the beginning. For him, it was also important to draw attention to the fact that the organizing process began "here!" "Aquí in Matamoros!" He pointed at the ground emphatically, and emphasized that the organizing had begun between him and the CFO workers without the influence of outsiders. His perception, at the time, was that it was a mere petition or *queja* (complaint), and he claimed to explicitly remember the meeting in which the workers voted for that. However, he then just as emphatically (and repeatedly) pointed out that his understanding of what the JPJ-JBW expressed in that meeting was that once the workers' complaints had been filed as a *petición,* they would then be filed as a *demanda* or lawsuit:

> Well, at one point we were meeting to talk about what was going on, and after that, well, we decided to make it a petition. But we wanted to sue. We wanted to get to the point that we could file a lawsuit. What we wanted really was to file a lawsuit so that they would punish the company, as well as to benefit the people who could no longer work—so that they would compensate them as well. If you can't work, they are supposed to compensate you for your arm, your hand . . . [he goes on to discuss his own hand injury]. But all I wanted was that they punish the company, or that they gave me, I don't know, some kind of blood test so that I would know how poisoned I might be. What we wanted more than anything though was to punish the factory. Clearly, if there had been some kind of

compensation or something like that, well, then, that would be better, right? But no, my motive was that they punish the company. And they [the company] go on working . . . the factory is now in Ramirez with the other factories. It continues to be open, and just goes on and on, and continues to do the same.[17]

When I asked him to go into greater detail regarding the aftermath of the petition, he said that he was mostly just disappointed that the organizers never returned to the workers to inform them of the status of the complaint. "Since they are the organizers, since they have information and technology," he said, "it makes sense that they would have kept us informed."

While Pedro and the other JPJ people I met blamed workers' confusion for discrepant accounts about whether it was a lawsuit, petition, or simple complaint in which they had participated, my interviews with workers led me to a different conclusion. There was a general lack of accountability within this transnational chain of events, people, and institutions. With the general turmoil that the border creates and the opacity created by digital divide, educational differences, linguistic obstacles, and class-associated capabilities (phone, computer, and Internet access), it seemed as though the JBW and JPJ had exploited these divides rather than attempt to bridge them. This seemed to be the inevitable conclusion of workers' testimonies. By all accounts, it seemed as though the JBW and JPJ simply collected information from the workers in order to serve their own alleged purposes (namely, proving that the NAALC did not work), and then disregarded any further responsibility—an easy thing to do since most, if not all, of the workers did not have phones, computers, visas, or other resources.

Once the workers were separated from the CFO by Pedro and the JPJ, they became mired in a transnational advocacy relationship with the JBW, which was similar to Brown and Fox's description of a transnational project campaign coalition (1998, 442–469). As the latter have described it, project campaigns can be extremely productive because "grassroots groups have information about actual on-the-ground impacts and the legitimacy to challenge noxious consequences" (1998, 442), meanwhile transnational advocacy organizations have the networks and policy understanding to operationalize grassroots groups' experience and knowledge. In order for a transnational coalition to function effectively, however, the following minimal standards should apply:

At a minimum, coalition members should be able to define their expectations for performance, monitor compliance with those expectations, and successfully press for changes in behavior that does not meet minimal standards. For coalitions organized around specific projects, agreements on these issues seldom exist at the outset, so accountability must evolve with the coalition. Shared goals, strategies, and responsibilities must be articulated before parties can implement coalition plans, let alone hold one another accountable for performance. (Brown and Fox 1998, 442)

Clearly, these minimal standards were not met in the case of the Spektra workers–JPJ-JBW entanglement. According to workers, the organization of the petition seemed to be a top-down affair that did not involve negotiations or contracts that would have resulted in local and cross-border accountability and trust. Moreover, although the JPJ and JBW may have had policy goals in mind with their filing of the petition—such as testing the labor accord's dispute resolution mechanism—the way in which it was done suggests that they harvested workers' experiences and observations as raw material to prepare the petition without the mutual collaboration necessary between two or more equal parties. For this reason, workers felt doubly victimized: first by Spektra plant and, later, by their own countrymen and the JBW.

A second reason for the lack of accountability has simply to do with the knowledge gap that existed between the JBW-JPJ and the grassroots Spektra workers. While this may seem too obvious to mention, it bears some elaboration because of specific border circumstances and because the NAALC petitioning process was constructed to ignore this knowledge gap, operating instead with an imagined uniform Habermasian public sphere in which all parties have equal access to information and communication technologies—and possess the scientific and legal literacy necessary to operationalize the NAALC dispute resolution processes.

There is a typical problem that plagues many transnational coalition-building efforts, which is that the northern NGO has ready access to information, networks, and policy level discussions that have direct relevance to the problems and concerns of the grassroots group. This produces a knowledge gap that can result in frustration, disagreement, distrust, and dissension. For this reason, Brown and Fox suggest it is necessary for "parties [to] develop capacities for communication and mutual influence that span vast gaps in experience and resources" (1998,

442). Not only did Spektra workers not have direct access to information about the NAALC dispute resolution process that guided the preparation of their petition by the JPJ-JBW but, equally important, the JBW and JPJ either deliberately misled the workers or failed to make the petitioning process and NAALC bureaucracy as transparent as possible to them. In the aftermath of the petitioning process, the JBW and JPJ failed on most measures of accountability given their negligence in not reporting back to the workers the status of the petition. Lack of accountability and blockages of informational flows were caused and exacerbated by the digital divide that separated Spektra workers from the other side.

Meeting with JPJ people

I continued to search for ex-Spektra workers with Rosalia but, for as many times as we tried to re-initiate the *cadena* ("chain" or Rosalia's version of "snowball sampling"), our efforts led increasingly to dead ends with reports that people had moved and could not be located. I had long since given up on the JPJ people talking with me because the calls I made were never returned. I had been told by several sources that they would want money in exchange for information, and that because they had "lied" to the petitioners, they would not want me to uncover their lies. After one final attempt to make contact and after I had met with all of the workers I could find, however, I was surprised when I finally received a call back from Ernesto, Pedro's right hand man. Ernesto and I arranged to meet that same week at a coffee shop in downtown Matamoros.

When I arrived for the meeting, Ernesto was there along with two more petition organizers, Roberto and his wife, Cristina.[18] Roberto was a former Spektra worker who had organized the workers through the JPJ. I explained again my interest in the Spektra petition, why I was there, what I hoped to give back to workers, and how I would use the information. When they asked if I hoped to influence policy, I responded that I would hardly be there otherwise. At that point, the tone shifted from interrogation to discussion. We talked about lawsuits and mass toxic torts. When I asked directly why the petition had not been turned into a lawsuit, given the tremendous JBW resources, they refused to answer, but wanted to know what workers had told me. I deflected. They claimed that a meeting had taken place in which all the workers voted on whether they wanted to file a petition or a lawsuit. The workers had voted to file a petition, a point that was specifically corroborated in an interview with Guillermo a few days later.[19]

This initial meeting with the JPJ appeared successful. At the conclusion, they determined that they would have another talk among themselves and with Pedro, then one of them would call me sometime over the weekend. In the interim, Roberto and I set up an appointment for an interview the following week. I left the meeting feeling inspired and hopeful, with the thought that perhaps the JPJ people were not scheming and corrupt at all, as I had been told by so many others.

On the following Tuesday, Roberto called to cancel his interview. I took the opportunity to ask him the status of their discussions, but they had not yet had the chance to meet. He told me that he would call back to reschedule, but I had a sinking feeling in my gut that he would not, that a wrench had been thrown into the seemingly good rapport that we had developed only a few days before. I was right.

Ernesto and I were finally able to arrange another meeting a month later. This time Pedro finally made an appearance.[20] Pedro was a handsome guy in his mid to late thirties with dark, curly hair and a pair of fashionable sunglasses perched high on his forehead. Throughout our meeting, he chain smoked nervously, stared at me suspiciously, guzzled Diet Coke, and talked excitedly.

The first two hours of the meeting were dedicated to Pedro chastising me. As this particular fieldwork drama played itself out, the tables were turned with the Mexicans at the table holding clear power over the *norteamericana* and, apparently, determined to see me grovel. I knew my role and played it as required. Pedro told me in no uncertain terms that they had known of my presence since I had been there and had been informed of my every move. When he asked why I had not contacted them, I told him that I had tried several times to contact Ernesto and he never returned my phone calls. I did not have his contact information until the meeting one month before with the JPJ people. Smoke signals had not worked either. When asked why I had not contacted Señor Portes, the Mexican-born leader of the US-based JBW or gone through him, I told him rather obliquely that I wanted to be sure to capture the workers' local level or grassroots perspective of the experience, rather than have the movement represented to me in ways orchestrated by the organizers.[21] I left unsaid the fact that I was an anthropologist, not an activist willing to do the bidding of any NGO. Ernesto remained silent throughout most of the evening, quietly watching me be pulverized by the vibrating Pedro.

Pedro warned me several times and in several different ways that I had been treading mined territory: "*Estás en tierra minada,*" "You are in mined territory," "You are on a mined road," "If you think you are in mined territory on the basis of what we are telling you, you don't know the half of it," and finally, "You are lucky that you have not stepped on a bomb." I listened politely. Apparently, the most damning evidence against me was my contacts: "*Cuando oigo de Rosalia and Javier, te desconfió immediatamente*" ("When I hear the names of Rosalia and Javier, I distrust you immediately").[22] Clearly, when I began fieldwork I had no way of knowing the potential influence of my preliminary contacts on the entire endeavor. While this is not an uncommon fieldwork scenario, it would behoove future fieldworkers and budding anthropologists to take note. It can take months or years for the unintended consequences of one's initial participant-observation efforts to become evident.

Oddly enough, in spite of this ongoing chastisement, which I humbly endured, he warmed up to me somewhat after a couple of hours. Soon the two of them were telling me long-winded and chummy stories about how "*mañoso*"[23] were Mexican border activist groups. Both of my evening companions seemed utterly oblivious that, even as they called the other kettle black, this was precisely the same character assassination I had been hearing about them for several months. Finally, I was able to ask why the workers were confused as to whether the action had been a petition or a lawsuit. We had at least agreed earlier on the fact that the workers were unsure whether it was a petition, a civil lawsuit, or just a complaint, but no reason had been offered for why. Nevertheless, they immediately began to lament the ignorance of the workers. Pedro shook his head, turned to Ernesto, and exclaimed, "How many countless hours and meetings have we gone through this trying to explain the difference?" Just as the other JPJ members had told me one month before, Pedro and Ernesto maintained that, in an early meeting, the workers themselves had made the decision to file a NAALC petition rather than a civil lawsuit. They insisted that at the time the workers seemed to clearly understand the difference between a petition and a lawsuit, as well as the possible rewards for each: filing a NAALC petition could result in a change in workplace health and safety measures, whereas filing a lawsuit could result in monetary compensation. They suggested, furthermore, that in good faith and in keeping with Mexican nationalism (and thus faith in the letter of the law and its institutions), the workers had preferred the former over the latter.

Once the meeting was finished, they said that I should prepare a set of documents for them, and then they would help me find more workers. The documents that they listed included the following: a proposal describing my project, my plan for carrying out the project, a list of my objectives, the benefits that I perceived to accrue to the workers as a result of the research, and a "contract" to be signed by interviewed workers. I prepared a proposal in Spanish for their benefit, as well as the contract, and emailed all of the documents to them within a few days. I never heard from them again. I later wondered if they secretly delighted in simply creating extra work for me that would result in nothing.

At the end of the evening, they reverted to the tired drama with which the evening had begun—Pedro, the (oddly, highly educated) "worker," Ernesto as factory drone (though obviously highly educated as well) and me, the daffy *gringa*. Instead of chiding me on my ethnographic methods, they now chided me on my choice of meeting spots (a downtown café). They told me that the next time we met they would take me to a popular place where I would presumably have my bourgeois tastes sullied and elbows dirtied by rubbing them with the unwashed masses. They seemed to have momentarily forgotten that I hardly could have collected the data they were so angry with me about had I spent my time in downtown bohemian cafés. We parted ways with Pedro tossing one final "mined territories" threat my way, but now in a kind of cheerful bonhomie kind of way, implicitly offering the consolation carrot stick that even mined territories could be negotiated with the appropriate guide: themselves.

El Grand Rechazo[24]

There are any number of possible reasons why the JPJ people were not interested in helping me with this study. Notwithstanding the fact that they were pretty angry with me for not following the proper chain of command (in their view), the most plausible ones involve the question of whether or not any benefit might accrue to them or the workers as a consequence of my study. Since one of the challenges of anthropology historically has been to prove its public utility, vague promises of producing an informative study that might eventually and circuitously reach policy circles sounded mildly unconvincing—both to my own ears and, possibly, to theirs. Other possible reasons included the ones that had been reiterated to me several times—namely, that they only sold the information and I would have to offer at least US$1,500 to them for access to additional information beyond that which I had already collected. They held within their grip a highly valuable commodity—a high-profile NAALC petition—about which any number of journalists, academics, and students were curious. Of course, there was also the simple possibility, as had often been suggested since the beginning: they had lied to workers and did not want me to find out.

Rosalia was more specific. She felt that it was because of my contacts. They had had their falling out with Javier over the organization of the petition itself. With her they had a longer history, involving not only the CFO but other matters. She attributed Pedro's adversarial attitude toward her (then me) to a specific event in donor history.

In the late 1990s, she had reported the abuse by JPJ and JBW of a donation to the donor organization, which was a US church. Apparently, this church had given Justice for Border Workers US$15,000 to construct two schoolhouses in one of the poorest *colonias* of Matamoros. The schoolhouses were to be built in the same neighborhood in which Rosalia and a Brownsville priest were helping to build a church (also with funds from a US religious organization). She was thus able to monitor the progress of the two schools' construction. When they were finished, they were simply tiny, cheap, unadorned shacks that might have cost US$2,000 to build, by her estimate, which left US$13,000 unaccounted for.

When Rosalia was giving a tour of the neighborhood to visitors from a church related to the donor church, she took them to see the shacks. At that time, the donor church was informed of the squandering of their monies. Father Gonzalez corroborated this story.[25] Since these shacks were on the same plot of land as the church she was helping to construct, I had the opportunity to see them. They looked like the clinics that Texaco had constructed in the Ecuadorian Amazon after they were accused of massive oil contamination. The problem with these so-called clinics was that if one rounded the back side, one found out relatively quickly there was no clinic, nor even a back side. In the same way, it was unclear how these unfinished shacks could possibly serve as schoolhouses. So Rosalia reported this to the donors. She was of the opinion that Pedro's venom toward me was due not only to the obvious CFO/Spektra history between them, but also to her report of donor fraud to the other side.

Early Identity Tensions within Las Caracaras

Similar to the Spektra workers, Las Caracaras also showed signs of stress fractures when US-based advocacy and financial resources were introduced into what had been, until then, a fairly harmonious organization. Many of the tensions that revealed themselves within Las Caracaras under this pressure were related to issues of identity, education, resources, and power. They were evident even at the organization's founding moments, with the initial collaborations between Rosalia and Nurse Felipa.

According to Rosalia, she and Nurse Felipa parted ways based on two different but related incidents. The first had to do with monies that had been donated to Nurse Felipa's clinic by a US church. Similar to Rosalia's denunciation of the JPJ's misuse of donations, Rosalia also denounced Nurse Felipa. In front of a larger group, Rosalia asked what had happened to these funds and donations, which were intended for the community, and Felipa had been unable to respond to the satisfaction of the group.

The second incident occurred when members of the recently convened Las Caracaras attended a border workgroup meeting organized by the Sierra Club in the spring of 2000. The group was sufficiently developed at the time to have a presence within the community and to make a presentation at the organized meeting. At this time, the Sierra Club was just beginning to develop the Beyond the Borders (BTB) program. In the spirit of developing relations with Tamaulipan environmental groups and inform itself of eastern border issues, so as to steer the emerging BTB program, the Sierra Club organized a regional forum in Brownsville, Texas. The meeting functioned as a workshop to showcase the various environmental problems and groups that were working in the region. For this unofficial launching of the BTB program, Rosalia and Las Caracaras were earmarked early on as a productive and informed border group.

Although Rosalia insisted that Nurse Felipa was the true founding person of Las Caracaras, other members of the group had chosen Rosalia, rather than the nurse, to represent them in the Brownsville forum. Upon conclusion of the meeting, the Sierra Club members awarded a monetary gift to Las Caracaras. Not only had they been impressed with Rosalia's presentation and with the other group members who were able to cross to the US side,[26] but Las Caracaras had also organized an elaborate and successful "toxic tour" of Matamoros for the representatives.

The US$5,000 donation was supposed to serve as seed money for the organization to move forward with its work and to help the Sierra Club begin to develop working relations with Mexican environmental groups for their new BTB program.

After this meeting, however, Rosalia and Nurse Felipa never spoke again, and Felipa stopped attending Las Caracaras meetings. Rosalia then took over effective leadership of the group and reoriented it toward the goal of cleaning and covering the *Dren Cinco de Marzo*. Somewhat ironically, and in a manner that would later become a pattern, the choices that the small organization made in order to succeed in the competition for a Sierra Club grant ultimately led to the first splintering within the group. This question of whether or how Rosalia functioned as a somewhat iconic representative of Mexico's poor and environmentally contaminated underclass would reverberate throughout the group's relations for a long time to come. Rosalia seemed, at once, to embrace the stereotype she knew herself to embody and could, in a sense, act out as an impassioned and justice-seeking activist. On the other hand, she deeply resented it because she knew that, ultimately, it was based on the absence of true power within her life in the sense of resources, technology, communication media, and education. This tension would become more pronounced in her later relations with the group's more educated and middle class PRD members as they vied for power over the future of Las Caracaras when Sierra Club funding became available again.

Transnational Influences and Grassroots Splintering

In this section, I describe the tumult that began to affect Las Caracaras as the organization entered more deeply into a relationship with the Sierra Club. As already noted, this relationship revolved largely around preparing Las Caracaras to apply for, and receive, a grant from the Sierra Club in order to continue its Matamoros-based environmental justice activities. The splintering of the group is evident in the series of events described below. However, it is important to note that this fractious parting of ways revolved largely around two themes.

The first had to do with increasing suspicions among Las Caracaras members that the committed and ambitious PRD members were attempting to hijack the group in order to fulfill their political, rather than environmental, ambitions. They hypothesized that this PRD take-

over could proceed in one of two ways: on the one hand, if Las Caracaras were to receive the grant—as was suspected they would—they feared
that the aspiring politicians would merely use the funds and the group
for their own political gain. On the other hand, Rosalia, in particular,
was aware of the extreme grassroots profile of the organization. Since
these same PRD politicians had used her and others in the past to extend their reach within the poorest *colonias* otherwise inaccessible to
them (because of their middle class status), she and others feared that
Las Caracaras would merely become a US-funded front for a local PRD
outreach campaign. The possible use of Las Caracaras as a political in-
strument was understood by many to be contrary to the terms of BTB
participation already stipulated by the Sierra Club.

The second theme that was essential to the splintering of the group
had to do directly with identity politics and Rosalia's prior experiences
with the PRD members in question. As she explained to me several
times, she had participated in many city-wide campaigns with Javier and
Eduardo; because of her relatively high profile within the community she
had brought them many votes. Without her, they would have been unable to reach many of the thousands—and tens of thousands—that lived
in the city's poorer *colonias*. I have also already mentioned Rosalia's suspicions that she was a mere figurehead in other people's eyes, yet she also
enacted a powerful stereotype that, ironically, was based on her general
powerlessness. Many of the frictions within the group revolved around
this tension. As the PRD members attempted this alleged takeover of the
group, Rosalia grew increasingly resentful of the fact that they seemed
pleased to put forward her dark and lined peasant face in order to get
funds, only to try to subjugate her to their control once the funds came
rolling in. There was clearly both a gender and class dimension to this
subjugation; gender, in the sense that they seemed ready to take over the
reins of the organization as it ceased to be merely a poor person's organization loosely based on environmental cleanup, *comunidades de base*,
"women's work," and became a professional entity; and class, in the sense
that they both had a university education, were well-spoken, drove de-
cent cars, and lived in nicer Matamoros neighborhoods. Unlike Rosalia
(and this was an ongoing bone of contention), they had regular access to
the Internet and phone; moreover, they knew how to express themselves
well in both of these media, while Rosalia was uncomfortable composing
an email. To her mind, the gradual professionalization of the organization was sadly equated with the takeover of the group by its more upper

working class and middle class members. Each of these tensions is amply evident in the following series of events.

Relations among members of Las Caracaras were frequently tense because of the unequal and contradictory power relations between Rosalia, the President, and those who were presumably secondary to her. At least four of the latter that were second to her within the organization were middle class and educated, thus wielding considerable more power than she economically, socially, and symbolically in Mexican society. Among them, two were ambitious politicians within the local PRD. The group's interactions with the Sierra Club through the spring, summer, and fall of 2002 set off a series of explosive incidents that were merely symptomatic of these deeper currents. Under stress, the tenuously binding structure of Las Caracaras gave way to factionalism, rivalries, and virtual chaos within the local political economy of scarce resources.

The first friction-producing incident coincided with the submission of the initial grant application in early April of 2002. Late in the afternoon of the day that the application was due, Rosalia and I set off in search of Eduardo, one of the PRD members who had been entrusted with the final draft of the application and responsible for ensuring that it was submitted online and on time. Since neither she nor I had heard from him, we wanted to make sure that the application had been sent. Unfortunately, Eduardo was not to be found in either home or office. We began to worry.

Father Gonzalez also had a next-to-final draft, as well as a telephone and Internet connection, so we knew that if he had heard nothing from Eduardo, the application likely had not been submitted. So we went to the *parroquia* in search of the priest and found him in his office, sweating bullets over the application. For the next several hours, the three of us sat and worked through the final details. Father Gonzalez and I alternated at the keyboard because Rosalia did not yet know how to type on a computer keyboard. The application was sent at precisely 11:45 p.m. (fifteen minutes short of the deadline), with Father Gonzalez feeling proud of his newly acquired skill of sending email attachments. Tequila was broken out in celebration, and the day's gossip began to roll.

Father Gonzalez proceeded to iterate the tribulations of the day for my sake, although he had already told Rosalia earlier in the day and she had filled me in during our search for Eduardo. At noon that day, he had received a surprise phone call from Carlos, the other aspiring politician in the group and a constant companion of Eduardo's. Carlos, who like

Eduardo had barely been present for the draft writing of the fifteen-page proposal and was scarcely aware of its contents, had told Father Gonzalez in no uncertain terms that he believed that he, rather than Rosalia, should be named on the grant as principal executor and director of the grant. Father Gonzalez responded in equally certain terms that the name of the principal executor could not be changed without a full consensus within the organization. They apparently had a little tête-à-tête and the phone call ended in argument.

Throughout this retelling of events, Rosalia sat silent, smoking and nodding at me as if to say, "Didn't I tell you this would happen?" I also listened silently, stunned by the betrayal. As it happened, Carlos's intervention was to open up an entire Pandora's box of underlying gender, class, race, and educational schisms. Additionally, it brought to the surface personal conflicts between Rosalia and the PRD politicians related to her longer history of assistance with PRD campaigns, a history that preceded and overlapped with her current Las Caracaras presidency.

Rosalia began to tell me about much of this later as we sat in the car in front of her house at two in the morning. Alternately crying and raging, she now explained to me in much greater detail the source of her conflicts with Eduardo and Carlos. She had known the local aspiring politicians for several years; they were both many years younger than she. They were driven primarily by naked political ambitions, according to her, and only cynically ascribed to the forward-looking and progressive agenda of the social democratic PRD party. They had been coming to her for years in order to garner her support for the Matamoros chapter. As I had been, they were attracted to her as a key informant and guide—someone who lived within one of the poorest *colonias* and possessed the considerable embodied and informed knowledge of a *pobre* who, for political purposes, had the power and personal charisma to mobilize popular support for a cause. As with many people, she felt disillusioned with the PRI, but still vowed support for a truly revolutionary government. She was equally disenchanted with the neoliberalizing policies of the Partido de Acción Nacional (PAN or National Action Party) and Fox administration, a party that she perceived to be only for the wealthy. The PRD was the new left alternative for true democracy and a more equitable distribution of wealth. She had, therefore, worked tirelessly for the PRD campaigns and, through her, Eduardo and Carlos could be assured of many of the votes of her and surrounding neighborhoods. Only two weeks before, Eduardo had won citywide elections to become president of the Matamoros chapter of the PRD.

She explained to me again, as she had many times, that in Mexico one could put little trust in friendships. Most relationships were about manipulating the other person to suit one's needs; one was always looking to get an advantage over the other person. This was, primarily, the view she held of Eduardo and Carlos and their relationship with her: they had used her in the past and were still trying to use her, but now the purpose was to get funds from the Sierra Club. As evidence, she noted that they did not come by to check on her when they did not need help with a campaign. When babies were born, cars broke down, and family members fell sick, they were nowhere to be found. She had since decided to no longer help with PRD election campaigns and had lost interest in the party.

With respect to Las Caracaras, she had come to the conclusion that they had named her as organizational president with the covert intention of displacing her once it became successful or began bringing in resources—much as Carlos had tried that day. More insidiously, she also thought that they had helped elect her as a puppet or figurehead president that could pull in more funds than they (with their pale, smooth skin) because of her peasant and indigenous-looking face: dark-skinned, deeply lined, and weary. She was quite certain that they saw her lack of education as an obstacle to the efficient running of the group and that, once established, they would want to be the ones at the forefront, especially in its dealings with other Mexican and non-Mexican NGOs. As a figurehead, she assumed that she fulfilled an important symbolic function for the group, allowing it to put forward the face of a peasant with the flaming desire for justice of a Rigoberta Menchu, but it still angered her. She assumed that they figured her a *tonta*,[27] but declared that she would get the last laugh.

In the midst of her anger, she also lamented the fact that, having known Rosalia for many years, they still could not see her or know her for who she was—a complicated person with mixed feelings and her own drives, ambitions, and concerns—but only as they themselves were raised to think about the poor: as illiterate, dim, and in constant need of guidance and direction. A more insidious effect of this latter conceptualization, of course, is that it reproduces the idea of a person like Rosalia as a person without a complicated mind, but with a passionate heart; body over mind or, more to the point, a body to their minds. It was based on this lengthy relationship with the two that she had concluded that their goal was to displace her from Las Caracaras and hijack the project funded by the Sierra Club for their own careers.

A Usurpation of Power?

In a meeting a couple of weeks later, Carlos and Eduardo together aggressively pursued the possibility of Carlos taking over as director of the Sierra Club project if it were funded. Father Gonzalez was out of town and in the days prior to the meeting, gossip flew as to why they would be so insistent about scheduling a meeting during Father Gonzalez's absence. The suspicion was that, if they had an agenda, they would try to pursue it while the priest was gone because he was their most formidable opponent among the remaining members—educated, eloquent, and fiery-tempered. Rosalia and other Las Caracaras members could be quickly overpowered by Eduardo and Carlos in Father Gonzalez' absence; after all, they were educated and they were politicians. She readily admitted to me that she did not always understand the words that they used. Her biggest fear was that they would push for a single, full-time salaried position that Carlos would occupy. Even worse, in her view, they might have to accommodate this attempted takeover by voting for two part-time positions, which meant she would have to occupy the office with the pushy Carlos. The latter was not an improvement over the former because, if she were in the office with him, she would never be able to suffer the indignity of having to ask him questions. He would shamelessly assert his superiority over her by wielding his higher education as a club. In short, if they were in the office together, he would treat her as an assistant while he steered the ship. After long months of hard work, Rosalia's dreams for Las Caracaras and what they could do with a Sierra Club grant seemed to be going up in smoke.

The meeting that Eduardo and Carlos had pressed for was finally scheduled. It started late in the evening in the yard of the *parroquia*. The sun had gone down and the air was beginning to cool. Several routine matters appeared on the meeting agenda, then came the final item to be discussed: whether or not to provide a single salary for one full-time position (as requested in the grant proposal), or two half salaries for two part-time positions. Eduardo and Carlos were staunchly in favor of a single salaried position and one person to staff it. Furthermore, they argued that a full-time salaried position should pay Mex$5,000 per month, which was more than originally indicated in the proposal. They proclaimed it was clear that the organization could not move forward until it had a steady and continuous presence, a mastermind to organize things and think strategically ahead.

The meeting grew heated in no time; some favored the full-time salaried position, others did not. Carlos argued in abstract and theoretical terms for the importance of a full-time position (to promote leadership, organizational development, etc.), while Eduardo made plugs for Carlos as the appropriate person to staff that position. Esperanza argued against having anyone, Mariceli came down in favor of a salaried position, Don Andres took the middle path and sought to avoid conflict by favoring both Rosalia and Carlos, and Tomas said nothing, except that the group should not be arguing.

By the end of the evening, a decision had been reached to include a full-time salary, but the decision was reached only out of sheer exhaustion. It was almost 11:00 p.m. The decision was made by Eduardo and Carlos who relentlessly pushed the codified statutes of Las Caracaras that stated the only votes that counted were those of the members who were present at the meeting at the time of a proposition. Although everyone knew that Father Gonzalez would have voted down any proposition that detracted from Rosalia's serving as the full-time director and president, he was not present and, therefore, he could not cast a vote. When Eduardo and Carlos were asked why this matter was so urgent and could not wait until Father Gonzalez returned, especially since he was so influential in making sure the grant was written and submitted in time (unlike them), they responded with: "Why wait? Would Father Gonzalez' vote really make a difference?" Of course it would have. In the end, the *PRDistas* won. The others had become complacent and tired of arguing. A vote was taken and all voted in favor of the need to pay a full-time salary, yet they remained undecided as to whether it should be for one or two people. That decision, at least, was postponed until another meeting.

Rosalia and the others now feared a complete PRD takeover. They viewed with irony the fact that these two members had scarcely, if at all, been present during the preparation of the grant application. Rosalia was firm in her conviction that her prophecy was being fulfilled: once Las Caracaras began to acquire some status and support, the *PRDistas* would want to use it as a vehicle for their own political ambitions and, more stinging to her, they would insist on having a middle class, educated, lighter skinned, and male face to represent and run the organization. The complication with this budding PRD takeover was the fact that, according to Sierra Club restrictions, BTB funding was not to go to any organization that had such strong political party connections that the interests of group members or group leadership could use BTB funds for political partisanship. In other words, the Sierra Club had safeguarded its funding program against precisely the type of political party hijacking that the PRD seemed to be attempting. The funds earmarked by the Sierra Club's BTB program were intended for grassroots environmental organizations only. Rosalia and Father Gonzalez subsequently used this funding stipulation in their attempt to dislodge the PRD members, Eduardo and Carlos, from their seats on the *mesa directiva* (executive board).

Splintering over Resources

Las Caracaras met the following week in its newly furnished office. Father Gonzalez' *parroquia* was able to lend it to the group as temporary quarters. It had been decided to use some of the monies that still remained from the original Sierra Club seed grant (from spring 2000) to furnish it with the rudiments necessary to running an office: hanging file folders, pens, paper, a desk chair to accompany the donated desk, a plastic bookshelf, and a very necessary fan. Rosalia and I had made a trip to Staples in Brownsville the week before in order to purchase these items, which were much cheaper on the US side of the border than on the Mexican side.

The group gathered in a circle in its sparkling new office. Rosalia calmly distributed the agenda, which included (1) Belen's renunciation, (2) discussion of whether or not someone with strong party or religious affiliations should be on the executive board, and (3) a reopening of the previous meeting's discussion of salaried positions. She quickly reviewed the previous meeting's discussion. Many of the core members were present: Maria, Esperanza, America, Alejandra, Don Andres, Maricela, Eduardo, Carlos, Belen, Tomas, Katerina, Arturo Grande, Arturo Chico, and others whose faces I had seen, but who were not always present at the meetings. Those who were opposed to having Carlos and Eduardo at the head of the organization had agreed privately to a script that was meant to oust the pair. Someone made the prudent suggestion that we name someone as mediator for the discussion. Three of us were nominated and I was selected.

Belen, a priest and the organization's secretary, had made his first appearance in months only to announce his resignation because of his religious affiliation. The hope was that this would spur Carlos to also to announce his resignation; instead, Carlos sat with arms crossed over his middle, smiling—presumably at the (admittedly, amusing) irony of someone showing up after months of absence only to announce his resignation. As it turned out, Belen's resignation was the only part of the evening that would unfold as planned.

When the second item of the agenda came up—which was the signal for people to begin renouncing their positions—the discussion was inconclusive and circled endlessly. This was aided by the fact that no one adhered to his or her previously prescribed roles and scripts. After all, what might be the real consequences of resigning? Perhaps this was not just a farce, would they then all be out of the organization and leave it to the PRD? Finally, Father Gonzalez jumped into the discussion, at which point it heated with remarkable rapidity to boiling temperature and remained there for the rest of the night, which is to say, for the next four hours. "Carlos and I have personal differences and I believe that it is impossible for us to work together anymore," Father Gonzalez proclaimed. Then, "If Carlos is to remain on the executive committee, I will renounce my membership in the organization." Others used this as an equal opportunity to unload their grievances against Carlos and the other PRD members (Eduardo and, somewhat less so, Maricela) and the general PRD influence within Las Caracaras. They did not want political influence, they said. This was a grassroots organization of poor people and politics had nothing to do with it. Someone brought up the rumor that Carlos had been seen in Nuevo Laredo a few days before with Oscar, the Sierra Club representative: Why had he met separately with Oscar? How did he represent Las Caracaras in that instance? Was it a private visit or was it with the intention of representing Las Caracaras? This led to bickering, with the PRD people on one side of the room and the rest of the group delivering an onslaught from the other side.

Eventually, the usually patient and even-tempered Esperanza announced her resignation as treasurer. Another intense discussion followed. By then it was ten o'clock at night. Other people began to half-heartedly renounce their positions, whether as members of the executive committee or as members of the organization, but without leaving the room or the discussion.

Two more hours passed. How to retain the grant money was something that Rosalia had already reviewed with Oscar, which the others knew nothing about. As the discussion wore on, Rosalia, having decided to change tactics at the last minute, refused to renounce her position. As often seemed to happen, the most important item up for discussion was the singular item to which no one would refer: the grant money. And so the performance continued: the throwing of gauntlets, laying down of cards, and the making and calling of bluffs. Throughout all of this, Belen continued to resign repeatedly.

This meeting's impasse resulted in the temporary disbanding of the group, and Rosalia withdrew Las Caracaras' grant application from the Sierra Club. She and the others agreed that they preferred to wait until the next grant-making cycle, rather than receive funds that would allow the PRD members to monopolize the organization.

The Second Sierra Club Grant-Making Cycle

Many months later, in October of 2002, Las Caracaras submitted a second grant application to the BTB program. In January of 2003, it was announced that the Las Caracaras had been selected by the Sierra Club to receive a grant of US$5,000. This money was intended as an organizational development grant that would allow the group to hold regular meetings, maintain an office, have a computer and Internet access, and to support them with miscellaneous office supplies throughout the next six months to one year. For example, included in the budget had been printing costs, since the organization frequently talked about printing flyers and leaflets for announcements and information—not least of which was about their meetings. The selection of Las Caracaras was made from a competition of approximately fifteen groups.[28] Rosalia, mysteriously, was not happy at the news that Las Caracaras group was scheduled to receive a grant.

"There is still the problem of Father Gonzalez," Rosalia claimed, "and how we are to receive the money. Father Gonzalez must not know that we won the grant," she said firmly.

"Why?"

"He came by here the other day and was asking questions, asking whether or not we had received any news yet."

"And what did you tell him?"

"I told him nothing, that it was all up in the air and we did not know when we would know." Then she explained that if he found out that they had received the grant, he would want to rejoin the group, and she could not tolerate his presence or influence any more. He was not PRD, but he was still more educated than she, *prepotente* (arrogant), and she was sure that he would try to bully her and treat her as a puppet figure, as the PRD folks had done. She did not want him to know that the grant had been won, as well, since he would then offer to receive the money into the church's account and that would put him in a one-up position. Since Las Caracaras were not yet registered as an *asociación civil,* they did not have a banking account into which they could receive the grant money. This would turn out to be a grave problem because the Sierra Club could not approve a check written to a personal name, and the group was experiencing long delays in having its *asociación* status approved.

Money-Related Suspicions and Losing the Comité Connection

Even though Father Gonzalez, who had attended at least a couple of the initial BECC/JPAC Comité Cuidadano (Citizens' Committee) meetings until Las Caracaras was inexplicably removed from their invitation list, might have shed some further light on the inner workings of the Comité Ciudadano, this did not happen. Around this period, he and other Las Caracaras members had suddenly begun to experience estranged relations. Perhaps because of or as a consequence of this, rumors began to circulate that he had been pilfering money from the little money they still had from the original donation made in the year 2000. Several meetings had taken place recently in which either he or the treasurer were expected to be present to inform the larger group about the status of its money, how much remained, and how it had been used. The group's treasurer, Esperanza, who usually did not oppose him in any way, had finally questioned him in his offices and he had thrown the checkbook onto the table between them. "There! Take the checkbook if you want it!" The checks would be useless, of course, without his signature. She and Rosalia had continued to ask for the money periodically with the excuse that they wanted to buy a computer. As of late 2002, he had yet to approve the purchase. For Rosalia, this was yet one more instance in which she felt overwhelmed and overpowered by middle class group members who had more opportunities and influence than she. She could not even control the organization's money since it was not yet registered as an *asociación,* and the money rested in the coffers of the temperamental Father Gonzalez' church.

Over two years after receiving the original US$5,000 seed grant from the Sierra Club, Rosalia estimated that US$1,800 had remained until recently. Until only a few months before, all of the expenditures could be accounted for as related to the organization: the purchasing of a communal meal when a Sierra Club representative came to visit, the money for the *Hacienda y Creditos* paperwork for *asociación civil* status, office supplies for the preliminary *parroquia* office, and small trees for a reforestation project on the banks of the *Dren Cinco de Marzo*. In the last few months, however, people had had to borrow from the account for various exigencies—the expenses of both Maria and Katerina having babies; bailing Katerina's brother, Emilio, out of jail; and, in the winter of 2002, funeral expenses for Katerina's infant that was buried in a paupers' cemetery across the road from Quimica Fluor. Even accounting for the borrowing that had recently occurred—and which was already being paid back by Katerina, at least, since Maria was not then earning money—it seemed to Rosalia and Esperanza that more should remain in the account. Thus they began to suspect Father Gonzalez of pilfering.

The Comité Ciudadano moved forward with its work and without the input of Las Caracaras. In late June of 2003, the BECC certified the *Plan Integral,* or Comprehensive Water and Wastewater Project of Matamoros. Although Las Caracaras had briefly held a nominal position on the Citizens' Committee, they had been unable to sustain their representation there partly because of internal politicking, and partly due to digital, social, and class divides that effectively excluded them.

This chapter has demonstrated that cross-border, US advocacy groups, whether intentionally or not, can have adverse effects on grassroots organizations in Mexico. In the case of the Spektra workers, the workers' petition, the CFO, JPJ, and JBW, the relationship was murky; there was not a lot of transparency in the relationship that the JPJ and JBW forged with the workers. The physical US-Mexico border can serve as a formidable obstacle to keeping lines of communication in coalitions and cross-border advocacy open. The digital border between those that are and are not digitally connected operates across different vectors, and it is unclear how the relationship between the JPJ, JBW, and Spektra workers might have turned out if even a handful of the latter had been digitally connected.

With regard to Las Caracaras, the underlying class, gender, and educational schisms within the organization became fully apparent and destructive as soon as the possibility of external funding from a powerful US NGO presented itself. Within the organization, Rosalia had often felt overshadowed and intimidated by the tiny minority middle class PRD members, as well as by Father Gonzalez. This was largely because of the education and class status that they wielded, but also because the latter had access to phones and the Internet, whereas she lived largely in a communications vacuum, only temporarily mediated and ameliorated by my presence. With the possibility of Sierra Club funding forthcoming, her worst fears had been confirmed as she and others struggled to keep the organization a grassroots environmental one and not allow its hijacking by political partisan interests. However, the sum total of the effect of transnational resources was to fracture Las Caracaras irreparably.

Conclusion

This book has argued that the passage of NAFTA relied on the creation of the North American labor and environmental side accords. It has argued, additionally, that the side accords were inextricably tied to Mexico's ongoing political democratization and economic transition efforts to reconcile trade, non-trade, and sustainable development interests, as all three of these rely discursively and practically on participation as the key to their success. The side accords were intended to encourage and guarantee participatory possibilities among Mexican, Canadian, and American populations. In Mexico, public participation in the side accords' petitioning and dispute resolution mechanisms was argued by the accords' crafters to encourage the growth of civil society, a robust sense of citizenship and responsibility among citizens of a democratizing nation, and accountability by the Mexican government. The accords were also intended to keep the spirit and substance of the pre-NAFTA debates alive even after the signing of NAFTA. Trade negotiators, policy-makers, Clinton's presidential campaign, and environmental and labor organizations were all in agreement that the debates had highlighted some of the most contentious points of conflict between free trade interests, on the one hand, and labor, environmental, and human rights concerns, on the other. Finally, it was believed that the environmental ills of the border region could be cured through the logic and practice of sustainable development because the *maquila* industry, until that point, had brought largely destructive development to the area. The sustainable development angle of the environmental side accord, evident most clearly in the mandates of the BECC and NADBank, conceptualized border communities as sustainable building blocks for a new and cleaner border region.

Participation was the key to ensuring the success of these three broad-based mandates. The empirical material in this book has demonstrated, however, how difficult it was for these border communities to participate, whether in a fledging or meaningful manner, in side accord institutions and processes—as well as in cross-border networks. US-Mexico cross-border advocacy is notoriously rife with basic and quotidian obstacles: language, cultural differences between nationalities and class, different organization building and advocacy techniques, and last, but not least, the border itself (Barry 1994; Bejarano 2002; Brooks and Fox 2002; Kelly 2002; Staudt and Coronado 2002). This did not start with NAFTA and it certainly has not ended with it—particularly with the United States' post-9/11 security measures and Mexico's unfolding drug cartel wars. The side accords introduced a new dimension, however, which was and is the emphasis on transparency as the key to securing participation and curing border ills. In doing so, they effectively added digital divide to the other social, cultural, linguistic, and territorial divides that fracture border life.

NAFTA and the side agreements went into effect around the same time that the Internet and worldwide web were beginning to take root as ineluctable aspects of a globalized and technologically advanced world. Popular perceptions of the new Internet Age oscillated between conspiratorial nightmares and optimistic visions of electronically supported democracies. Optimists believed that "electronic communications would have inherently democratic impacts, facilitating equal access to data and knowledge regardless of social standing or geographic location" (Warf 2001, 4; cf. Norris 2002). The fact that the Internet exists and that institutions can post documents on web pages, make announcements via mail discussion lists, maintain online discussions or a "civil society comment box" (as the Free Trade Area of the Americas or FTAA negotiators maintained for several years), and otherwise behave in an ostensibly transparent manner, means that the Internet can also be manipulated for what might be called the "performance of participation." Performances of this type are now pandemic, as a perusal of the civil society-oriented web pages posted by the World Bank, IADB, FTAA, and other global development actors demonstrate. Once a document is online, it is officially public. However, this is a highly circumscribed public that effectively excludes those digitally disenfranchised by a host of social and economic reasons that predate the Digital Age. As Warf (2001) has argued, the geographies of power in the non-cyber world are replicated in the world of the Internet which, in turn, reproduce and reinforce inequalities of the material and social worlds. Anzaldúa's description of the US-Mexico border as a place where "the third world grates up and bleeds against the first" is redolent even of the digital border where "all the existing social categories of wealth and power are replicated in cyberspace" (Warf 2001, 16–17).

Early crafters and supporters of the side accords seem to have embraced the potential democratic qualities of the Internet, their beliefs buttressed by the economic conviction germane to NAFTA that "the market alone [would] take care of any perceived" digital disparities (Mariscal 2005, 10). For that reason, the imagined public sphere of the border, as it has been produced by environmental and labor side accord institutions, is mediated primarily through the Internet. During the time of my fieldwork in Matamoros, I never saw a newspaper used to announce or invite people to attend public forums in which potential development projects or other border infrastructure health issues might be discussed. In cases of the Good Neighbor Environmental Board, Border 2012, and Citizens' Committee meetings, the events drew a public that was already digitally and socially connected and, in some cases, seemed to be there by invitation only. They were largely from the successful and well-established business sectors, as well as the local social elite. Therefore, the fact that "the NAAEC contains mechanisms for public participation and transparency that are unparalleled in any other international agreement or institution" (Ferretti 2002, 85; see also Goldschmidt 2002) does not really matter if these mechanisms are fundamentally inaccessible to the very populations for which they were ostensibly created.

The digital divide on the Mexican side of the border mirrors the digital divide in the rest of Mexico. Per thousand inhabitants, the "United States has more than ten times as many personal computers" than does Mexico, so there are few computers; a home computer is a luxury typically reserved for the middle to upper middle classes. A 2004 study of the number of people in Mexico with home PCs and Internet access put that number at only 11.18 percent of the population.[1] The poor and rural areas of Mexico have significantly less Internet access than do urban areas and, in recent years, the digital divide has been increasing rather than decreasing relative to other developing countries (Mariscal 2005). The problem of Internet access is a rural-urban and economic one. NAFTA did not remedy this problem on the border, as Molloy has noted of the region's Internet haves and have-nots: "[T]he benefits of Internet development are thus accruing to the business classes, not to public education, labor, and other grassroots development efforts" (Molloy 1999, 14).

Digital connectedness and literacy versus digital obstacles affected all levels of cross-border organizing—at least from the perspective of those who did not have routine Internet access. Clustered and crowded border cities like Matamoros that essentially live off or barely on the grid are not only short on potable water, indoor plumbing, or paved roads, but also are short on telephone wires and Internet access. At one point, Las Caracaras used part of the funds awarded to them through the Sierra Club grant to buy its own telephone pole and wires. They hoped that this would encourage the local Telmex office to establish telephone service for the neighborhood, but to no avail.

Digital divides caused increasing friction within Las Caracaras, particularly when they started networking across the border with the Sierra Club and Brownsville's Coalition Against Contaminated Communities. Inadequate communication produced allegations of misrepresentation and conspiracy on the part of the Brownsville group and Javier, although they might have been a useful ally and source of support. My role was often that of an unbiased digital conduit, even while I simultaneously engaged in capacity building so that Las Caracaras would be connected to the Internet and computer literate when my fieldwork period ended. The Spektra workers' petition faltered at a number of points that might have been remedied by efforts to mitigate the digital divide at the time the accords were crafted. The Spektra case is particularly dramatic because much that happened during the course of preparing, filing, and waiting for the US National Administrative Office response took place on the American side of the physical border, and was thus exacerbated by the digital border between the haves and have-nots. As a consequence, the petition—which was supposed to be an exercise in transparency, participation, and accountability (like all petitions)—was, instead, shrouded in opacity. It was for that reason that, when I met the workers, they were understandably mystified.

In sum, the logic behind the side accords and the democratizing linchpin they supposedly provided rested almost entirely on the ideals of transparency and participation. If documents were made public by being posted to the Internet, Mexican border and nonborder populations could seemingly participate, strengthening a grassroots democratic cosmopolitanism and cultivating dedicated border denizens. Such was not the case, largely because the side accords' creators, whether through benign neglect or lazy oversight, failed to take the digital divide and economic disparities of the borderlands seriously enough to implement immediate measures. For example, NAALC and NAAEC offices could have been established as government offices in each of the border cities. They could have been economically staffed with one or two permanent personnel. These personnel could have been deemed responsible for educating citizens about the side accords and their petitioning processes. Cyber stations could have been established so that those who were computer and digitally literate could help train others, so that the accords could be operationalized by all. These would have been easy and affordable measures to implement, but they were not. Instead, the accords' crafters and implementers lackadaisically relied on the logic of the market, which was presumed to trickle down and economically support a robust, grassroots democratization. It is impossible to have democratic participation in a process, institution, or democracy when the majority of the target population is unaware of the participatory possibilities.

Not only did NAFTA fail to create the type of thriving economic development opportunities that would allow those lowest on the socioeconomic ladder to participate in the side accords but, as I have argued in this book, it prolonged the duration of some *maquila* environmental and labor practices as essentially wasting processes. I have argued that the *maquila* sector is the primary mechanism through which waste is disproportionately produced among people and in places along the Mexican side of the US-Mexican border, thus defining it as a marginal zone. The social, economic, and demographic marginality of the northern Mexican frontier helps to reproduce the Mexican national state at the ideological and economic level (*maquila* sector revenues are third only to oil and tourism, in terms of GDP generation) and it contributes to global capitalism and the persistence of core-periphery relations. Marginality is socially reproduced and economically productive.

The history of the environmental wasting of the borderlands by the *maquila* sector is a well-known history. However, I have tried to apply this wasting filter to an analysis of working bodies in the *maquila* production process, as well as to my analysis of Spektra workers' and their labor conditions. The search for cheaper labor has been a driving force behind the spread of offshore assembly plants since the 1970s. Equally important in the case of Mexico and other developing nations, their comparative advantage has often consisted of selling cheap labor that can be performed under conditions of poor health, inadequate safety regulations, and limited enforcement (Denman 1992; Graubart 2005; Kourous 1998; Simon 2007). This is especially true for the *maquila* enclave, but it is also clearly evident in two separate and recent incidents in

Dhaka, Bangladesh: the November 2012 garment factory fire in which 112 workers were killed and the May 2013 collapse of a garment factory complex in which more than 1100 workers died. In the case of Spektra workers, the failure to provide appropriate safety equipment or to limit mandated higher production quotas puts workers' bodies at risk in the same way that the natural environment is put at risk when injected with toxins at dangerously high levels. The failure to safeguard against workers' health opens their bodies to wasting processes as they are exposed to chemicals, glues, solvents, and other unsafe toxins.

In *The Body as an Accumulation Strategy* (2000), Harvey describes the laboring body as an "unfinished project" whose production is embedded within commodity production processes themselves. The effect of this Marxist perspective is to displace the notion that bodies (and peoples) in capitalist economies exist a priori as atomistic and discrete units whose relations to commodity production processes are secondary to their original and, allegedly, fully formed identities and bodies. This perspective draws attention to how bodies function as nodes within commodity production processes, and how social identities are forged partly as a consequence of where laboring bodies are situated within broader social relations of production. In short, bodies are produced alongside commodities; they are not coherent units that maintain discrete boundaries and physical existence separate from the production processes of which they are a part. As part of the assembly of parts that form the conditions of production, human bodies become conduits through which forces of capitalist accumulation wind, at the same time that they are reproduced as marginal. According to Harvey, this requires a "relational-dialectical view in which the body (construed as a thing-like entity) internalizes the effects of the processes that create, support, sustain, and dissolve it. The body which we inhabit and which is for us the irreducible measure of all things is not itself irreducible" (Harvey 2000, 98).

How does the damaging of workers' bodies serve capital accumulation? Foreign-owned assembly plants have migrated to southern countries for the past forty years precisely because failure to enforce labor or environmental laws is a guaranteed revenue multiplier that, naturally, gets folded back into profits and capital accumulation. In addition to ongoing exposure to glues and solvents, Spektra workers were regularly harassed into higher production quotas. Accumulation and profitability, as noted by Cooney (quoting Marx), is typically achieved by "(1) lengthening the working day, (2) increasing productivity, and (3) increasing the intensity of work" (2001, 70), all of which caused a range of enduring muscular-skeletal injuries among existing and former Spektra workers. In short, laboring bodies become repositories for the negative externalities that are figured into production costs and, in fact, are hidden sources of surplus value.

I used the ecological economics' concept of negative externalities in this volume because it highlights the ways in which wasting processes— whether environmental or labor—are inherently economically productive. That is why the factory owners choose to waste. Negative externalities are waste, but not just any kind of waste. Rather, they are waste produced alongside commodities through modern, industrial mechanisms that are then housed in local bodies and ecologies. The Mexican side of the US-Mexico border is saturated with such externalities in the form of damaged bodies and contaminated environments. Its function as a marginal (and marginalized) cultural and environmental area bears direct relevance to its four-decade history as a pollution haven and safe harbor from regulatory controls. The august Raymond Williams anticipated the insights from ecological economics with the following words that merit quoting at length here:

> In our complex dealings with the physical world, we find it very difficult to recognize all the products of our own activities. We recognize some of the products, and call others by-products; but the slaghead is as real a product as the coal, just as the river stinking with sewage and detergent is as much our product as the reservoirs. (. . .) Furthermore, we ourselves are in a sense products: the pollution of industrial society is to be found not only in the water and in the air but in the slums, the traffic jams, and not these only as physical objects but as ourselves in them and in relation to them. In this actual world there is then not much point in counterposing or restating the great abstractions of Man and Nature. We have mixed our labor with the earth, our forces with its forces too deeply to be able to draw back and separate either out. Except that if we mentally draw back, if we go on with the singular abstractions, we are spared the effort of looking, in any active way, at the whole complex of social and natural relationships which is at once our product and our activity. (Williams 1980, 83)

The side accords were created to halt the largely unfettered wasting practices of the *maquila* industry in the pre-NAFTA era. These wasting practices were evident in both the environmental contamination and destruction, which the industry unleashed in a relatively brief period, and in the wasting of *maquila* workers' bodies, as male and female laborers were routinely exposed to occupational health and safety risks ranging from chemical exposure to plant fires.

The NAFTA side accords were also proffered as a model that subsequent trade negotiations (particularly those of the FTAA, see Deere and Esty 2002; Estevadeoral et al. 2004; Smith 2002) sought to emulate as the new gold standard for resolving conflicts between trade and environmental, labor, and human rights interests. This early optimism is evident in the following comment: "The NAFTA experience can be considered as a paradigmatic case for the renewed interest in issues of civil society vis-à-vis international institutions. It has been regarded as a test run for future trade agreements" (Thomas and Weber 1999, 134). The labor and environmental side accords of NAFTA promised a lot and they failed to deliver. The vision of a truly participatory, sustainable and transparent democracy was, however, a laudable one. They failed to deliver because of the absence of appropriate enforcement and implementation mechanisms; one hopes this will be taken into account when the side accords are revisited in the future as potential tools for harmonizing trade and non-trade interests.

Notes

Introduction

1. With the exception of the Sierra Club and official US Government and international agencies, personal and organizational names used in this book are pseudonyms.
2. This and all other *colonia* names are pseudonyms.
3. There are twin formations on the southern and northern sides of the US-Mexico border. On the Texas side, there is the well-protected Padre Island and Laguna Madre corridor. In fact, the coast of Padre Island is one of the longest continuous stretches of protected coastal lands in all of the United States. On the Tamaulipan side, there is a similar formation with an internal lagoon (the Laguna Madre) and an outer coastal barrier. The private Mexican environmental organization, ProNatura, has been working for years to preserve the Laguna Madre—which has unique ecological formations due to its brackish waters—but the outcome of its efforts remains uncertain. At the time of this fieldwork, Laguna fishing communities had already been adversely affected by the declining fish populations.
4. The complete name for the accord is the North American Agreement on Environmental Cooperation (NAAEC). It was one of two passed with NAFTA. The second is the North American Agreement on Labor Cooperation (NAALC). Information about each can be found at *www.cec.org* and *www.clc.org,* respectively.

Chapter 1

1. The *dedazo* describes the customary practice of the incumbent PRI president to "finger-point" (handpick) his successor.
2. Confederación de Trabajadores Mexicanos (CTM).
3. While Claudio Lomnitz-Adler (1995) has argued that corruption has functioned as an important tool of "pragmatic accommodation" in Mexican public life since the colonial period, I refer here to the more common popular association of Mexican corruption with PRI rule (cf. Morris 1999, 2003).
4. Frente Auténtico de Trabajo (FAT).
5. Labor activist, Ron Blackwell, of the Amalgamated Clothing and Textile Workers Union chronicles the shift of this organization's increasing recognition that workers in the United States or Canada could not be protected without protecting workers elsewhere, particularly "in the South." Like Evans, he cites this as a "permanent accomplishment" of the NAFTA struggle (Blackwell 2002, 70–71).

6. The side accords go by a number of different names. The NAALC is alternately called the labor side agreement, labor side accord, LSA, labor accord, or "on labor cooperation." The same is true of the NAAEC. In this manuscript, the agreements are referred to either by their proper acronyms (NAALC or NAAEC) or by the more common terms, labor side accord or environmental side accord.

7. See essays in *Greening the Americas* (Deere and Esty 2002).

8. The texts of each agreement can be located at *www.naalc.org* and *www.naaec.org.*

9. In the case of a labor dispute, sanctions are only available in cases of child labor, work at below minimum wages, and occupational safety violations.

10. Guidelines for submissions and the review processes for each commission can be found at their respective websites: *www.cec.org* for the Commission on Environmental Cooperation and *www.clc.org* for the Commission on Labor Cooperation.

11. The entire text of the NAALC agreement can be found in French, Spanish, and English on the Commission for Labor Cooperation website *www.naalc.org.*

12. Office of the United States Trade Representative, *Study on the Operation and Effect of the North American Free Trade Agreement,* available at the Organization of American States website *www.sice.org/geograph/north/chap3_1.asp.*

13. March 20, 2002 letter to US Labor Secretary Elaine Chao protesting her refusal to convene an evaluation committee of experts, accessed July 3, 2006, *mhssn.igc.org/nafta6.html.*

14. For a discussion of the conferences and conventions that set the stage for the WCED report, see Adams (1990, 54–69).

Chapter 2

1. More specifically, Mexican businesses can often be dependent on the tourist economy, meanwhile both poor and more well-to-do Mexicans might shop on the US side for nontourist items. Poor people often go to the grocery or dollar stores on the US side that, ironically, often provide goods at cheaper prices than in Mexico. The better-off seem to be attracted to the upscale shopping malls in the US towns.

2. Ginger Thompson, "Fallout of US Recession Drifts South into Mexico," *New York Times,* December 26, 2001, *www.nytimes.com/2001/12/26/business/worldbusiness.* Daniel Wood, "Border Factories Hit Hard By Recession, Winds of Trade: Maquiladores, A Symbol of Growing US-Mexican Economic Ties, See Fortunes Plunge for the First Time," *Christian Science Monitor,* January 23, 2002, *www.csmonitor.com/2002/0123/p02s02-woam.html.*

3. Joe Cantlupe, "EPA Ends Database Tracking Hazardous Waste from Mexico, *San Diego Union Tribune,* October 26, 2003.

Chapter 3

1. "Backward" linkages means that a particular industry uses local or national resources like raw materials. "Forward" linkages refer to an industry's contribution to local or national technological development and transfer. Regarding the

maquilas, Slaiken has argued that "third generation" factories are generating the technology and knowledge transfers (forward linkages) that were supposed to be generated in the initial generations.

2. Citing recent studies, the authors go on to note that third generation Mexican *maquilas* have had more luck with this integration: "Mexican *maquiladora* establishments have begun to incorporate their own design elements and research and development, giving rise to 'third-generation' *maquiladoras.* These coexist with first- and second-generation plants, which focus, respectively, on assembly or industrial processing without engaging in technological endeavors. Although this dualism demonstrates the disparity that exists in the *maquiladora* industry, it also indicates the sector's potential to evade the trap of long-term specialization based solely on comparative advantages stemming from unskilled labor" (Mattar, Moreno-Brid, and Peres 2003, 153).

3. Bensusan does note that there has been a turnaround in manufacturing wages since 1999.

4. Author's field notes from the Semarnat-EPA Border public comment session 2012 meeting at Brownsville Public Library, Brownsville, TX, November 12, 2002.

5. Anencephaly is a neural tube defect in which babies are born without brains, or with partial or deformed ones. It is one of three major categories of neural tube defects: anencephaly, spina bifida, and encephalocele.

6. Danielle Knight, "Health: Birth Defects Continue in US-Mexico Border Areas," *Inter Press Service,* June 18, 1998, *www.oneworld.org/ips2/june98/19_57_093. html.* Tony Vindell, "Environmental Issues Thorny," *Brownsville Herald,* October 15, 1996. Dane Schiller, "Families Settle *Maquila* Suit for $15 Million," *Brownsville Herald,* January 25, 1995.

7. Laura Beil, "Corn Toxin Examined in Border Birth Defects: Diet May Have Put Hispanics at Risk," *The Dallas Morning News,* March 8, 2001.

8. Ibid.

9. Ibid.

10. Ibid.

11. James Pinkerton, "Parents of Deformed Babies, Sue, Claim 88 Companies Contaminated Valley," *Houston Chronicle,* March 27, 1993; "GM Settles Border Suit; Auto Maker Averts Trial in Brain Defects Case," *Houston Chronicle,* August 25, 1995; "Birth Defect Suit Settled," *Houston Chronicle,* July 29, 1995; "The Spoils of Tragedy, Profiting on Disaster, Unscrupulous Lawyers Solicit Victims in Valley," *Houston Chronicle,* August 2, 1992; "Environmental Nightmare on US-Mexican Border Debates: Some Credit NAFTA, Texas Lawsuit for Slow Shift Toward Less Pollution by *Maquiladoras,*" *Los Angeles Times,* March 12, 1996.

12. Gregg Wilkinson, Carmen Rocco, Gregoria Rodriguez, Dennis Daniels, and Lei Meng. 1995. *Epidemiologic Study of Neural Tube and Other Birth Defects in the Lower Rio Grande Valley.*

13. Danielle Knight, "Health: Birth Defects Continue in US-Mexico Border Areas," *Inter Press Service, www.oneworld.org/ips2/june98/19_57_093.html.* Tony Vindell, "Environmental Issues Thorny," *Brownsville Herald,* October 15, 1996, page 1, Sec. A. Dane Schiller, "Families Settle Maquila Suit for $15 Million," *Brownsville Herald,* January 25, 1995, page 1, Sec. A.

14. Erick Muñiz, "Los Niños Mallory: Un Calvario Que No Termina y Una Lección Para No Olvidar," *Hora Cero* (February 2002): 5–8.

15. Schiller, "Families Settle *Maquila* Suit for $15 Million."

16. Erick Muniz, "Los Niños Mallory: Un Calvario Que No Termina y Una Lección Para No Olvidar" 5–8.

17. Tape recorded interview conducted in the home of Catalina, Colonia Blanca, May 23, 2002.

18. The Ley Federal de Trabajo (1931) contains within it strict guidelines regarding the amount of former salary with which a worker should be compensated depending on the loss that the worker has suffered in the workplace, for example, movement of a finger or limb, or the loss of limb entirely.

19. This point was made by Luiza in her interview, January 26, 2002. She claimed that this was because the supervisors knew that the work would be too difficult for women to perform.

20. Tape recorded interview conducted with Jose in his home, December 13, 2001.

21. Tape recorded interview conducted with Luiza in her home in Colonia Naranja, January 26, 2002.

22. Hospital.

23. Tape recorded interview conducted with Ava in her home, Colonia Amarillo, June 9, 2002.

24. Neuropraxia affects a radial nerve located in the upper body and results from a blockage in the nervous system.

25. Non-tape recorded interview conducted with Juan, Colonia Azul, June 10, 2002.

26. Non-tape recorded interview conducted with Gilla, Colonia Negro, February 17, 2002.

27. Tape recorded interview with Ana, conducted in the home of Rosalia, Colonia Verde, November 28, 2001.

28. Tape recorded interview with Ana on November 28, 2001.

29. Tape recorded interview conducted in the home of Pablo, Colonia Naranja, January 29, 2002.

30. A slang expression meaning "screwed" or "fucked."

31. From Alejo's affidavit that was shared with the author and submitted in support of the Spektra workers' petition.

32. Tape recorded interview conducted with Catalina in her home, Colonia Blanca, December 7, 2001.

33. Ibid.

34. Tape recorded interview conducted with Catalina in her home, Colonia Blanca, May 23, 2002.

35. Ibid.

36. Ibid.

37. Ibid.

38. Tape recorded interview conducted with Catalina in her home, Colonia Blanca, May 23, 2002, in which she reiterates portions of her December 7, 2001, interview.

39. Tape recorded interview conducted with Catalina in her home, Colonia Blanca, May 23, 2002.

40. Cited in the workers' petition and workers' testimony, as well as in individual

interviews (e.g., Marta, December 15, 2001; Ana, November 28, 2001; Martin, February 2, 2002).

41. Tape recorded interview conducted with Marta in her home, Colonia Verde, December 15, 2001.

42. Tape recorded interview conducted with Martin and Adelia in their home, Colonia Naranja, February 2, 2002.

43. Tape recorded interview with Ana in Rosalia's home, Colonia Verde, November 28, 2001.

44. Martin, in tape recorded interview with Martin and Adelia in their home, Colonia Naranja, February 2, 2002.

45. Tape recorded interview with Martin and Adelia in their home, Colonia Naranja, February 2, 2002.

46. Ibid.

47. Tape recorded interview with Ana in her home, Colonia Verde, November 28, 2001.

48. Martin, in tape recorded interview with Martin and Adelia in their home, Colonia Naranja, February 2, 2002.

49. Both organizational names are pseudonyms.

50. Based on conversations and interviews with the CFO workers, Rosalia and Ava, professionals who know of the organization, as well as the CFO's own publications (e.g., *Six Years of NAFTA: A View from Inside the Maquiladoras*, A Report by the Comité Fronterizo de Obreras (Border Committee of Women Workers), October 1999, Piedras Negras, Coahuila, and Philadelphia, PA; Rachel Kamel and Anya Hoffman (eds.), *The Maquiladora Reader*, 1999, Philadelphia, PA: American Friends Service Committee).

51. Based on continuous conversations with Rosalia, and tape recorded interview with Ava in her home, Colonia Rosa, February 2, 2002.

52. Extract from Guillermo's affidavit.

53. Based on tape recorded interview conducted with Guillermo in his home, Colonia Naranja, June 2, 2002.

54. Tape recorded interview with Catalina in her home, Colonia Blanca, May 23, 2002.

55. Ibid.

56. Ibid.

Chapter 4

1. Because the Laguna Madre of Tamaulipas was not officially protected at the time, fishing communities inhabited its banks and *maquila* and municipal wastes fed into it via the *Dren Cinco de Marzo*. It was reported by Rosalia and others that fishing opportunities in recent years had radically declined because of *maquila* runoff and pollution. She had in years past gone down there to sell used clothing. At a later date, Las Caracaras had the opportunity to meet up with members of ProNatura (which at the time was lobbying to have the Laguna Madre turned into a conservation zone) and members of an emerging US-Mexico Coalition that included the World Wildlife Fund and the Texas Center for Policy Studies.

2. Much of this early Caracaras history was told to me in conversations with

Rosalia through December of 2001 and January of 2002, but was also corroborated by other early members of Las Caracaras, such as Katerina, Esperanza, and Father Gonzalez.

3. Sewage.

4. Civil engineer from the Juntas de Agua y Drenaje who came and gave a MS PowerPoint presentation of the Matamoros *Plan Integral* (which was part of the larger application for a NADBank loan) to Las Caracaras in its office in the *parroquia*, May 20, 2002.

5. Tape recorded interview with Tomas, Colonia Rojo, October 26, 2002.

6. Executive board.

7. I heard this story in various forms at different times informally. Formal taped interviews were also conducted with Rosalia regarding her and her family's history—one on December 10, 2001, in her home in Colonia Verde and a second one, also tape recorded, in the new office of Las Caracaras in Colonia Negra, November 7, 2002.

8. Under Salinas, the parceling up and selling of individual plots of *ejido* lands was legalized and many people did this. The selling of *ejido* lands legalized under Salinas was part of the general opening up of the economy to more foreign influence, the breaking up of the state monopoly of key sectors of the economy, and a move toward privatization. These were the years of a sea change in the overall structure and organization of the Mexican economy, as well as a dismantling and disintegration of the previously cohesive PRI regime. Salinas's aggressive restructuring of the economy was also part of the anticipation that preceded NAFTA, discussions about which he had participated in with then-President Bush (George senior).

9. Although the Colonia Cuauhtémoc had been a well-established and seemingly incorporated community (with roads, electricity, and some indoor plumbing) the city had forcibly removed it in 2002, claiming that it was an illegal squatter settlement. The *colonia* had been located next to Los Tomates, one of three international bridges that connected Matamoros with Brownsville. The city claimed that it wanted to build a new shopping center there, as well as more offices to support the international customs offices. When municipal authorities built a new neighborhood that consisted of homes the size of sheds in a field on the outskirts of Matamoros, the community refused to move and, instead, moved much of their furniture into and around the pagoda of Matamoros' central square. For many months, they lived there in complete living rooms, bedrooms, and kitchens.

10. Respectively, Arturo Senior and Arturo Junior.

11. Tape recorded interview with Maria in her home, Colonia Verde, Oct. 29, 2002.

12. Ibid.

13. Octavio Junior.

14. National Autonomous University of Tamaulipas.

15. Informal interview conducted April 17, 2002, and formal interview conducted November 6, 2002.

16. Tape recorded interview with Katerina in her home, Colonia Verde, November 6, 2002.

17. Ibid.
18. Tape recorded interview with Gabriela in her home, Colonia Azul, October 16, 2002.
19. Tape recorded interview with Luis and Virginia in their home, Colonia Roja, October 20, 2002.
20. Virginia, in tape recorded interview conducted with Luis and Virginia in their home, Colonia Roja, October 20, 2002.
21. Tape recorded interview with Felipe in Las Caracaras' office, Colonia Negra, November 2, 2002.
22. Ibid.
23. Tape recorded interview with Martin and Adelia in their home, Colonia Naranja, February 2, 2002.
24. Tape recorded interview with Luiza in her home, Colonia Naranja, January 26, 2002.
25. Tape recorded interview with Marta in her home, Colonia Verde, December 15, 2001.
26. Tape recorded interview with Tomas in his home, Colonia Roja, October 26, 2002.
27. Ibid.
28. Tape recorded interview with Gabriela in Rosalia's home, Colonia Verde, October 16, 2002.
29. Tape recorded interview with Katerina in her home, Colonia Verde, November 6, 2002.
30. Tape recorded interview with Felipe in Las Caracaras' office, Colonia Negra, November 2, 2002.
31. Roughly translated, a campaign for a "culture of cleanliness" or to encourage people to "put trash in its place."
32. Tape recorded interview with Felipe in Las Caracaras' office, Colonia Negra, November 2, 2002.
33. Ibid.
34. Tape recorded interview with Oscar in his home, Colonia Azul, October 20, 2002.
35. Sierra Club, *Beyond the Borders, Mexico Project, A Joint Project of the Sierra Club and the Sierra Club Foundation.* See also *www.sierraclub.org/beyondborders/mexicoproject.*

Chapter 5

1. "We're Third Worlders!"
2. Presentation given to Las Caracaras by engineer in their *parroquia* offices. May 20, 2002.
3. "The Creation of the Executive and Citizens' Committee for Matamoros' Plan Integral," *El Bravo,* September 5, 2002.
4. National Chamber of Transformational Industries.
5. "Proyecto de Saneamiento, El Más Importante: COCEF Certificará en Diciembre, Asegura Zolezzi," *El Bravo,* September 6, 2002.
6. Hoja de Envió de la Propuesta de Donación del Proyecto, April 15, 2002. Hoja de Envió de la Propuesta de Donación del Proyecto, October 15, 2002.

7. Tape recorded interview with Luis and Virginia in their home, Colonia Roja, October 20, 2002.

8. North American Development Bank, "Matamoros Signs US$15 Million Grant Agreement with North American Development Bank," 22 July 2003, *beccnet@ listserv.arizona.edu.*

Chapter 6

1. Both of these names are pseudonyms. "Justice for Border Workers" is a famous US-based NGO that lobbies for workers' rights in Mexico, particularly *maquila* workers; it also lobbies for other issues connected with social justice.

2. This story was reiterated to me several times by Rosalia, as well as in the author's tape recorded interviews with Ava, Colonia Rosa, February 2, 2002, and with Guillermo, Colonia Naranja, June 2, 2002.

3. Social climber.

4. According to Pedro and Ernesto, JPJ was a grassroots community action and religious group that also dedicated itself to helping and educating workers. Like Las Caracaras, it was described as a self-empowerment movement based some-what loosely on the philosophy of Brazilian educator Paulo Freire. Completely unlike Las Caracaras, it was also, as described by Ernesto, "rhizomatic" in a man-ner then fashionable among anti-globalization movements.

5. A slang expression for crooked or corrupt.

6. Tape recorded interview with Ava in her home, Colonia Rosa, February 2, 2002.

7. Ibid.

8. Tape recorded interview with Guillermo in his home, Colonia Naranja, June 2, 2002.

9. Ibid.

10. Non-tape recorded interview with Javier in Brownsville, November 14, 2001.

11. Local media and border networks had been saturated with stories about abuse of workers, union threats and harassment, and the most shocking stories of anen-cephalic and spina bifida births during the filing of the petition.

12. Non-tape recorded interview with Juan in his home, Colonia Azul, June 10, 2002.

13. Tape recorded interview with Catalina in her home, Colonia Blanca, May 23, 2002.

14. Tape recorded interview with Adelia in her home, Colonia Naranja, June 9, 2002. Much of this had also been discussed in the original interview with her and her husband, but she iterated it here.

15. Non-tape recorded interview with Marta, Colonia Verde, December 17, 2001.

16. Tape recorded interview with Pablo in his home, Colonia Naranja, January 29, 2002.

17. Tape recorded interview with Guillermo in his home, Colonia Naranja, June 2, 2002.

18. Meeting conducted with JPJ members in downtown Matamoros coffee shop, May 29, 2002.

19. Tape recorded interview with Guillermo in his home, Colonia Naranja, June 2, 2002.
20. Meeting held in Matamoros coffee shop, June 29, 2002.
21. In actual fact, I was building on my previous experience studying an Ecuadorian mass toxic tort, in which the lead lawyer controlled with whom I spoke, thus obstructing my capacity to collect unfiltered the experiences of the plaintiffs themselves, including their experiences with the lawyer in question.
22. Direct quote from Pedro in meeting, June 29, 2002.
23. Twisted, corrupt.
24. The Great Rejection.
25. Based on tape recorded interview with Father Gonzalez, in his parish, January 25, 2002, in which he iterates a conversation he had with Señor Portes at their first meeting.
26. At the time, this included only Arturo (her husband), Katerina, Maria, and Father Gonzalez.
27. Ignorant or stupid person.
28. Personal communication with Sierra Club representative, January 2003.
29. North American Development Bank, "Matamoros Signs US$15 Million Grant Agreement with North American Development Bank," 22 July 2003, *beccnet@ listserv.arizona.edu.*

Conclusion

1. Oscar Contreras, "Technological Training: The Digital Economy and Information Workers in Northern Mexico," talk given at the Center for US-Mexican Studies, University of California at San Diego, CA, May 19, 2004.

Bibliography

Abbott, Frederick M. 2001. "NAFTA and the Legalization of World Politics: A Case Study." In *Legalization and World Politics*, edited by Judith L. Goldstein, Miles Kahler, Robert O. Keohane, and Anne-Marie Slaughter. Cambridge, MA: MIT Press.

Abrams, H. K. 1979. "Occupational and Environmental Health Problems Along the US-Mexico Border." *Southwest Economy and Society* 4: 3–20.

Abrams, Philip. 1988. "Notes on the Difficulty of Studying the State." *The Journal of Historical Sociology* 1(1): 58–89

Adams, W. M. 1990. *Green Development: Environment and Sustainability in the Third World*. (2nd edition). New York: Routledge.

Alvarez, Robert. 1995. "The Mexican-US Border: The Making of an Anthropology of Borderlands." *Annual Review of Anthropology* 24: 447–470.

Anderson, Benedict. 1983. *Imagined Communities*. London: Verso.

Andreas, Peter. 1998. "The Political Economy of Narco-Corruption in Mexico." *Current History* 97 (618) 160–165.

Anzaldúa, Gloria. 1987. *Borderlands: The New Mestiza = La Frontera*. San Francisco: Aunt Lute Books.

Appadurai, Arjun. 1996. *Modernity at Large*. Minneapolis: University of Minnesota Press.

Araya, Monica. 2002. "Mexico's NAFTA Trauma: Myth and Reality." In *Greening the Americas: NAFTA's Lessons for Hemispheric Trade*, edited by Caroline Deere and Daniel Esty, 61–78. Cambridge, MA: MIT Press.

Arreola, Daniel D. 2002. *Tejano South Texas: A Mexican American Cultural Province*. Austin: University of Texas Press.

Baerresen, Donald. 1971. *The Border Industrialization Program of Mexico*. Washington, D.C.: Heath Lexington Books.

Barenberg, Mark, and Peter Evans. 2004. "The FTAA's Impact on Democratic Governance." In *Integrating the Americas: FTAA and Beyond*, edited by Estevadeordal et al., 755–789. Cambridge, MA: Harvard University Press.

Barkin, David. 1987. "The End to Food Self-Sufficiency in Mexico." *Latin American Perspectives* 14 (3): 271–297.

Barry, Tom. 1994. *The Challenge of Cross-Border Environmentalism: The US-Mexico Case*. Albuquerque, NM: Resource Center Press.

Beck, Ulrich. 1992. "From Industrial Society to the Risk Society: Questions of Survival, Social Structure and Ecological Enlightenment." *Theory, Culture and Society* 9: 97–123.

Behre, Christopher. 2003. "Mexican Environmental Law: Enforcement and Public Participation Since the Signing of NAFTA's Environmental Cooperation Agreement." *Journal of Transnational Law and Policy* 12: 327.

Bejarano, Fernando. 2002. "Mexico-US Environmental Partnerships." In *Cross-Border Dialogues: US-Mexico Social Movement Organizing,* edited by David Brooks and Jonathan Fox, 113–132. San Diego: Center for US-Mexican Studies.

Bensusan, Graciela. 2002. "NAFTA and Labor: Impacts and Outlooks." In *NAFTA in the New Millenium,* edited by Edward Chambers and Peter Smith, 243–264. San Diego: Center for US-Mexican Studies.

Blackwell, Ron. 2002. "Labor Perspectives on Economic Integration and Binational Relations." In *Cross-Border Dialogues: US-Mexico Social Movement Organizing,* edited by David Brooks and Jonathan Fox, 69–76. San Diego: Center for US-Mexican Studies.

Brenner, Joel, Jennifer Ross, Janie Simmons, and Sarah Zaidi. 2000. "Neoliberal Trade and Investment and the Health of Maquiladora Workers on the US-Mexico Border." In *Dying for Growth: Global Inequality and the Health of the Poor,* edited by Jim Yong Kim, Joyce Millen, Alec Irwin, and John Gershman, 261–292. Monroe, ME: Common Courage Press.

Brooks, David and Jonathan Fox. 2002. "Movements Across the Border: An Overview." In *Cross-Border Dialogues: US-Mexico Social Movement Organizing,* edited by David Brooks and Jonathan Fox, 1–68. San Diego: Center for US-Mexican Studies.

———. 1998. "Accountability within Transnational Coalitions." In *The Struggle For Accountability: The World Bank, NGOs and Grassroots Movements,* edited by Jonathan Fox and David Brown, 439–484. Cambridge, MA: MIT Press.

Brown, Phil. 1997. "Popular Epidemiology Revisited." *Current Sociology* 45 (3): 137–156.

———. 1987. "Popular Epidemiology: Community Response to Toxic Waste-Induced Disease in Woburn, Massachusetts." *Science, Technology and Human Values* 12 (3&4): 78–85.

Bullard, Robert. 1990. *Dumping in Dixie: Race, Class, and Environmental Quality.* Boulder: Westview Press.

Buchanan, Ruth. 2001. "Border Crossings: NAFTA, Regulatory Restructuring, and the Politics of Place." In *The Legal Geographies Reader,* edited by Nicholas Blomley, David Delaney, and Richard T. Ford, 285–297. Malden, MA: Blackwell Publishers.

Camacho, David.1998. *Environmental Injustices, Political Struggles: Race, Class, and the Environment.* Durham, NC: Duke University Press.

Campbell, Howard. 2011. "No End in Sight: Violence in Ciudad Juarez." *NACLA Report on the Americas* 44 3: 19–22.

Carlos Vasquez, Xavier. 1993. "The North American Free Trade Agreement and Environmental Racism." *Harvard International Law Journal* 34 (2): 357–379.

Carlsen, Laura and Hilda Salazar. 2002. "Limits to Cooperation: A Mexican Perspective on the NAFTA's Environmental Side Agreement and Institutions." In *Greening the Americas,* edited by Caroline Deere and Daniel Esty, 221–243. Cambridge, MA: MIT Press.

Castañeda, Jorge. 2010. What's Spanish for Quagmire? *Foreign Policy,* no. 177 (January/February), 76–81.

———. 2003. "Introduction." In *Mexico's Politics and Society in Transition,* edited by Joseph Tulchin and Andrew Selee, 5–25. Boulder: Lynne Reinner Publishers.

Cech, Irina and Amelia Essman. 1992. "Water Sanitation Practices on the Texas-Mexico Border: Implications for Physicians on Both Sides." *Southern Medical Journal* 85 (11): 1053–1064.

Centeno, Miguel Angel. 1995.*Democracy within Reason: Technocratic Revolution in Mexico.* University Park, PA: Pennsylvania State University Press.

———. 1994. "Between Rocky Democracies and Hard Markets: Dilemmas of the Double Transition." *Annual Review of Sociology* 20: 125–147.

Chambers, Edward and Peter H. Smith. 2002. "NAFTA in the New Millennium: Questions and Contexts." In *NAFTA in the New Millennium,* edited by Edward J. Chambers and Peter H. Smith, 1–24. San Diego: Center for US-Mexican Studies.

Cleaver, Frances. 2001. "Institutions, Agency and the Limitations of Participatory Approaches to Development." In *Participation: The New Tyranny?* edited by Bill Cooke and Uma Kothari, 36–55. London: Zed Books.

Cockcroft, James. 2010. "Mexico: 'Failed States, New Wars, Resistance.'" *Monthly Review* 62 (6): 28–41.

Conger, Lucy. 2001. "Mexico's Long March to Democracy." *Current History* 100 (643): 58–64.

Cooke, Bill and Uma Kothari (editors) 2001. *Participation: The New Tyranny?* London: Zed Books.

Cooney, Paul. 2001. "The Mexican Crisis and the Maquiladora Boom: A Paradox of Development or the Logic of Neoliberalism?" *Latin American Perspectives* 28 (3): 55–83.

Cornelius, Wayne. 2002. "Impact of NAFTA on Mexico-to-US Migration." In *NAFTA in the New Millennium,* edited by E Edward J. Chambers and Peter H. Smith, 287–304. San Diego: Center for US-Mexican Studies.

Couto, Richard.1986. "Failing Health and New Prescriptions: Community-Based Approaches to Environmental Risks." In *Current Health Policy Issues and Alternatives: An Applied Social Science Perspective,* edited by Carole Hill. Athens, GA: University of Georgia Press.

Curtin, Deane. 2003. "Ecological Citizenship." In *Handbook of Citizenship Studies,* edited by Engin Fahri Isin and Bryan S. Turner. London: Sage Publications.

Cronon, William. 1996. "The Trouble with Wilderness; or Getting Back to the Wrong Nature." In *Uncommon Ground: Rethinking the Human Place in Nature,* edited by William Cronon. New York: W. W. Norton.

Das, Veena, and Deborah Poole. 2004. "State and Its Margins: Comparative Ethnographies" In *Anthropology in the Margins of the State,* edited by in Veena Das and Deborah Poole, 3–33. Santa Fe: School for American Research Press.

Davis, Charles. 1998. "Mass Support for Regional Economic Integration: The Case of NAFTA and the Mexican Public." *Mexican Studies/Estudios Mexicanos* 14 (1): 105–130.

Deere, Carolyn, and Daniel Esty. 2002. *Greening the Americas: NAFTA's Lessons for Hemispheric Trade.* Cambridge, MA: MIT Press.

Delgado Wise, Raúl, and James M. Cypher. 2007. "The Strategic Role of Mexican Labor under NAFTA: Critical Perspectives on Current Economic Integration." *The Annals of the American Academy of Political and Social Science* 610 (1): 120–142. March.

Delp, Linda, and Marisol Arriaga, Guadalupe Palma, Haydee Urita, and Abel Valenzuela. 2004. *NAFTA's Labor Side Agreement: Fading Into Oblivion?* Los Angeles: UCLA Center for Labor Research and Education.

Denman, Catalina. 1998. "Salud y Maquila: Acotaciones del Campo de Investigación en Vista de las Contribuciones Recientes." *Revista Relaciones,* 19 (74).

———. 1992. "Productos Toxicos y Potencialmente Peligrosos en la Industria Fronteriza." In *Ecologia, Recursos Naturalies y Medio Ambiente en Sonora,* edited by Jose Luis Moreno. Hermosillo, Sonora: Gobierno del Estado de Sonora, Secretaría de Infraestructura Urbana y Ecologica y el Colegio de Sonora.

Desai, Vandana. 2002. "Community Participation in Development." In *The Companion to Development Studies,* edited by Vandana Desai and Robert B. Potter, 117–120. New York: Oxford University Press.

Dobson, Andrew. 2003. *Citizenship and the Environment.* New York: Oxford University Press.

Dreiling, Michael. 1998. "Remapping North American Environmentalism: Contending Visions and Divergent Practices in the Fight over NAFTA." In *The Struggle for Ecological Democracy: Environmental Justice Movements in the United States,* edited by Daniel Faber, 218–247. New York: Guilford Press.

Drezner, Daniel. 2001. "Globalization and Policy Convergence." *International Studies Review* 3 (1): 53–78.

Dwyer, Augusta. 1994. *On the Line: Life on the US-Mexico Border.* Nottingham, England: Russell Press.

Eaton, David. 1996. "NAFTA and the Environment: A Proposal for Free Trade in Hazardous Waste Between the United States and Mexico." *St. Mary's Law Journal* 27: 715.

Ellis, Elizabeth. 1996. "Bordering on Disaster: A New Attempt to Control the Transboundary Effects of Maquiladora Pollution." *Valparaiso Law Review* 30: 621.

Englehart, Fredrick. 1997. "Withered Giants: Mexican and US Organized Labor and the North American Agreement on Labor Cooperation." *Case Western Reserve Journal of International Law,* 29: 321–388.

Escobar, Arturo. 1996. "Constructing Nature: Elements for Poststructural Political Ecology." In *Liberation Ecologies: Environment, Development and Social Movements,* edited by Richard Peet and Michael Watts, 46–68. New York: Routledge.

———. 1995. *Encountering Development: The Making and Unmaking of the Third World.* Princeton, NJ: Princeton University Press.

Escobar, Arturo, and Sonia Alvarez (editors). 1992. *The Making of Social Movements in Latin America: Identity, Strategy, and Democracy.* Boulder: Westview Press.

Estevadeordal, Antoni, Dani Rodrik, Alan M. Taylor, and Andrés Velasco (editors). 2004. *Integrating the Americas: FTAA and Beyond.* Cambridge, MA: David Rockefeller Center for Latin American Studies and Harvard University Press.

Esty, Daniel. 2001. "Bridging the Trade-Environment Divide." *The Journal of Economic Perspectives* 15 (3): 113–130.

——"The Environmental Dimension of Economic Integration." 2004. In *Integrating the Americas: FTAA and Beyond*, edited by Antoni Estevadeordal et al., 673–694. Cambridge, MA: Harvard University Press.

Evans, Peter. 2000. "Fighting Marginalization with Transnational Networks: Counter-Hegemonic Globalization." *Contemporary Sociology* 29 (1): 230–241.

Fatemi, Khosrow, (editor). 1990. *The Maquiladora Industry: Economic Solution or Problem?* New York: Praeger Press.

Fernandez-Kelly, Maria Patricia. 1983. *For We Are Sold, I and My People: Women and Industry in Mexico's Frontier*. Albany: State University of New York Press.

Fischer, Frank. 2000. *Citizens, Experts, and the Environment: The Politics of Local Knowledge*. Durham: Duke University Press.

Fox, Claire. 1999. *The Fence and the River: Culture and Politics on the US-Mexico Border*. Minneapolis: University of Minnesota Press.

Fox, Jonathan, and Luis Hernández. 1992. "Mexico's Difficult Democracy: Grassroots Movements, NGOs, and Local Government." *Alternatives* 17 (2): 165–208.

Friedman, Elisabeth, Kathryn Hochstetler, and Anne Marie Clark. 2001. "Sovereign Limits and Regional Opportunities for Global Civil Society in Latin America." *Latin American Research Review* 36 (3): 7–35.

Fuentes Muñiz, Manuel. 1995. "The NAFTA Labor Side Accord in Mexico and Its Repercussions for Workers." *Connecticut Journal of International Law* 10: 379–401.

García-Johnson, Ronie. 2000. *Exporting Environmentalism: U.S. Multinational Chemical Corporations in Brazil and Mexico*. Cambridge, MA: MIT Press.

Garcia Urrutia, Manuel. 2002. "The Authentic Labor Front in the NAFTA-Era Regional Integration Process." In *Cross-Border Dialogues: US-Mexico Social Movement Organizing*, edited by David Brooks and Jonathon Fox, 77–86. San Diego: Center for US-Mexican Studies.

Garvey, Jack. 1995. "Current Development: Trade Law and Quality of Life—Dispute Resolution under the NAFTA Side Accords on Labor and the Environment." *The American Journal of International Law* 89: 439–453.

Gehlbach, Frederick. 1993. *Mountain Islands and Desert Seas: A Natural History of the US-Mexican Borderlands*. College Station: University of Texas Press.

Grayson, George. 2010. *Mexico: Narco Violence and a Failed State?* New Brunswick, NJ: Transactions Press.

Goldschmidt, Mark. 2002. "The Role of Transparency and Public Participation in International Environmental Agreements: The North American Agreement on Environmental Cooperation." *Boston College Environmental Affairs Law Review* 29: 343.

Graubart, Jonathan. 2005. "'Politicizing' a New Breed of 'Legalized' Transnational Political Opportunity Structures: Labor Activists Uses of NAFTA's Citizen-Petition Mechanism." *Berkeley Journal of Employment and Labor Law* 26: 97–142.

Graves, Scott. 1999. "Citizen Activism and BECC Policymaking." *Borderlines* 7 (2): 1–4.

Green, Duncan. 1995. *Silent Revolution: The Rise of Market Economics in Latin America*. London: Cassell and Latin American Bureau Press.

Guerra, Maria Teresa, and Anna Torriente. 1997. "The NAALC and the Labor Laws of Mexico and the United States." *Arizona Journal of International and Comparative Law* 14: 503–526.

Guerrero-Miller, Alma Yolanda, and Cesar Leonel Ayala. 1993. *Por Eso! Historia de El Sindicato de Jornaleros y Obreros Industriales de Matamoros, Tamaulipas.* Matamoros, Tamp., MX: Centro de Investigacion Multidisciplinaria de Tamaulipas/Sindicato de Obreros y Jornaleros de Matamoros.

Gutierrez Najera, Raquel. 1999. "The Scope and Limits of Mexican Environmental Law." *Borderlines* 7 (10): 1–5.

Hale, Charles. 2005. "Neoliberal Multiculturalism: The Remaking of Cultural Rights and Racial Dominance in Central America." *Political and Legal Anthropology Review* 28 (1): 10–28.

Hanson, Gordon. 2004. "What Has Happened to Wages in Mexico since NAFTA? Implications for Hemispheric Free Trade." In *Integrating the Americas: FTAA and Beyond,* edited by Antoni Estevadeordal, Dani Rodrik, Alan Taylor, and Andres Velasco, 505–538. Cambridge: Harvard University Press.

Harrigan, Stephen. 2004. "Highway One." In *Rio Grande,* edited by Jan Reid, 175–179. Austin: University of Texas Press.

Harris, Jonathan. 2000. "Free Trade or Sustainable Trade? An Ecological Economics Perspective." In *Rethinking Sustainability,* edited by Jonathan Harris, 117–140. Ann Arbor: University of Michigan Press.

Hart-Landsberg, Martin. 2002. "Challenging Neoliberal Myths: A Critical Look at the Mexican Experience." *Monthly Review* 54 (7): 14–27.

Harvey, David. 1989. *The Condition of Postmodernity.* Cambridge, MA: Blackwell Press.

———. 2000. *Spaces of Hope.* Berkeley: University of California Press.

Herzog, Lawrence. 1990. *Where North Meets South: Cities, Spaces, and Politics on the US-Mexico Border.* Austin, TX: Center for Mexican American Studies.

Heyman, Josiah. 1991. *Life and Labor on the Border: Working People of Northeastern Sonora, Mexico, 1886–1986.* Tucson: University of Arizona Press.

———. 1994. "The Mexico-United States Border in Anthropology: A Critique and Reformulation." *Journal of Political Ecology* 1: 43–65.

———, ed. 1999. *States and Illegal Practices.* Oxford: Berg Press.

Hiskey, Jonathan. 2005. "The Political Economy of Subnational Economic Recovery in Mexico." *Latin American Research Review* 40 (1): 30–55.

Hofrichter, Richard. 2000. "Introduction: Critical Perspectives on Human Health and the Environment." In *Reclaiming the Environmental Debate: The Politics of Health in a Toxic Culture,* edited by Richard Hofrichter, 1–14. Cambridge: MIT Press.

———. 1993. *Toxic Struggles: The Theory and Practice of Environmental Justice.* Philadelphia: New Society Publishers.

Hogenboom, Barbara. 1996. "Cooperation and Polarisation beyond Borders: The Transnationalization of Mexican Environmental Issues During the NAFTA Negotiations." *Third World Quarterly* 17 (5): 989–1005.

Horowitz, Joel. 2005. "Corruption, Crime, and Punishment: Recent Scholarship on Latin America." *Latin American Research Review* 40 (1): 268–277.

Irwin, Alan. 1995. *Citizen Science: A Study of People, Expertise and Sustainable Development.* New York: Routledge.

Isa, John P. 1999. "Testing the NAALC's Dispute Resolution System: A Case Study." *American University Journal of Gender, Social Policy and the Law* 7: 179.

Janetti-Díaz, María Emilia, Jose Mario Hernandez-Quezada, and Chadwick Benjamin DeWaard. 1995. "National Environmental Policy and Programs in Mexico." In *Environmental Policies in the Third World,* edited by O.P. Dwivedi and Dhirendra Vajpeyi, 175–203. Westport: Greenwood Press.

Karl, Terry Lynn. 1990. "Dilemmas of Democratization in Latin America." *Comparative Politics* 23 (1): 1–21.

———. 2003. "The Vicious Cycle of Inequality in Latin America." In *What Justice? Whose Justice? Fighting for Fairness in Latin America,* edited by Susan Eva Eckstein and Timothy Wickham-Crowley, 133–157. Berkeley: University of California Press.

Kearney, Milo, and Anthony Knopp. 1991. *Boom and Bust: The Historical Cycles of Matamoros and Brownsville.* Austin: Eakin Press.

Kelly, Mary. 2002. "Cross-Border Work on the Environment: Evolution, Successes, Problems, and Future Outlook." In *Cross-Border Dialogues: US-Mexico Social Movement Networking,* edited by David Brooks and Jonathan Fox, 133–144. San Diego: Center for US-Mexican Studies.

Kelly, Mary. 1993. "NAFTA and the Environment: Free Trade and the Politics of Toxic Waste." *Multinational Monitor* 15 (10).

Kopinak, Kathryn. 1995. "Gender as a Vehicle for the Subordination of Women Maquiladora Workers in Mexico." *Latin American Perspectives* 22 (1): 30–48.

Kothari, Uma. 2001. "Power, Knowledge and Social Control in Participatory Development." In *Participation: The New Tyranny?* edited by Bill Cooke and Uma Kothari, 139–152. London: Zed Books.

Kourous, George. 1998. "Workers' Health is On the Line: Occupational Health and Safety in the Maquiladoras." *Borderlines* 6 (6): 1–4.

La Botz, Dan. 1995. *Democracy in Mexico: Peasant Rebellion and Political Reform.* Boston: South End Press.

Lawson, Chappell. 2000. "Mexico's Unfinished Transition: Democratization and Authoritarian Enclaves in Mexico." *Mexican Studies/Estudios Mexicanos* 16 (2): 267–287.

Leonard, H. Jeffrey. 1998. *Pollution and the Struggle for the World Product: Multinational Corporations, Environment, and International Comparative Advantage.* Cambridge: Cambridge University Press.

Levinson, Jerome. 1993. Symposium: "Comments on Labor Law in Mexico: The Discrepancy Between Theory and Reality." *United States-Mexico Law Journal* 1: 225–228.

Lewis, Sanford, Marck Kaltofen and Gregory Ormsby. 1991. "Border Trouble: Rivers in Peril: A Report on Waste Pollution due to Industrial Development in Northern Mexico." Boston: National Toxics Campaign Fund.

Lofgren, Don J. 1989. *Dangerous Premises: An Insider's View of OSHA Enforcement.* Ithaca: Cornell University Press.

Lorena Cook, Maria. 1997. "Regional Integration and Transnational Politics: Popular Sector Strategies in the NAFTA Era." In *The New Politics of Inequality in Latin*

America, edited by Douglas Chalmers et al., 516–540. Oxford: Oxford University Press.

———. 1995. "Mexican State-Labor Relations and the Political Implications of Free Trade." *Latin American Perspectives* (22) 1: 77–94.

Loustaunau, Martha Oehmke, and Mary Sanchez-Bane. 1990. *Life, Death, and In-Between on the Border: Así es la Vida.* Westport: Bergin and Garvey Press.

MacArthur, John. 2000. *The Selling of Free Trade: NAFTA, Washington, and the Subversion of Democracy.* Berkeley: University of California Press.

MacDonald, Laura. 2004. "Civil Society and North American Integration." *Options Politiques.* (Juin-Juillet): 4–8.

Mancillas, Manuel Rafael. 2000. "Transborder Collaboration: The Dynamics of Grassroots Globalization." In *Globalization on the Line: Culture, Capital, and Citizenship at U.S. Borders,* edited by Claudia Sadowski-Smith, 201–220. New York: Palgrave Press.

Mariscal, Judith. 2005. "Digital Divide in a Developing Country." *Telecommunications Policy* 29: 409–428.

Mattar, J. J. C. Moreno-Brid and W. Peres. 2003. "Foreign Investment in Mexico after Economic Reform," in *Confronting Development: Assessing Mexico's Economic and Social Policy Challenges,* edited by K. J. Middlebrook and E. Zepeda, 123–160. Stanford: Stanford University Press.

Mayer, Frederick. 2002. "Negotiating the NAFTA: Political Lessons for the FTAA." In *Greening the Americas,* edited by Caroline Deere and Daniel Esty, 97–118. Cambridge: MIT Press.

Mazuyer, Emmanuelle. 2001. "Labor Regulation and Trade: Labor Regulation in the North American Free Trade Area: A Study on the North American Agreement on Labor Cooperation." *Comparative Labor Law and Policy Journal* 22: 239.

McAslan, Erika. 2002. "Social Capital and Development." In *The Companion to Development Studies,* edited by Vandana Desai and Robert B. Potter, 139–144. New York: Oxford University Press.

Meed, Douglas. 1992. *Bloody Border: Riots, Battles and Adventures Along the Turbulent US-Mexico Borderlands.* Tuczon: Westernlore Press.

Merry, Sally Engle. 1992a. "Anthropology, Law, and Transnational Processes." *Annual Review of Anthropology* 21: 357–359.

———. 1992b "Legal Pluralism." In *Law and Anthropology,* edited by Peter Sack and Jonathan Aleck, 131–158. New York: New York University Press.

———. 1997. "Legal Pluralism and Transnational Culture: The Ka Ho'okolokolonui Kanaka Maoli Tribunal, Hawaii, 1993." In *Human Rights, Culture and Context,* edited by Richard Wilson, 28–48. Chicago: University of Chicago Press.

Middlebrook, Kevin. 1989. "The Sounds of Silence: Organized Labour's Response to Economic Crisis in Mexico." *Journal of Latin American Studies* 21 (2): 195–220.

———. 1995. *The Paradox of Revolution.* Baltimore: Johns Hopkins University Press.

Middlebrook, Kevin, and Cirila Quintero Ramírez. 1998. "Protecting Workers' Rights in Mexico: Local Conciliation and Arbitration Boards, Union Registration, and Conflict Resolution in the 1990s." *Labor Studies Journal* 25 (1): 21–51.

Mies, Maria. 1986. *Patriarchy and Accumulation on a World Scale: Women in the International Division of Labor.* London: Zed Books.

Mikulas, Nicole. 1999. "Comment: An Innovative Twist on Free Trade and International Environmental Treaty Enforcements: Checking in on NAFTA's Seven-Year Supervision of US-Mexico Border Pollution Problems." *Tulane Environmental Law Journal* 12: 497.

Molloy, Molly. 1999. "Researching the Border Environment: An Information Professional's Perspective." *Borderlines* 7 (8): 14–15.

Morris, Stephen. 1999. "Corruption and the Mexican Political System: Continuity and Change." *Third World Quarterly* 20 (3): 623–643.

———. 2003. "Corruption and Mexican Political Culture." *Journal of the Southwest* 23 (3): 671–703.

Mosse, David. 2001. "'People's Knowledge,' Participation and Patronage: Operations and Representations in Rural Development." In *Participation: The New Tyranny?*, edited by Bill Cooke and Uma Kothari, 16–35. New York: Zed Books.

Moure-Eraso, Rafael, Meg Wilcox, Laura Punnett, Leslie MacDonald, and Charles Levenstein. 1997. "Back to the Future: Sweatshop Conditions on the Mexico-US Border. II. Occupational Health Impact of Maquiladora Industrial Activity." *American Journal of Industrial Medicine* 31 (5): 587–599.

Moure-Eraso, Rafael, Meg Wilcox, Laura Punnett, Leslie Copeland, and Charles Levenstein. 1994. "Back to the Future: Sweatshop Conditions on the Mexico-US Border. I. Community Health Impact of Maquiladora Industrial Activity." *American Journal of Industrial Medicine* 20: 311–324.

Mumme, Stephen. 1999. "NAFTA's Environmental Side Agreement: Almost Green?" *Borderlines* 7 (9): 1–4.

———. 1992. "Systems Maintenance and Environmental Reform in Mexico: Salinas's Preemptive Strategy." *Latin American Perspectives* 72 (19) 1: 123–143.

Mumme, Stephen, Richard Bath, and Valerie J. Assetto. 1988. "Political Development and Environmental Policy in Mexico." *Latin American Research Review* 23 (1): 7–34.

Nash, June, and Patricia Fernandez-Kelly. 1983. *Women, Men, and the International Division of Labor.* New York: SUNY Press.

Nef, Jorge. 1995. "Demilitarization and Democratic Transition in Latin America." In *Capital, Power and Inequality in Latin America,* edited by Sandor Halebsky and Richard Harris, 81–108. Boulder: Westview Press.

Nevins, Joseph. 2002. *Operation Gatekeeper: The Rise of the "Illegal Alien" and the Making of the U.S.-Mexico Boundary.* New York: Routledge.

Norris, Pippa. 2002. *Digital Divide: Civic Engagement, Information Poverty, and the Internet Worldwide.* New York: Cambridge University Press.

Olvera, Alberto J. 2010. "The Elusive Democracy: Political Parties, Democratic Institutions, and Civil Society in Mexico." *Latin American Research Review* 45: 79–107.

Ong, Aihwa. 1987. *Spirits of Resistance and Capitalist Discipline: Factory Women in Malaysia.* Albany: State University of New York Press.

Oppenheimer, Andre. 1996. *Bordering on Chaos.* Boston: Little, Brown and Company.

Ortiz, Victor. 1999. "Only Time Can Tell if Geography is Still Destiny: Time, Space, and NAFTA in a US-Mexican Border City." *Human Organization* 58 (2): 173–181.

———. 2001. "The Unbearable Ambiguity of the Border." *Social Justice: A Journal of Crime, Conflict, and World Order* 28 (2): 96–112.

Oxhorn, Philip and Pamela K. Starr. 1999. *Markets and Democracy in Latin America: Conflict or Convergence?* Boulder: Lynne Reinner.

Paredes, Américo. 1958. *With His Pistol in His Hand: A Border Ballad and Its Hero.* Austin: University of Texas Press.

Pastor, Manuel and Carol Wise. 1997. "State Policy, Distribution and Neoliberal Reform in Mexico." *Journal of Latin American Studies* 29 (2): 419–456.

Peña, Devon Gerardo. 1993. "Letter from Mexico: Mexico's Struggle Against NAFTA." *Capitalism, Nature, Socialism* 4 (4): 123–128.

———. 1997. *The Terror of the Machine: Technology, Work, Gender, and Ecology on the US-Mexico Border.* Austin: Center for Mexican American Studies, University of Texas at Austin Press.

Peters, Pauline, ed. 2000. *Development Encounters: Sites of Participation and Knowledge.* Cambridge: Harvard Institute for International Development.

Pomeroy, Laura Okin. 1996. "The Labor Side Agreement Under the NAFTA: Analysis of Its Failure to Include Strong Enforcement Provisions and Recommendations for Future Labor Agreements Negotiated with Developing Countries." *George Washington Journal of International Law and Economics* 29: 769–801.

Postero, Nancy Grey, and Leon Zamosc. 2004. *The Struggle for Indigenous Rights in Latin America.* East Sussex: Sussex Academic Press.

Quintero-Ramírez, Cirila. 1997. *Restructuración Sindical en la Frontera Norte: El Caso de la Industria Maquiladora.* Tijuana: El Colegio de la Frontera Norte.

Quintero-Ramírez, Cirila, and Maria de Lourdes Romo Aguilar. 1999. "Riesgos y Prevención Laboral: La Industria Maquiladora Electronica en la Frontera Tamaulipeca:" *Reporte de Investigacion.* Matamoros: El Colegio de la Frontera Norte.

Rahnema, Majid. 1992. "Participation." In *The Development Dictionary: A Guide to Knowledge as Power,* PAGES, edited by Wolfgang Sachs. London: Zed Books.

Rajagopal, Balakrishnan. 2003. *International Law from Below: Development, Social Movements and Third World Resistance.* Cambridge: MIT Press.

Reblin, Kelly. 1996. "Comment: NAFTA and the Environment: Dealing with Abnormally High Birth Defect Rates Among Children of the US-Mexico Border Towns." *St. Mary's Law Journal* 27: 929.

Reed, Cyrus. 1998. "Hazardous Waste Management on the Border: Problems with Practices and Oversight Continue." *Borderlines* 6 (5): 1–5.

Reid, Jan. 2004. "Prologue." In *Rio Grande,* edited by Jan Reid, xiv-xxiii. Austin: University of Texas Press.

Richardson, Chad. 1999. *Batos, Bolillos, Pochos, and Pelados: Class and Culture on the South Texas Border.* Austin: University of Texas Press.

Rivera-Batiz, Francisco L. 1986. "Can Border Industries be a Substitute for Immigration?" *The American Economic Review* 76 (2), Papers and Proceedings of the Ninety-Eighth Annual Meeting of the American Economic Association: 263–268.

Robinson, William. 2003. *Transnational Conflicts.* London, UK: Verso Press.

Rodríguez-Garavito, César. 2006. "Nike's Law: The Anti-Sweatshop Movement,

Transnational Corporations, and the Struggle Over International Labor Rights in the Americas." In *Law and Globalization from Below: Towards a Cosmopolitan Legality,* edited by Boaventura de Sousa Santos and César A. Rodríguez-Garavito, 64–91. New York: Cambridge University Press.

Ruiz, Ramón Eduardo. 2000. *On the Rim of Mexico: Encounters of the Rich and Poor.* Boulder: Westview Press.

Russell, Philip. 1994. *Mexico Under Salinas.* Austin: Mexico Resources Center.

Sachs, Wolfgang. 1992. "Environment." In *The Development Dictionary,* edited by Wolfgang Sachs, 26–37. London: Zed Books.

Saldivar, José David. 1997. *Border Matters: Remapping American Cultural Studies.* Berkeley: University of California Press.

Salzinger, Leslie. 2003. *Genders in Production: Making Women Workers in Mexico's Global Factories.* Berkeley: University of California Press.

Sanders, Todd, and Harry West. 2003. "Power Revealed and Concealed in the New World Order." In *Transparency and Conspiracy: Ethnographies of Suspicion in the New World Order,* edited by Harry West and Todd Sanders, 1–37. Durham: Duke University Press.

Seligson, Mitchell, and Edward Williams. 1981. *Maquiladoras and Migration: Workers in the Mexico-United States Border Industrialization Program.* Austin: University of Texas Press.

Shore, Chris, and Dieter Haller. 2003. "Introduction—Sharp Practice: Anthropology and the Study of Corruption." In *Corruption: Anthropological Perspectives,* edited by Dieter Haller and Chris Shore. Ann Arbor: Pluto Press.

Simon, Joel. 1997. *Endangered Mexico: An Environment on the Edge.* San Francisco: Sierra Club Books.

Simon, Suzanne. 2007. "Framing the Nation: Law and the Cultivation of National Character Stereotypes in the NAFTA Debate and Beyond." *Political and Legal Anthropology Review* 30 (1): 22–45.

Simonian, Lane. 1995. *Defending the Land of the Jaguar: A History of Conservation in Mexico.* Austin: University of Texas Press.

Slater, David. 1995. "Power and Social Movements in the Other Occident: Latin America in an International Context." *Latin American Perspectives* 21 (2): 11–37.

Smith, Michael Peter. 1994. "Can You Imagine? Transnational Migration and the Globalization of Grassroots." *Social Text* 39: 15–33.

Smith, Neil. 1984. *Uneven Development: Nature, Capital and the Production of Space.* Oxford: Basil Blackwell.

Smith, Peter. 2002. "From NAFTA to FTAA? Paths Toward Hemispheric Integration." In *NAFTA in the New Millennium,* edited by Edward Chambers and Peter Smith, 471–496. San Diego: Center for US-Mexican Studies at UCSD.

Specht, Patrick. 1998. "The Dispute Settlement Systems of WTO and NAFTA—Analysis and Comparison." *The Georgia Journal of International and Comparative Law* 27: 57.

Speth, James Gustave. 2008. *The Bridge at the End of the World.* New Haven: Yale University Press.

Staudt, Kathleen, and Irasema Coronado. 2002. *Fronteras no Más: Toward Social Justice at the U.S.-Mexico Border.* New York: Palgrave Macmillan.

Stebbins, Kenyon Rainier. 1992. "Garbage Imperialism: Health Implications of Dumping Hazardous Waste in Third World Countries." *Medical Anthropology* 15: 81–102.

Stein, Eric. 2001. "International Integration and Democracy: No Love at First Sight." *American Journal of International Law* 95: 489–534.

Steinhart, Peter. 1994. *Two Eagles/Dos Aguilas: The Natural World of the United States-Mexico Borderlands.* Berkeley: University of California Press.

Stemp-Morlock, Graeme. 2007. "Pesticides and Anencephaly." *Environmental Health Perspectives* 115 (2): A78.

Stern, Peter. 1998. "Marginals and Acculturation in Frontier Society." In *New Views of Borderlands History,* edited by Robert Jackson, 157–188. Albuquerque: University of New Mexico Press.

Szasz, Thomas. 1984. "Industrial Resistance to Occupational Safety and Health Legislation: 1971–1981." *Social Problems* 32 (2): 103–116.

Teichman, Judith. 1997. "Neoliberalism and the Transformation of Mexican Authoritarianism." *Mexican Studies/Estudios Mexicanos* 13 (1): 121–147.

Thomas, Caroline, and Martin Weber. 1999. "New Values and International Organizations: Balancing Trade and Environment in the North American Free Trade Agreement." In *Global Trade and Global Social Issues,* edited by Annie Taylor and Caroline Thomas, 135–150. New York: Routledge Press.

Truett, Samuel. 1997. Neighbors by Nature: Rethinking Region, Nation, and Environmental History in the US-Mexico Borderlands. *Environmental History* 2 (2): 160–178.

Tybout, Richard A. 1967. "Pricing Pollution and Other Negative Externalities." *The Bell Journal of Economics and Management Science* 3 (1): 252–266.

Visvanathan, Shiv. 1991. "Mrs. Bruntland's Disenchanted Cosmos." *Alternatives* 16 (3): 377–384.

Walsh, Casey. 2004. "'Aguas Broncas': The Regional Political Ecology of Water Conflict in the Mexico-U.S. Borderlands." *Journal of Political Ecology* 11: 43–58.

———. 2008. *Building the Borderlands: A Transnational History of Irrigated Cotton on the Mexico-Texas Border.* College Station: Texas A&M University Press.

Warf, Barney. 2001. "Segues into Cyberspace: Multiple Geographies of the Digital Divide." *Environment and Planning B: Planning and Design* 28: 3–19.

Warnock, John. 1995. *The Other Mexico: The North American Triangle Completed.* New York: Black Rose Books.

Warren, Kay, and Jean Jackson, eds. 2002. *Indigenous Movements, Self-Representation, and the State in Latin America.* Austin: University of Texas Press.

Wilkinson, Gregg S., Carmen Rocco, Gregoria Rodríguez, Dennis Daniels, and Lei Meng. 1995. "Epidemiologic Study of Neural Tube and Other Birth Defects in the Lower Rio Grande Valley." Unpublished Report. Galveston: University of Texas Medical Branch.

Williams, Raymond. 1980. "Ideas of Nature." In *Problems in Materialism and Culture,* 67–85. London: Verso Press.

Williams, Edward J., and John T. Passé-Smith. 1992. *The Unionization of the Maquiladora Industry: The Tamaulipan Case in National Context.* San Diego: Institute for Regional Studies of the Californias.

Wilson, Patricia. 1992. *Exports and Local Development: Mexico's New Maquiladoras.* Austin: University of Texas Press.

Wise, Carol. 1998. "Introduction." In *The Post NAFTA Political Economy: Mexico and the Western Hemisphere,* edited by Carol Wise, 1–37. University Park: Pennsylvania State University Press.

Worcester, Donald. 1988. "The Significance of the Spanish Borderlands to the United States." In *New Spain's Far Northern Frontier: Essays on Spain in the American West, 1540–1821,* edited by David Weber, 1–16. Dallas: First Southern Methodist University Press.

World Commission on Environment and Development. 1987. *Our Common Future.* Oxford: Oxford University Press.

Wright, Melissa. 2001. "The Dialectics of Still Life: Murder, Women and Maquiladoras." In *Millennial Capitalism and the Culture of Neoliberalism,* edited by Jean and John Comaroff, 125–146. Durham: Duke University Press.

———. 2006. "Public Women, Profit and Femicide in Northern Mexico." *South Atlantic Quarterly* 105 (4): 681–698.

Wrobel, Paulo. 1998. "A Free Trade Area of the Americas in 2005?" *International Affairs* 74 (3): 547–561.

Zárate-Ruiz, Arturo. 2001. *A Rhetorical Analysis of the NAFTA Debate.* Lanham: Free Press of America.

Zavaleta, Antonio. 1986. "The Twin Cities: An Historical Synthesis of the Socio-Economic Interdependence of the Brownsville-Matamoros Border Community." In *Studies in Brownsville History,* edited by Milo Kearney, 125–171. Brownsville: Pan American University Press.

Index

aguas negras, 51, 56, 97
anencephaly
  border cluster, 50, 67–70
  definition, 195n5
  Spektra plant cluster, 71, 83, 87, 89, 92
  See also neural tube defects (NTDs)
asociación civil, 124, 140, 181–82
Authentic Labor Front, 25, 193n4

backward and forward linkages, 61–63, 91, 104, 194nn1–2
Border Environmental Cooperation Committee (BECC)
  certification process, 142–44, 147–49, 182
  complaints about, 36
  and JPAC, 181
  and NADBank, 128, 148–49, 185
  participation requirements, 138–40
  structure, 30–31
Border Industrialization Program (BIP), 46–49, 62

Las Caracaras
  class differences within, 150–51, 163, 170–83, 186–87
  and Coalition against Contaminated Communities (CCC), 13, 128–36
  and Comité Ciudadano (Citizens' Committee), 143–44, 181–82
  Dren Cinco de Marzo and area beautification, 98–100
  environmental justice goals, 2, 96, 98–99, 119–21
  founding of, 66, 95–97
  gender differences within, 124, 151, 171–76, 182–83
  JAD and BECC/NADBank participatory requirements, 13, 128, 138–43, 198n4
  membership, 97–98
  organization, 93, 97, 193
  place-making, 12, 99–100
  place-making and migration, 100–114
  PRD influence, 123–24, 140, 171–75, 177–83
  Sierra Club and Beyond the Borders, 1, 10, 14, 121–25, 150–54, 170–71, 188
  transnational advocacy impacts on, 150–54, 171–81, 182
carpal tunnel syndrome, 71–73, 75, 81, 161
Citizens' Committee (Comité Cuidadano)
  and BECC and JAD, 128, 141, 143, 147, 199n3
  and Las Caracaras, 142–44, 181–82
  and environmental side accord, 125, 187
  and NADBank loan, 124, 139
citizens' petitioning mechanisms
  in environmental side accord, 21, 30
  and participation, 3, 38
  and transparency, 6, 34
  See also dispute resolution mechanisms; participation
civil society
  and BECC, 138, 148–49
  global, 17, 151

civil society, *continued*
    growth in Mexico, 5–6, 17–19, 22–23
    and side accords, 3–5, 185–86
    and trade treaties, 21, 192
    and transparency, 20
Coalition Against Contaminated Com-
    munities (CCC), 13
    and Las Caracaras, 128–40, 153
Comité Cuidadano. *See* Citizens' Com-
    mittee
Comité Fronterizo de Obreros (CFO),
    2, 27
    and Spektra workers, 62, 71, 87, 150,
    154–63, 169, 197n50
Commission on Environmental Coop-
    eration (CEC)
    and NAFTA, 4, 125, 194n10
    petitioners' concerns, 35–36
    structure and function, 30
Commission on Labor Cooperation
    (CLC)
    and Spektra workers, 160
    structure and function, 31–32,
    194n10
Confederación de Trabajadores Mexica-
    nos (CTM), 18, 157
    repression by, 26
corruption
    grassroots allegations of, 14, 150–51
    and the JAD, 145–48
    lax law enforcement, 24
    and Mexican political culture, 5–6,
    18, 26, 59, 193n3
    and transparency, 19–21, 34
cross border advocacy
    in border context, 127–28, 182, 186
    coalition-building and accountability
    within, 152–54, 157, 163–65
    in NAFTA era, 22, 25, 121
    and Spektra workers, 154
    See also transnational advocacy

democratization
    and free trade, 5, 7, 22, 185, 189
    and Mexican civil society, 23
    in Mexico and Latin America, 16–18

    and participation, 38
    and sustainable development, 33, 39
    and transparency, 33
    See also dual transition governments;
    participation; transparency
digital divides, 7, 13, 34, 143–45,
    186–88
    and Las Caracaras, 102, 171–73, 188
    (*see also* Las Caracaras: class differ-
    ences within)
    and side accords, 11, 32, 164
    in Spektra petition, 87, 150, 163
dispute resolution mechanisms (DRMs)
    and side accords, 15, 30, 38, 185
    as soft law, 3
    See also citizens' petitioning mecha-
    nisms; participation
Dren Cinco de Marzo
    beautification of, 182
    and Las Caracaras, 94–98, 123–24,
    129, 143, 171
    description of, 1–2
    and Laguna Madre, 1–2, 197n1
    pollution, 4
    public health problem, 67, 141
dual transition governments
    in development and neoliberalism,
    11, 16
    in Mexico and Latin America, 16–21
    and side accords, 16
    See also democratization; participa-
    tion; transparency

ecological economics
    and environment, 65, 125
    negative externalities, 61–65, 87,
    91–92, 104, 191
ejido
    definition, 18
    in Mexican Revolution, 27
    migration from, 50, 102, 109, 111–15
    and reform of Article 27 of Mexican
    Constitution, 101, 198n1
environmental citizenship
    and environmental side accord, 126
    and border environment, 148–49

environmental justice
  and Las Caracaras, 1, 4, 9–10, 99, 122
  as place-making, 12, 99–100
  and popular epidemiology, 88,
    99–100, 131
  and the Sierra Club, 122–23, 171
Environmental Protection Agency
    (EPA)
  and Coalition against Contaminated
    Communities, 128–31, 133, 135,
    137
  Matamoros grant, 147
  hazmat tracking, 194n3
environmental side agreement/accord
  and border environment, 2, 4, 9, 12,
    30, 53
  citizen petitioning within, 21
  definition and purpose, 2, 194n6
  enforcement of environmental law,
    52, 121
  and environmental citizenship, 126,
    159
  role in NAFTA approval, 3, 29, 185
  and participation, 13, 126–27, 138,
    149, 192
  and sustainable development, 185
  See also North American Agreement
    on Environmental Cooperation
    (NAAEC)
Evaluation Committee of Experts
    (ECE), 31, 194n13

Federal Labor Law, 27, 196n18
  and Comité Fronterizo de Obreros,
    154–57
  and Spektra workers, 90
  See also Ley Federal de Trabajo (LFT)
Free Trade Area of the Americas
    (FTAA), 3, 186
Frente Auténtico de Trabajo, 25, 193n4

Import Substitution Industrialization
    (ISI), 17, 52, 101
Instituto Mexicano de Seguro Social
    (IMSS), 26
  and Spektra workers, 31, 80

Joint Public Advisory Committee (JPAC)
  and environmental side accord, 30,
    125
  and participation, 128, 181
Jóvenes Pro Justicia (JPJ)
  and Las Caracaras, 170
  description of, 200n4
  and Justice for Border Workers
    (JBW), 154–65
  meeting with, 165–69
  and Spektra workers, 91, 154–65, 182
Junta de Aguas y Drenaje (JAD)
  application for NADBank Loan, 13,
    145–48, 182
  and BECC participatory require-
    ments 128, 139–43, 145–47
  and Las Caracaras, 99
Justice for Border Workers (JBW)
  allegations of corruption, 169
  and Comité Fronterizo de Obreros
    (CFO), 71, 156–58
  description of, 200n1
  and Jóvenes Pro Justicia (JPJ), 154–65
  and Spektra workers' petition, 87,
    151, 154–56, 159–60, 162–66
  and transnational advocacy, 152–53,
    182

labor side agreement/accord
  deficiencies, 36, 187
  objectives, 34–35
  petitioning processes, 149, 164–65,
    188
  and Spektra petition, 5, 31, 70, 74,
    156–58, 163, 167, 169
  structure and function, 28, 31, 148,
    193n4, 194nn6–11
  and transnational advocacy, 87, 151,
    154
  transparency and labor law enforce-
    ment, 33
  See also North American Agreement
    on Labor Cooperation (NAALC)
Laguna Madre, 1–2, 56, 101
  and the *Dren Cinco de Marzo*, 95, 97,
    197n1

Laguna Madre, *continued*
  protection of, 124, 193n3
La Paz Agreement, 28, 30, 53, 131, 140
legal pluralism, 33. *See also* soft law
Ley Federal de Trabajo (LFT), 27, 196n18
  and Comité Fronterizo de Obreros,
    154–57
  and Spektra workers, 90
  See also Federal Labor Law
Limpieza Pública (LP), 99
Lower Rio Grande Valley
  environmental pollution in, 53–56,
    128, 195n12
  history of, 43–46

maquilas
  backward and forward linkages,
    62–64, 104, 194n1–2
  and Comité Fronterizo de Obreros
    (CFO), 87–88, 197n50
  and economic liberalization, 19,
    22–23, 152
  and environmental pollution, 2, 55,
    57, 95–97, 141, 185
  and environmental racism, 23
  female labor force in, 49
  history of, 48
  and "labor turnover narrative," 61
  and Laguna Madre, 197n1
  in NAFTA debates, 24
  and negative externalities, 64–66
  and NTD cluster, 67–70, 195n6,
    195nn11–13
  occupational health and safety condi-
    tions in, 26, 83, 116
  wasting practices of, 189, 191
Mexican environmental laws, 28, 51–52
  lack of enforcement of, 52–53
Mexican labor laws, 27–28
  and CFO, 88
  deformation of, 26
  and Spektra workers, 77, 154–56
Mexican Miracle, 18, 100
migrant histories
  Las Caracaras, 100–111, 114–19
  Spektra workers, 111–14

migration
  and NAFTA, 48, 64
  to Tamaulipas, 45, 48, 50
  to United States, 47–48

NADBank. *See* North American Development Bank
negative externalities, 61–65, 87, 91–92,
  104, 191
  and wasting practices, 189–92
  See also ecological economics
neutral tube defects (NTDs)
  border cluster, 50, 67–70
  Spektra plant cluster, 71, 83, 87, 89, 92
  types and definition, 195n5
  See also anencephaly
los niños Mallory, 70, 196n14
  and founding of Las Caracaras, 95
North American Agreement on
    Environmental Cooperation
    (NAAEC)
  and border environment, 2, 4, 9, 12,
    30, 53
  citizen petitioning within, 21
  definition and purpose, 2, 194n6
  enforcement of environmental law,
    52, 121
  and environmental citizenship, 126,
    159
  and participation, 13, 126–27, 138,
    149, 192
  role in NAFTA approval, 3, 29, 185
  and sustainable development, 185
  See also environmental side agree-
    ment/accord
North American Agreement on Labor
    Cooperation (NAALC)
  deficiencies of, 36, 187
  objectives of, 34–35
  petitioning process, 149, 164–65, 188
  and Spektra workers' petition, 5, 31,
    70, 74, 156–58, 163, 167, 169
  structure and function, 28, 31, 148,
    194nn6–11
  and transnational advocacy, 87, 151,
    154

transparency and labor law enforcement, 33
See also labor side agreement/accord
North American Development Bank (NADBank), 13, 30, 66, 124
and participation, 128, 138–144, 148–49, 198n4
and sustainable development, 185
North American Free Trade Agreement (NAFTA)
and civil society inclusion, 3, 6
and cross-border advocacy, 5–6, 12–13, 25–26, 35, 46, 87, 121
debates about, 16, 22–28, 51, 127, 185
and environmental side accord, 2–4, 52–53, 61, 97, 125–26, 138–39
and labor side accord, 5, 51
and Mexico's dual transition, 16–21
negotiation of, 22
and neoliberalism, 7, 58–59, 111–12, 187, 189
novelty of, 5–6, 192
and sustainable development, 37–39

participation
absence of, 148, 189
and democratic transition, 3, 5, 185–88
and environmental side agreement, 126–28
and labor side agreement, 36
in Matamoros' application for NADBank loan, 128, 138–44, 149
and participatory ideal, 126
performance of, 36, 128, 186
and side accords, 7, 11, 16, 32, 185
and sustainable development, 37–39, 126, 149, 185
and transparency, 186–88
See also sustainable development; transparency
Partido de Acción Nacional (PAN), 18–19, 174
Partido de la Revolución Democrática (PRD), 123
PRD membership in Las Caracaras, 123–24, 140, 171–75, 177–83

Partido Revolucionario Institucional (PRI), 18–20, 22–24, 52, 174, 193n1, 193n3
Plan Integral de Aguas Potables y Saneamiento (PIAPS), 128
and JAD and BECC, 139–40
and Matamoros' Citizens Committee 144–48, 199n3
popular epidemiology, 4
and Las Caracaras, 88, 131–32
and Spektra workers, 87–91, 154
Programa Fronterizo XXI, 140
Programa Nacional Fronterizo (PRONAF), 47

Quimica Fluor, 4, 66, 132

Red Mexicana ante el Libre Comercio (RMALC), 22, 25

Salinas de Gortari, Carlos, 19, 22, 26, 101, 198n8
Secretaría de Desarrollo Urbano y Ecologia (SEDUE), 53
Secretaría de Medio Ambiente y Recursos Naturales (SEMARNAT), 52, 66
Secretaría de Trabajo y Prevision Social (STPS), 26
and Spektra workers, 31, 154
Sierra Club
Beyond the Borders campaign, 1, 10, 14, 121–25, 150–54, 170–71, 188
representatives, 1–2, 103, 123, 133, 179, 182
soft law, 3, 21, 29
and legal pluralism, 32–34
Spektra
anencephaly cluster in factory, 70–71, 151
chemical health and safety hazards in factory, 82–87, 151
and Comité Fronterizo de Obreros, 62, 150, 154–58, 169
Jóvenes Pro Justicia (JPJ) and Justice for Border Workers (JBW), 154–58, 159–65, 182

Spektra, *continued*
workers and Justice for Border
Workers, 151, 153, 159
workers as *jonkeados*, 71
workers' injuries, 62, 70, 71–82, 151
workers' labor side accord petition,
31–32, 128, 151, 153, 159, 188
workers' local and cross-border organizing, 87–92, 151
spontaneous abortions
and Spektra workers, 62, 71, 87,
89–90, 151
sustainable development
and the BECC, 139–41, 149
and democracy, 5, 38, 127, 185
and environmental side accord, 30,
126, 139
and free trade, 5, 15
in *Our Common Future* (WCED), 37,
126
and participation, 5, 16, 37–39,
126–27, 149
and side accords, 6, 11, 13, 20
and transition governments, 15, 185
and transparency, 13, 20
See also participation; transparency

tirar la basura campaign, 119–21
transnational advocacy
in border context, 127–28, 182, 186
coalition-building and accountability
within, 152–54, 157, 163–65
in NAFTA era, 22, 25, 121

and Spektra workers, 154
TAN (transnational advocacy networks), 152
See also cross-border advocacy
transparency
absence of, 14, 35–36, 182, 186–88
and citizen participation, 34, 187–88
(*see also* citizens' petitioning
mechanisms)
and corruption, 19–20
and cross-border advocacy, 150, 182,
188
in democratic transitions, 16, 19, 20,
39, 188
and digital divides, 7, 34, 186 (*see
also* digital divides)
discourse, 20–21, 34
and law enforcement, 33, 35
and Matamoros' application for
NADBank loan, 145–48
and side accords, 7, 11, 20–21, 34, 39,
188
and sustainable development, 37, 39
and Vincente Fox administration,
19
See also participation; sustainable
development

US environmental advocacy, 23, 24,
28–29. *See also* Sierra Club
US labor advocacy, 25–26, 28–29, 35,
51, 193n5. *See also* Justice for Border
Workers